Skiffle

Skiffle

The Definitive Inside Story

Chas McDevitt

Robson Books

FIRST published in Great Britain in 1997 by Robson Books Ltd, Bolsover House, 5-6 Clipstone Street, London W1P 8LE

British Library Cataloguing in Publication Data
A catalogue record for this title is available from the British Library

ISBN 1 86105 140 9

Typeset by FSH, Ltd., London
Printed in Great Britain by St Edmundsbury Press
Bury St Edmunds, Suffolk

Contents

For my daughter, Kerry, who may have missed it all the first time round, but who is catching up fast. To the memory of Ken, Russell, Alexis, Bob, Denny, Les, Bill, Marc, John, Redd, Wally, *et al.*, who enriched our lives with their enthusiasm for the music.

Forewords

Before I was a kid in Newcastle I was a smaller kid in Glasgow, birthplace of many a king of skiffle including Lonnie Donegan, the music's biggest star. Lonnie made the first records I owned, the songs which threw my switch and thrilled me so much I knew I had to be a part of it. I was another young victim, one of hundreds of boys with their heads in the stars dreaming of guitars.

Being asked to write these words is another thrill for me, like the one I had a few years ago when Hank Marvin asked if I'd write an introduction to his guitar tuition method; it completes a circuit with the past.

At last the definitive (as far as I know) book about skiffle has been written. It achieves many things, one of which is to explain in an entertaining way how kids in the British Isles tried to make sense of American roots music in the days before records were put under so many different headings, before the demographics, marketing and radio promotion people had invented themselves. In the days before rock and roll.

I opened a *Billboard* magazine for the last time in a studio a few years ago – at a page where white and black gospel records were displayed on separate charts. Last year in Nashville I opened another paper to read about a new term some business genius had coined: Positive Country. What the hell is that you ask. Well it rules out Hank Williams I know that much, and Don Gibson and a whole lot more. If you're so lonesome you could cry you won't be crying on the airwaves. They decided the listeners of this station didn't want to hear sad songs (it might stop them ordering one of those new pick-up trucks being advertised). So give 'em Forever and Ever Amen. Positive. Don't you love it.

When I was four feet tall I didn't know or care if it was black or white, happy or sad, Burl Ives or Big Bill Broonzy. I didn't know what a hobo or a revenue officer was and I'd never eaten cornbread. The music was rare and precious and I wanted it all. I think I still know all the words to 'Big Rock Candy Mountain'.

Maybe Chas picked me for this because he suspects I'm still an addict. Because I played 'Jimmy Brown the Newsboy' and 'Darling Corey' four thousand times between the ages of six and nine. Because 'Freight Train' still gives me a lump in the throat. Because I started with a radio for an amplifier. Because I can honestly claim to know what the original Fender catalogue smelled like. Because I definitely know all the words to 'The Battle of New Orleans' . . .

But I'm too young for this. The year I was born Chris Barber was forming his first band long before he made those great skiffle records. Put on 'Rock Island Line' by Donegan and crank it right up. That's Barber thrashing away on bass and a mighty sound it is. I don't know how I know that but you can always check it in this book.

Mark Knopfler
London

I have a lot to thank skiffle for. Without it being so simple I may not have put in so much time with the guitar, enabling me to learn more of the instrument as I progressed, and without the guitar I would not have had a career!

Being in a skiffle group allowed me to meet other musicians and get the feel of playing in small clubs and coffee houses. But most importantly, the music itself introduced me to folk, country, blues and traditional songs and people like Leadbelly who, to this day, is still one of my favourite singer/songwriter/guitar players.

Of course Lonnie Donegan was the major reason so many of us loved this music for he was full of vitality and I saw him 'live' at the Liverpool Empire on many occasions. I even knocked on the door of a house in the next road to mine where he was visiting and got his autograph. Others too, like the Vipers, I saw at the Locarno Ballroom Liverpool . . . and who could resist Chas and Nancy when they did 'Freight Train'? I loved it then and I still think it's pretty cool now! It certainly beats Rap, Hip Hop and Techno!

With great memories and love from

George Harrison
Henley-on-Thames

The number of times that people in the pop business have called me and said, 'Do you know the words to "Nobody's Child" or "John Henry"? We are thinking of recording some skiffle songs.'

My answer is always the same. 'If you want to know anything about skiffle, ask Chas McDevitt.' Chas is a mine of information, and if anyone is qualified to write about the most important two years in British pop history, he's the man.

There is no doubt in my mind that the phenomenon we know as skiffle was the most influential force in the formation of today's pop music scene, quite simply it started us all off.

Lonnie Donegan was Jesus and we were his disciples. He still thinks he's Jesus (sorry Lon), and today's pop music fans are the followers, whether they know it or not.

Joe Brown
Henley-on-Thames

Acknowledgements

In the preparation of this book I must acknowledge the guidance, advice and encouragement provided by so many.

Particularly I would like to thank: Holger Lührig, from Unna in Germany, who has prepared his own skiffle discography and John R. Cowling for background information, also Dave Radcliffe with his complete Lonnie Donegan discography and Darren Vidler who is researching the Saturday Skiffle Club sessions.

Sean Killeen, of the Lead Belly Society, was of particular assistance through his articles for the *Lead Belly Newsletter*.

Richard Wieze of Bear Family and John Beecher of Rollercoaster Records provided sound advice.

Both Chris Burke and Barry Martyn in New Orleans together with Diane Rose of the Hogan Jazz Archive at Tulane University, New Orleans, helped trace important information. Thanks go to Eddie Armer and Derek Mason of the Southern Skiffle Society and to Bill Varley who has the fortuitous habit of filing and recording copies of almost everything.

I am indebted to all the authors who over the years have touched on this subject and would suggest that the bibliography provided would reward further reading.

Most of all I am grateful to all the skifflers, past and present, whose anecdotes, dedication and enthusiasm for the music help it live on.

Introduction

It is now over 40 years since skiffle hit the headlines. The effect that this musical style has had on the British rock scene has been neglected for far too long. Passing references have acknowledged the debt owed to skiffle by the beat musicians, but little of that period has been chronicled or documented. Virtually nothing has emerged over the years to chart the development of skiffle or even give a hint of the climate and atmosphere of that post war era. Its American influences and ancestry have been ignored. The roots must be recognized, revered even.

As long ago as 1957, I produced an illustrated *Skiffle Souvenir*, but the music press at that time was more interested in the new *enfant terrible*, rock and roll.

Luckily I retained many of the photographs and memorabilia from this project: and these, together with other items supplied by many of my contemporaries, I feel should be shared with a wider audience, hence this book.

In recent years we have seen the demise of many skiffle luminaries. The 'Guv'nor' Ken Colyer, and skiffle kings Russell Quaye and Bob Cort were among the first to pass on; to be followed by Denny Wright, Marc Sharratt and Les Bennetts. The founding leader of the Vipers Skiffle Group, Wally Whyton, succumbed to cancer at the end of January 1997. Before too many of us are recruited to join Gabriel's Big Band, I have tried to get as much information as possible from the 'survivors', both factual and anecdotal; in itself, not an easy task. These survivors are spread worldwide: Ray Bush in Palm Springs, Diz Disley in Hollywood (where else!), Shirley Bland in Holland, Dick Bishop in Germany, Johnny Duncan in Australia and Lonnie Donegan in Spain. Lonnie, though a frequent visitor to these shores, is hard to pin down; his trips usually coincide with a recording session or a TV appearance. Of the original skiffle boomers, only Lonnie and myself still regularly front our own skiffle groups. Though a few are still in the business, as either amateurs or professionals, most have drifted into careers away from music, or they are enjoying a quiet rural retirement.

So as to be all embracing, and as a preamble, I have given a concise history of skiffle's American roots and their influence, the reason for skiffle's birth, popularity and sudden collapse.

I have produced a biographical A–Z of those groups that gained national prominence, either through their recordings or broadcasts. Where appropriate, I have included anecdotes received first hand from original group members; at other times I have had to rely on hearsay and sleeve notes for the more obscure entries.

Throughout the biographical section I have tried not to intrude too much and hope that the facts and details will be sufficiently entertaining in themselves. Consequently, most of the pen pictures are written in the third person, as an observer rather than as a participator.

In order to contrast with this reportage and as an extension to this introduction, I have given a brief resumé of my early days and recalled some incidents and events experienced with the group – and not always musical experiences. These escapades probably appear very tame when compared to the wild actions of the Who, the Rolling Stones and the Sex Pistols, but in those innocent times, to the Establishment, we were equally rebellious and obnoxious. The mere fact that we had the audacity to appear on stage in sneakers and jeans gave the showbiz hierarchy apoplexy.

My own story can be echoed in and multiplied by all the groups, but I have intentionally kept a rein on this aspect and restricted it to the opening paragraphs. I hope that the skiffle fan who just wants the facts, lists and discographies, will appreciate this point; a taste of life behind the glitz but not too much to obscure the intent of the historical accuracy and flavour of that era.

Until the post-war period, popular music was not the pastime of the very young. The record-buying public was to be found among the wage earners not the schoolkids. All this was to change. Many a paperround salary was soon to be spent on the latest record heard on the radio or at the movies.

As far as I was concerned, George Formby was to blame, well, George Formby and his ukulele or, to be more precise, his ukulele-banjo.

Like thousands of kids my age I was bored with the dreariness

'It's Tight Like That', High Curley Stompers 1952 – Chas McDevitt, banjo; Neil Manders, bass.

Muddy Waters and Otis Spann dispensing advice.

of the popular music of the immediate post-war years. 'The Dream of Olwen' and 'The Warsaw Concerto' were as dull as dishwater and so sentimental, as were most of the dance-band tunes of the day.

George Formby's records and films, made in the late 1930s and wartime years, cut a swathe through all this romantic candyfloss. As my peer group and I grew up, this string-driven music found its full expression in the skiffle music of the 1950s. We realized that music could be made quite easily, and bright and cheerful music it was.

Many a youngster in that post-war decade would have been given a uke, as I had been, and would also have graduated to banjo and guitar. The initial interest in music, aroused by Formby and his ilk, was nurtured by the jazz and blues of the late 1940s and 1950s that was gradually filtering on to the airwaves. Jack Payne, Jack Jackson, Wilfrid Thomas and Alan Lomax – the 1950s version of a disc jockey – all played a part in this dissemination of information.

While still at college it was assumed that I would probably take up football as a career, but my plans were interrupted by a prolonged illness at the age of 16. Football didn't enter the equation again until, in the late 1950s, I was playing with the Showbiz XI and it was suggested that I might get a chance to play for QPR. After recovering from pleurisy and a TB shadow, I returned to college to complete my education and threw myself into my new hobby. I lived and breathed jazz and blues; the *Melody Maker* was my bible.

I was often accused by my tutors of being vacuous. They said my constant whistling was a sign of being brain dead. Perhaps they were right. In the same way as Bunk Johnson, when talking to Bill Russell at a recording session at Grunewalds in New Orleans, could illustrate his trumpet solos and all their modulations by whistling them note for note, I could whistle Louis Armstrong's hot 'licks' and took a delight in whistling the clarinet solo from 'High Society'. In the late 1980s I remember confronting Monty Sunshine during a band break, whistling a 32-bar phrase, and asking him if he recognized the piece. It was his clarinet solo from the 1952 Crane River Jazz Band recording of 'Lily of the Valley'. Monty was not impressed and looked at me as if I was a trainspotter in an anorak, or someone whose hobby was memorizing the matrix numbers on obscure recordings. But I had become inured to such reactions. After all, I was a banjo player.

Having borrowed a chord book from Neil Manders, the banjoist with the local band, the High Curley Stompers, I proceeded to increase my repertoire. One Saturday night at the White Hart Hotel in Blackwater, Neil discovered that the velum on his banjo was split. I was in the audience; he knew I had been rehearsing nearby and pleaded with me to take his place. His banjo was a tenor, mine a G. The tuning was completely different so he could not use my instrument. I was terrified at being thrown in at the deep end, but all turned out well, for from that night on the band featured twin banjos playing in unison, 'um ching a ching, um ching a ching.' This was to be the favoured rhythm and the basic skiffle beat of the massed coffee-bar groups. It must have been from such situations that the banjo gags were born – one banjo was bad enough, but two! Neil eventually took up the double bass, always a difficult chair to fill.

It was during this period, 1952–3, that I began singing with the rhythm section of the band: banjo, piano, bass and drums or washboard. In hindsight this was contemporary to the Colyer and Barber set-up, but until Colyer started calling the inner combo a skiffle group, we had no specific name for this line-up.

When I began working in London, I took over the banjo spot with the New Crane River Jazz Band, and before long I had introduced a skiffle group into the band. We had started playing in the coffee bars of Chelsea and Soho, the Fantasie, the Breadbasket, the Gyre and Gimble, and included regular spots at Cy Laurie's Jazz Club in Windmill Street. Our repertoire at this time was all embracing; we did not regard ourselves as purists. We were being bombarded by the records of not only Muddy Waters and Bo Diddley, but Freddy Bell and the Bellboys, Mitchel Torok and finally Bill Haley. All this fused with our first love of jazz standards, blues and work songs and created the hybrid that became recognized as the new skiffle music. We even sang 'Giddy up a Ding Dong', the Freddy Bell and the Bellboys' hit, as part of our programme in Cy Laurie's and included it on our original demo record for Oriole Records.

It was during the Chelsea days that we had the time of our lives and our music gradually gained wider recognition. We were the darlings of the coffee-bar set, and were booked for many debutante parties and student bashes. Our local following proved useful when we crammed them into the Chelsea Palace and used them as a 'claque' for our first Radio Luxembourg talent competition, winning hands down.

On one occasion, Eddie Chapman, a West End villain, who had been involved in the infamous wire-cutting scam at a racecourse in Ireland, took over an empty house in Chelsea and threw an open-house party, one of many he sponsored. He booked the Mick Mulligan Band and our group, providing free beer for all from strategically placed barrels. Marc Sharratt and I discovered a massive selection of free bottles of wine, but these were disappearing rapidly. We decided that we couldn't do justice to these on the night, so we planned to hide a few bottles away till it was time to leave. In one of the rooms at the top of the house, we found a cupboard set at arm's height in a small recess, and decided to stash our loot in there. Half way through the evening we tried to retrieve a bottle and discovered to our horror that this in fact was a service hatch to the dumb waiter; our bottles were all lying smashed to pieces in the basement. At last we found a solution and hid our bottles from the scavenging hoards by hanging them on pieces of string out of the rear window behind where we were playing. An ideal arrangement that produced fifteen bottles that were eventually to lie empty for weeks on end together with the dirty dishes floating in the bath of our flat in the King's Road.

The flat in the King's Road was an ideal pad in an ideal position. It provided a haven for many an itinerant jazzer, visiting American folkies and unsuspecting embryo groupies. Chelsea at that time was full of coffee bars that later became fashion boutiques. Lucian Freud, Quentin Crisp, and Annegoni were often to be seen in these establishments along with a host of posers and debutantes, the antecedents of the yuppies and Sloanes of the 1980s and 1990s.

The West End too had its attractions. The jazz clubs and coffee bars were better placed to cash in on the potential commercial success of the new music. Soho was beginning to regain its pre-war allure.

One of the all-night coffee bars that I would frequent, because of its music, its food and its female clientele, was the Nucleus in Monmouth Street, at the top end of Shaftesbury Avenue. One night my manager, Bill Varley, and I spent the evening there in the company of our publicist, Fraser White, a Fleet Street journalist who had the Scotsman's love of the grain, in excess of the norm. Bill and I pulled a couple of mysteries and took them back to our office, round the corner in Denmark Street where we all spent the night. We were discovered the next morning *in flagrante delicto*, by the group's secretary Christine Addey; she was close to tears. It was only then that I discovered that she held a torch for me. Apart from this disturbing facet of the situation, the whole event slipped my mind until about five years later.

Having acquired a coffee bar of my own in 1958, I often served late night behind the counter after coming back from a gig. One morning about 2 am. Fraser White came staggering into the premises, obviously the worse for drink. He drew my attention to an attractive working girl swinging her handbag in a doorway just across the road from the coffee bar in Berwick Street.

'Don't you recognize her, she's the girl that Bill pulled that night at the Nucleus.'

My recollection of Bill's girl was of a plain, snub-nosed teenager. This was an attractive but streetwise professional. I said, 'How on earth can you be certain of that?'

'She called me over and said, "Hi! Fraser, why don't you come up and have one on the house, for old times' sake?" I couldn't even raise a smile, I'm so pissed. She said, "Never mind Fraser, put it on the slate and come back when you are good and ready." That's how I know,' he replied.

Memories of these 'romantic' escapades abound. The music seems incidental to the story of that era. When I mentioned to Wally Whyton, the leader of the Vipers Skiffle Group, that I intended to write this book and asked him if he could he give me any relevant information, he said, 'Don't forget to mention Roma from Sheffield.'

Initially, not a word about the music; he tried to remind me that I had said Roma was a very attractive and friendly girl, but that he had to be aware of her false teeth. He said that everything I had told him about her was true, right down to the false teeth. I have no recollection of this advice or of the obviously delectable Roma and her false teeth. Yet when I mention Roma's name to our contemporaries, like Freddie Lloyd of the Worried Men and later of the Vipers, he says, 'Oh yes, I remember Roma!' And his eyes mist over.

How could I have possibly forgotten such a popular girl as Roma? I was not that caught up in the music and touring to have missed out on such a find. Perhaps in my case she used a pseudonym; maybe, Helen, Wendy or even Marguerite, but definitely not Jean. Jean who featured prominently in George Melly's book *Owning Up*, provided a service all of her own. The package shows that passed through Leeds would invariably pass through Jean as well – in the back of the tour bus.

Leeds was one of the livelier spots on the one-night-stand circuit. A favourite after-hours haunt was the club run by Bob Barclay, the tuba player with the Yorkshire Jazz Band. I have a vivid picture in my mind of Denny Wright, then playing the guitar with Johnny Duncan, and not yet on the wagon, lying on his back in the middle of the room well in his cups, yet still playing some great licks.

All the major cities, Leeds, Glasgow, Manchester, Liverpool, Birmingham and Newcastle, had big theatres, the Moss Empires, and many dance halls. These venues also gave birth to thousands of skiffle groups, for a few years providing a ready-made audience for the touring name bands.

Newcastle was always a date we looked forward to. We indulged in the practice, nothing new in showbusiness, of sneaking the girls into our digs for the night. In the morning, one of the group, usually myself, would keep the landlady occupied in the rear kitchen, while the others sneaked the girls out the front door. They would then return to their homes, cold and dishevelled, while we returned to the kitchen for a greasy fry-up. On occasion we would take a chance and introduce a more presentable 'mystery' as 'the wife'. This was all very well but entailed the keeping of a kind of diary, so that new 'wives' were not introduced too often to the already suspicious landladies.

Lennie Harrison, our bass player (he had replaced John Paul who didn't want to turn professional), had a technique with the ladies that had to be admired by us youngsters. Obviously years on the road had honed his art. The oldest member of the group, he had played in Paris before the war with such giants as Benny Carter and Django Reinhardt. He had grown up in the company of Ray Ellington, for a while playing in his Quartet, and shared many of Ray's mannerisms, even down to the stylish cigarette holder. He wore American gabardine suits from Cecil Gee's, sported a Ronald Coleman moustache and really looked the business.

He was one of the real characters of Archer Street, where every Monday morning it seemed all of London's musical community would be milling around doing deals and fixing dates. It was amusing to pick out the drummers, who usually had a pair of drumsticks poking from their pockets, advertising their calling and their availability. Lennie obviously couldn't carry his double bass around all the time, so he no doubt developed the ebullient personality to compensate.

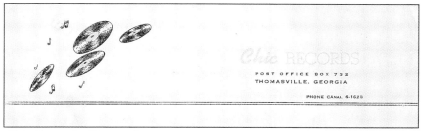

Chic Records. Here today, gone tomorrow.

On stage Lennie was a showman to the tip of his toes. He knew all the tricks. Although a solid bass player, his florid technique masked his limitations. Fast runs, twirling and slapping the bass, constant vocal interpolations, all helped to ignite what often might have been a dismal gig.

On many occasions, in mid song, I would notice that the audience's attention had been diverted away from me at the central mike, and all heads were turned towards my right-hand

Ed Sulivan Show, June 1957, (from left) Marc Sharratt, Nancy Whiskey, Chas McDevitt.

side. Looking over my shoulder I would see that Lennie had manoeuvred himself from the back-line of bass, drums or washboard, and was practically alongside me, one foot on the footlights, winking and chatting up the girls in the first few rows.

One night seconds before we were due to start our dance-hall engagement, Lennie was nowhere to be found. Then right on cue, he emerged from a broom cupboard wearing a broad smile of satisfaction, holding the hand of a red-faced dolly bird who was busily trying to adjust her skirt. We desperately tried to find the secret of his success. In the end we came up with two main solutions. Firstly, before almost any conversation he'd ask the girl, 'Do you fuck?' Nine times out of ten he would be rejected, but he would not have to waste time on the non-starters. Secondly, he had a story that he would lay on the more gullible, and it seemed to work every time, he'd say, 'When I was in the forces, serving in Italy, I got a bullet through my private parts. Consequently, darling, you have nothing to fear, because now when I reach a climax, all you get is whoosh! a little gush of air.'

Life on the road was not all birds and booze. I did have the odd hairy experience that brought a chill to my spine.

At the end of June 1957, Nancy Whiskey, Marc Sharratt and I flew to New York to promote 'Freight Train' on the prestigious Ed Sullivan show. Chic Thompson, the owner of Chic Records, had put us into suites at the Park Sheraton Hotel. A press reception was held in the suite Marc and I were occupying. TV cameramen, radio and newspaper reporters were all taking full advantage of the free drinks and snacks on offer. Then proceedings stopped abruptly as all heads turned to see this stunning blonde wiggle into the room on her stiletto heels. In a pale-blue two-piece suit enveloping her neat figure and topped by a bouffant hair style, in the Jayne Mansfield manner, she entered, followed by a little old man in his late seventies. It was Chic's wife, a real Georgia peach. She introduced the old man to the assembled company and he left the room. As he was going she said to Chic in her Southern drawl, 'Chic, I hayed ta bring him in. He tried ta kiss me in the elevator.'

With that Chic rushed out of the room, grabbed the old man by the scruff of the neck, made him apologize, kneel at his wife's feet, kiss her shoes and then crawl out of the room on his hands and knees. The entourage was dumbfounded.

When it was hinted that Nancy might sign to a rival company while we were still in the USA, Chic threatened to kill me if she left. He said he had killed before and wouldn't hesitate to do so again. Whether he meant in Korea or on the streets of New York, having seen him at work, I had no doubt that he was capable of carrying out such a promise.

This was the only black spot on our US trip. The rest of it was a dream come true. We got to meet and hear American musicians and rock artists that until now had only been names on a record sleeve: George Lewis and Tony Parenti among the jazzers and backstage at the Paramount Theatre on 3 July 1957, we were introduced to Alan Freed and the cast of his *Summer Festival*. Backed by the Alan Freed Big Band that featured both Sam 'The Man' Taylor and Al Sears on saxes, the show included Chuck Berry, Frankie Lymon, the Everly Brothers, the Kalin Twins, LaVern Baker, Jodie Sands, Ruth Brown, Clyde McPhatter, Big Joe Turner, the Moonglows, the Cadillacs, Teddy Randazzo of the Chuckles, a 15-year-old Paul Anka, and in my opinion the hit of the show, Screamin' Jay Hawkins. We had never seen such a bevy of hit makers. We were promised inclusion in the next edition of this show, but working visas could not be arranged in time and in any case we were contracted to a big tour back in the UK.

Screamin' Jay had such a profound effect on me that on my return home I went to a large undertaker's in the Tottenham Court Road and stood inside a coffin while giving instructions to have it lined and hinged like the one Screamin' Jay used on stage. Luckily good sense prevailed and, realising I didn't have the *chutzpah* to carry this through, I abandoned the idea, leaving such innovations to the likes of Wee Willie Harris and Screaming Lord Sutch, who were both aware of my stories about the originator.

When Nancy left the group in August 1957, she was replaced by Shirley Douglas. After about a year on the road, the group underwent another metamorphosis. Shirley took up the bass-guitar, Les Bennetts came in on lead guitar and Red Reece occupied the drum stool: a short-lived combo that nevertheless had its moments. When we discovered that on our one-night tours the billing was often wrong, we insisted that Bill Varley should circulate all the promoters with a detailed guide to drawing up the posters. He compiled a rough, giving my name 100 per cent billing with the Freight Train Boys 25 per cent and Shirley Douglas 50 per cent. Imagine the reaction when we rolled into one northern venue only to discover that the promoter had followed instructions to the letter. The posters actually printed out the complete instructions, Chas McDevitt 100 per cent etc.

Les and Red had come from the now defunct Les Hobeaux Skiffle Group, and brought with them some of the schoolboy pranks prevalent in that group. An enduring, but not endearing, memory is when I had the misfortune to share a bedroom with them on tour. They were opposite me in a double bed and after a liberal consumption of curry and beer, they kept me awake all night setting light to each other's farts. For what seemed like an eternity I would hear, 'Here comes another one!' The cigarette lighter would click and this was invariably followed by a blue flash that would illuminate the dark room.

Les was eventually poached by Lonnie Donegan. At first Donegan had approached Darrell Lyte, the other guitar player with Les Hobeaux, but Darrell realized that it was Les's guitar virtuosity that was being sought and pointed Lonnie in my direction. Consequently, Les was soon replaced by Roy Powell, an aggressive Mancunian pianist. Roy had a nasty habit of dragging the back of his hand across his runny nose and, while surreptitiously wiping it down his trouser leg, would say, 'Bloody Chas, *sniff*, I want more money!'

He suffered from asthma, but in spite of this, or perhaps because of this, he was always trying to prove himself. In so doing he often accepted the most ridiculous wagers. On one occasion he raced our burly manager, Bill Varley, through a remote Highland village in mid-winter; on another for a 10s. dare he stripped down to his underpants, a pair of football shorts, and submerged himself in the icy black waters of Loch Lomond. All this did nothing for his asthma.

An excellent rock pianist, he was later to join Tony Crombie's Rockets; his speciality was to play the piano from a standing position, à la Jerry Lee Lewis. 'Bony Moronie' was his solo piece and between the phrases he would beam at the girls standing round the foot of the stage. Once in full flight his false teeth came shooting across the stage. Undeterred he carried on singing, albeit tight lipped. Nobody in the audience had really noticed, but, concerned for the safety of his choppers, I moved across the stage, bent down and picked them up, handing them back to Roy in mid song. The follow spot had indeed followed my every move, and the entire audience erupted when they realized Roy's predicament. He never forgave my tactless act; it ruined his chances that night.

About that time we used to play dates at American bases in Suffolk and Norfolk. We would hire a mini-van and driver to take the whole show to the gig and bring us back, dropping us at the Freight Train in the early hours. For all this effort, the driver, a sometime film extra and stunt man, was paid £11. His name was Peter Grant, soon to become the legendary manager of the supergroup Led Zeppelin. Peter died in November 1995, just as preparations were being put in hand for the filming of his life story. His experiences in the heyday of rock and roll would have made my New York brush with Mafia look like child's play.

But all these experiences and amusing episodes would never have come about without the music. Where did skiffle come from, why and how did it crash through the formal barriers of the established entertainment world?

PART
ONE
Supernova

1

In the Beginning

A supernova: A star that explodes catastrophically . . . becoming for a few days up to one hundred million times brighter than the sun. The expanding shell of debris . . . creates a nebula that radiates radio waves, x-rays and light for hundreds or thousands of years.

Collins English Dictionary

Skiffle had all the attributes of a supernova. It exploded into the hit parade in January 1956. In a few days, its expanding shell of groups had created the nebula that would radiate and develop into the folk and rock groups of the 1960s and 1970s. Bright yet short-lived, this music became the social phenomenon of the late 1950s.

Although skiffle had been around for three or four years it did not become a craze until the supernova exploded. The ingredient that provided the catalyst for this rapid popularity was Lonnie Donegan's recording of 'Rock Island Line'. It had stormed into the hit parade in January 1956 and from that instant popular music was never to be the same. During the last couple of months of 1955, the number one tunes were provided by such family favourites as Jimmy Young and Dickie Valentine: 'The Man from Laramie' and 'The Christmas Alphabet'. Sentimental ballads and love songs were the norm. Skiffle songs hardly ever mentioned love; being very impersonal and down to earth, they were usually about trains or travelling, bad men and gamblers. At the time they were classified as novelty songs. In itself this was not enough to make the form so popular. How did this record suddenly appear from out of the blue? In reality, the ground had been prepared for this phenomenon during the previous five years.

The first traditional jazz revival had taken place in the late 1940s and early 1950s. Humphrey Lyttelton, the Crane River Jazz Band with Ken Colyer, the Manchester Saints, Freddy Randall and a host of similar bands, catered for the ever-increasing interest in New Orleans style jazz. One concert held at the Royal Albert Hall featured twelve trad bands and just one modern jazz quartet. A subculture of young fans followed the bands – youth was beginning to have its fling. The restrictions and constrictions of the immediate post-war years were at last being jettisoned. It is hard to believe that some forms of rationing had continued right into the early 1950s. The overall greyness of those austere years was being coloured by the music and a liberal consumption of Merrydown cider.

At one time a jazz club was strictly for the connoisseur, what one might describe as a jazz fan was more a student of jazz, essentially an enthusiastic listener. With the arrival, at the turn of the decade, of Graeme Bell and his Australian Jazz Band, and his association with the Humphrey Lyttelton Band, dancing to the music was encouraged. The result of this was that the music now reached a younger and more diverse audience. Many jazz clubs met on unlicensed premises, so age was no barrier for involvement.

In July 1951 as part of the Festival of Britain celebrations, a monster jazz concert was held at the Royal Festival Hall in the presence of Princess Elizabeth. Now that jazz had received the royal stamp of approval it became more acceptable to the Establishment. Parlophone Records issued a series of singles recorded live at this performance. One of these, 'I Want a Girl' by the Manchester Saints backed by 'I'm Travellin'' by the Crane River Jazz Band, could by today's standards be described as a hit. It received a tremendous amount of airplay. The duffel-coated jazz fan had arrived and made his mark. It would not be too long before he would transmogrify into a skiffle fan.

Of all the bands playing at the concert, only the Mick Mulligan Band, with George Melly on vocals, failed to make it on to record. Mick Mulligan had conceded the two arrangements they had decided on were a little ambitious and complicated. As George Melly put it in his book, *Owning Up*: 'They sounded ragged and unconvincing.'

Whatever the reason for their omission, it would have been

very interesting to hear the reaction of the audience to George Melly singing 'Rock Island Line', a full four years before Lonnie was to record the song.

It was appropriate that Ken Colyer, the leader of the Crane River should be part of this renaissance; for it was Colyer who a few years later would incorporate his embryo skiffle group into the band that included both Chris Barber and Lonnie Donegan.

By 1952 Ken Colyer had left the Crane River and rejoined the Merchant Navy, jumping ship in Mobile, Alabama. He made a story-book journey to New Orleans and achieved a lifetime's ambition: to play in the Land of Dreams with some of the few surviving legends of New Orleans music. He was able to sit in with such luminaries as George Lewis, Percy Humphries, 'Big' Jim Robinson, Lawrence Marrero, Alcide 'Slow Drag' Pavageau and Joe Watkins. For a while he was in seventh heaven, sending first-hand reports back to the *Melody Maker* and through the BBC reaching millions of listeners to 'The World of Jazz'. Suddenly he found himself in prison. His visitor's permit had expired on Christmas Day and he was arrested as he tried to renew it on 29 December. He was denied bail and treated like a common criminal. Dr Edmond Souchon, the president of the New Orleans Jazz Club was extremely vexed at this uncompromising attitude from the authorities. The truth was that some of these authorities were glad to get Colyer out of the limelight; he was causing too much of a stir – a white musician playing with black bands who looked as if he was about to take up permanent residence. Colyer's association with Dr Souchon could have stimulated his interest in skiffle, for as a young lad Dr Souchon had played in a skiffle band.

When Colyer eventually returned to the UK he was hailed as a folk hero. His reputation enhanced by his imprisonment in the New Orleans jail, he was welcomed back to a ready-made band that included Chris Barber, Monty Sunshine and Lonnie Donegan. This band originally had the 17-year-old Pat Halcox on trumpet. However, Halcox could not turn professional like the rest of the band because of scholastic commitments, so Colyer stepped in.

The band built up a fantastic following playing in such venues as the Bryanston Street Jazz Club, held in the basement of a church near Marble Arch. In late 1953 they recorded some tracks in Copenhagen for Storyville Records. These were not issued in this country until 1993 on the Bear Family Records compilation of Lonnie Donegan's material *More Than Pye in the Sky*. Colyer and

Donegan duet on 'Midnight Special'. Hearing this today one realises that this was not a very happy marriage of talents. It became plain that all was not well in the band, musical differences surfaced and Colyer left. He then formed his own band including Acker Bilk in the line-up. He also featured the skiffle group with brother Bill Colyer on washboard and a variety of other musicians including Alexis Korner on guitar and mandolin, Bobby Kelly on piano (later to marry Nancy Whiskey); on bass was Jim Bray who was to be replaced by Ron Ward, formerly with the new Crane River Jazz Band that included the first Chas McDevitt Skiffle Group.

With the success of the groups that were recording, the skiffle craze blossomed and groups were formed from Land's End to John o'Groats. Every town could muster a dozen groups; every barrack room, youth club and church hall echoed to the pounding of the washboard.

Most coffee bars, a relatively new phenomenon themselves, played host to the new groups. There was already a tradition of live music in coffee bars. To give the customer the impression of being in Italy or Spain, a guest guitar player would be featured to blend in with the overall decor. At least this provided a change to the ubiquitous muzak newly imported from the USA. The Moulin Rouge in Hanway Street, just off Tottenham Court Road, had a Spanish guitarist, Tony, who would serenade the young shop assistants with 'Arrivederci Roma' while they sipped their espresso coffee. However, he and many other troubadours were gradually ousted by the new skifflers. It would start off so innocently; a young guitar player would ask the manager if he could sing a couple of songs, other friends or the occasional customer would turn up the following night with a guitar and within days another group had been created. This practice continued right into the R&R era; even Cliff Richard took his newly formed group the Drifters into the Freight Train coffee bar to find new fans. And there were fans aplenty, as seen from the number of records sold. To put your record at the top of the hit parade you would need sales of 150,000. Whereas today a sale of 25,000 would guarantee a top place, in 1957 you would barely get into the lower reaches of any chart. The sale of records was also mirrored in the sale of guitars.

At one point in 1957, it was estimated that there were between 30,000 and 50,000 groups in the British Isles. The sale of guitars was booming and it was reported that more music shops than

jewellers were being broken into. Ben Davis, managing director of one of Britain's biggest wholesale and retail firms, commented:

> The demand is so great that no country in the world can hope to keep up with it. Since last September it has increased more than 10 times.
>
> At Christmas people were walking around Charing Cross Road with bunches of notes in their hands looking for guitars. At the moment I have 20,000 on order and wish I could get more. I estimate that this year over 250,000 will be imported into this country, compared with about 6,000 in 1950.

Considering that this all took place almost six years before the big beat era, the popularity of this new music is really put into perspective by such statistics.

Adam Faith described this phenomenon:

> Skiffle hit Britain with all the fury of Asian flu. Everyone went down with it. Anyone who could afford to buy a guitar and learn three chords was in business as a skiffler. It grew in cellars, nice dark cellars, and it shot up like mushrooms.

Although many jazz bands had a skiffle interlude, it was the coffee bar that became the breeding ground for the skiffle groups and this change in venue brought about a change in the music.

Now, by attracting a wider audience, the groups catered for a wider taste in musical content. It was not only the blues and jazz standards that were played but folk songs, calypsos and popular hits, even the newly emerging R&R tunes, all were given the skiffle treatment. Skiffle had again become party music, less serious and more youth orientated than its 1920s ancestor. The popularity of the music warranted the opening up of specialist clubs and these sprung up all over London's West End: notably the Skiffle Cellar, the Princess Louise and the 44 Club in Gerrard Street. Some, like the 44 Club, leaned a little to the left and one was sure to hear a smattering of union or protest songs, particularly those associated with the legendary Woody Guthrie. Others like the Skiffle Cellar, hosted by Russell Quaye and the City Ramblers, favoured the spasm and jug music as created by the original hokum bands. Elsewhere, when no specific club could be found, special skiffle sessions were performed in existing jazz clubs. The Cavern in Liverpool was one such venue, and as is well documented, this became the home of Merseybeat, the phenomenon of the 1960s.

Most of the major groups now had recording contracts and followed Lonnie Donegan into the hit parade. The Vipers, the Chas McDevitt Group with Nancy Whiskey and Johnny Duncan and the Bluegrass Boys all had high chart entries.

A national skiffle competition was started prompting the promotion of thousands of other contests throughout the land. Both radio and television fired the flames of this enthusiasm by jumping on the bandwagon with such shows as 'Saturday Skiffle Club' on the BBC Light Programme and the 'Six-Five Special' on BBC Television.

Straight musicians, who had originally derided this amateur music, now cashed in by forming their own combos or including skiffle in their repertoire. One well-established band leader looked favourably on skiffle and showed considerable foresight. Eric Delaney, ever the showman, not only booked skiffle groups as support to his big band but even played the washboard himself. Instead of the usual thimbles he would place the old-fashioned copper pennies between his fingers – somewhat reminiscent of the knuckledusters used by one or two of the 1920s groups.

In July 1957, Basil and Ivor Kirchin discontinued their big band format in favour of a smaller more lively combo. They realized

Hammersmith Palais, 28 April 1957, Eric Delaney playing washboard with a fistful of pennies.

that the big bands were losing favour with the public: it was years since a big band had featured in the hit parade. Kirchin blamed this falling popularity partly on the attitude of the musicians in the big bands. He pinpointed their presentation:

> They slouch on to the stand, and the way they sit, so bored with it all. Naturally the skifflers and rock and rollers have dethroned the big bands. The impact of seeing musicians suddenly come alive and throbbing with vitality was enormous.
>
> What it amounts to is this: today the public wants to be entertained, and if any form of music wants to flourish, it must do just that. Like skiffle and rock and roll it must be sold.

It was refreshing to hear such views from the hardened professional musician. It was true, the enthusiasm and boundless energy of the skiffle group was soon to acquire the polish and musicianship that was originally lacking, and this would propel it further into the mainstream of entertainment. Still played for fun by the young amateurs, it swiftly developed a showbiz gloss.

The new groups, prompted by Lonnie Donegan's use of a lead guitar, provided work for many a pro musician. Well-respected guitar players like Denny Wright, Bill Bramwell, Jimmie Currie, Diz Disley, Ken Sykora, Bryan Daly, and Neville Skrimshire; bass players like Micky Ashman, Jim Bray, Jack Fallon and Lennie Harrison and notable drummers like Lennie Hastings, Nick Nicholls and Pete Appleby, all lent their talent to the up and coming groups. As the renewed interest in the guitar was such a sudden and unforeseen occurrence, good lead guitar players were like gold dust. However, it was very difficult to tame these guitar players who often wanted to adorn the music with a sophistication it did not require. Nevertheless, whatever complaints one might have had, it cannot be denied that their contribution was invaluable. To hear either Denny Wright or Bill Bramwell in full flight, swinging like mad, was a pleasure not to be missed.

Although some musicians embraced this new music wholeheartedly, or at least as an extra source of income, it was still derided by some professional musicians, who were fearful of redundancy. Critics mocked the nasal noises of the 'three-chord wonders' as mere caterwauling; and even respected names like Humphrey Lyttelton (himself reaping rewards from dues paid by early jazz pioneers) joined the chorus: 'Why was it left to local imitators to reap the harvest sown through the years by popular singers from Frank Crummit to Burl Ives.'

In spite of all these brickbats skiffle remained popular. Jazzers would delight in pooh-poohing the phoney American accents, yet they themselves all tried to sound like Louis Armstrong when singing. And if the trombone sounded like Kid Ory and the clarinet like Johnny Dodds or George Lewis, the more they were esteemed. It wasn't really the phoney accents or the enthusiasm of the skifflers that got their goat, it was their easy path to success.

With this constant sniping from the Establishment, it was a wonder that skiffle hadn't been killed off earlier. Its popularity gradually waning, it survived a while longer, at least long enough to have an impact on future musical trends. In the end its demise was partly of its own making.

The influences that had gone into the melting pot to create skiffle, in the end, swamped it. Donegan, striving to become the all-round entertainer, became more music hall than Mahogany Hall, only returning to his roots in recent years. The McDevitt Group, with the advent of Shirley Douglas, moved more into the mainstream, featuring compositions by Buddy Holly and other R&R artists. The Vipers had changed their style to record such numbers as Eddie Cochran's 'Summertime Blues'. Both Johnny Duncan and Dickie Bishop, who already relied strongly on country and western material, went further in that direction. The

Dickie Bishop Group could lay claim to having been one of the first skiffle groups to feature the electric bass guitar. Quite an avant-garde thing to do. Even Dickie's voice, instead of having the nasal skiffle twang, was in the Elvis Presley mould. Uh, huh, huh!

The popularity of rock and roll was taking over and those groups that did not disband or drift into R&R concentrated on their folk roots and helped establish the folk boom of the early and mid 1960s. Other groups had a profound influence on the rhythm and blues vogue that was to follow. Alexis Korner, Cyril Davies, Long John Baldry, Chris Farlowe and Van Morrison had all experienced playing in a skiffle group.

By October 1962 Lonnie Donegan's last hit record, 'Pick a Bale of Cotton', had dropped out of the charts, just as the Beatles' first hit, 'Love Me Do', was coming in. It was ironical that 'Pick a Bale' by the Vipers was one of the first skiffle songs recorded in 1956 and Donegan's version the last to enter the ratings.

Only Ken Colyer persisted with his original concept. As late as December 1968, when the Beatles were in the charts with such hits as 'Lady Madonna' and 'Hey Jude', Colyer recorded two skiffle songs at a concert in Hamburg University: 'Grey Goose' and 'Take This Hammer'. He was still playing undiluted skiffle. Affection-ately known as the 'Guv'nor', he had eschewed commercial success to stick to his principles. He had lamented:

> I make no bones about it, certain ideals had been lost. I viewed it all with great distaste. I never deviated from my original intentions. Instead of a beautiful scene being created, that was genuine and good, it just didn't work that way. I should have known better than to naively think it would. I was aghast at the way things were all going wrong. Instead of trying to get the true sound, you were left with a pastiche that really had very little to do with the real thing.

But what was 'the real thing'? How did it become so commercial and so popular? To discover this we need to get back to the roots and reveal the influences on the home-bred exponents of the music.

2

Roots

During the 1920s and 1930s, migrant workers had left the southern states in their thousands, seeking work and prosperity in the supposedly more affluent and less racially prejudiced cities of the north – Chicago, Kansas City, St Louis and New York. They carried with them their musical heritage, be it the Mississippi blues, the work song, the barrelhouse ballad or the simple songs they learnt at their father's knee. These migrants tended to stick together in their new environment and in troubled times would rally round to help each other. Rent parties were often organized to help raise a few dollars. Music was an essential part of these events and all the aforementioned musical influences fused to form a unique and lively type of party music. A wealth of household instruments augmented the ever-present piano and guitar – washboard, jug, gut bucket or teachest bass, in fact anything that would provide rhythm and liven up the proceedings was commissioned into service.

Perhaps the most precise description of this music was offered by Paul Oliver in his outstanding book *The Story of the Blues*:

'The parlour social' and the 'struggle', the 'gouge' and the 'percolator', the 'skiffle' and the 'too terrible' party, were all names for the function most commonly termed 'boogie' or 'house rent party'. At the height of the prohibition era these provided a substitute for open saloons, being mounted in back rooms and in 10,000 apartments all over the South Side. The House Rent Party, a Southern custom which was transported with equal effectiveness to

Harlem, was a means of meeting the rent when money was low. Spending the last few dollars on jars of 'moonshine' and 'home brew', the host would engage a piano player, if he wasn't one himself, and throw a party for which admission was a quarter! It was at these parties that Montana Taylor, Romeo Nelson, Dan Burley and scores of other pianists played.

In 1925 Jimmy O'Bryant recorded with his Chicago Skiffle. The name seemed to disappear for a couple of decades only to be revived again in 1946 by Dan Burley and his Skiffle Boys. Burley made his recordings in New York for Rudi Blesh's Circle label. Dan Burley was accompanied by Brownie and Globe-trotter McGhee on guitars and Pops Foster on bass. The process seemed to have gone full circle when, in 1958, Brownie McGhee recorded a version of the McDevitt/Whiskey 1957 hit 'Freight Train'. Dan Burley was a well-known newspaper man who, apart from being editor in chief of *The Amsterdam News*, had written a book in the 1940s entitled *Burley's Handbook of Harlem Jive*. So it is no surprise that he was 'hip' when it came to finding a name for the music he loved to play at Jimmy's Chicken Shack.

In 1928, Paramount issued a record called *Hometown Skiffle*,

Dan Burley, encouraged by Al Rose. (A. Rose)

HOME TOWN SKIFFLE

Here's the record everybody's been waiting for, six of the great Paramount artists on one record - each one playing or singing for you at their big get-together party. Hear how they celebrate by getting this record from your dealer or sending us the coupon.

{ 12806----Hometown Skiffle. Part I and II. Descriptive Novelty featuring Blind Lemon Jefferson, Blind Blake, Will Ezell, Charlie Spand. The Hokum Boys. Papa Charlie Jackson. }

12072 -- Bed Springs Blues, and Yo Yo Blues Vocal guitar acc. Blind Lemon Jefferson

12052 -- Bakershop Blues and Long Distance Moan, Vocal guitar acc. Blind Lemon Jefferson

12792 -- Pony Blues and Bandy Rooster Blues, Vocal. guitar acc.. Charley Patton

12077 -- Pea Vine Blues and Tom Mashan Blues, Vocal, guitar acc., Charley Patton

12078 -- My Lovin' Blues and Weary Heart Blues, Vocal, piano acc., James Wiggins

12060 -- Forty Four Blues and Frisco Bound, Vocal, piano acc., James Wiggins

12002 -- I Was Afraid of That Part 1 and 11, Vocal, piano-guitar acc., The Hokum Boys.

12079 -- Chase 'em Down and Louisiana Glide, Piano Solo, Blind Leroy Garnett.

12075 -- Badcrease Stomp and Some Do and Some Don't, Orchestra, Barrell House Five

SPIRITUALS

12074 -- Take Your Burden to the Lord and Telephone to Glory, Vocal. inst acc., Blind Arthur Groom and Brother.

12217 -- Ezekiel Saw de Wheel and Crying Holy Unto the Lord, Norfolk Jubilee Quartette

The New York Recording Laboratories

SEND NO MONEY: If your dealer is out of the records you want, send us the coupon below Pay postman 75 cents for each record, plus small C. O. D. for when he delivers records. *We pay postage on shipments of two or more records.*

(Note bare feet and prominent display of local newsheet.)
Razzy Dazzy Spasm Band, New Orleans 1897.

Part 1 and 2, a descriptive novelty recording featuring Blind Lemon Jefferson, Blind Blake, Will Ezell, Charlie Spand, the Hokum Boys and Papa Charlie Jackson. Big Bill Broonzy, who was to have such a profound influence on the British skiffle scene, claimed to have been taught the guitar by Charlie Jackson, who played the six-string banjo. The publicity for *Hometown Skiffle* read:

> Here's the record everybody's been waiting for, six of the great Paramount artists on one record, each one playing or singing for you at their big get-together party. Hear how they celebrate by getting this record from your dealer, or sending us this coupon.

Other notable recording artists from that era were: Tampa Red's Hokum Band, the Memphis Jug Band who recorded for RCA Victor and Gus Cannon's Jug Stompers; Cannon was the writer of 'Walk Right In', a top ten hit for the Rooftop Singers in 1963.

In 1897 Emile 'Stalebread Charley' Lacoume (1885–1940) formed a skiffle band of boy performers playing homemade instruments. He called his group the Razzy Dazzy Spasm Band and they performed in the streets of Storyville (from 1897 the red-light district of New Orleans, closed down in 1917 due to its detrimental effect on the navy). Stalebread, though blind, was an active performer in the New Orleans jazz bands of the 1920s and 1930s.

In 1936, Herbert Asbury wrote a book about New Orleans, *The French Quarter*, described on its cover as: 'A gay account of the most sinful section of New Orleans when it was considered "The Wickedest City in the World".'

Asbury includes a reference to Lacoume's spasm band and lists the personnel of the band as:

> Willie Bussey, better known as Cajun, harmonica; Charley Stein, who manipulated an old kettle, a cowbell, a gourd filled with pebbles, and other traps and in later life became a famous drummer; Chinee, who smote the bull fiddle, at first, half a barrel and later a coffin-shaped contraption built by the boys; Warm Gravy; Emile Benrod, called Whisky, and Frank Bussey, known as Monk.

It's amusing to note that there was a 'Whisky' in one of the original skiffle groups, and with the Scottish spelling!

In his book *I Remember Jazz*, Al Rose recalls interviewing Lacoume in 1938 when he was in his early 50s. Asking him about the claims that others often made that he had been the originator of jazz, Lacoume said:

> Me? Not me! We had this little spasm band – you know – most all homemade instruments. We were really lousy but we had good rhythm – just kids, you know. I guess I was ten, twelve years old. We played around in the district and people used to throw us money. Even them whores. Sarah Bernhardt – you know – the French actress – she come by an' give us a dime. The whores tipped better than that.
>
> There was plenty kids before us done that. We copied off somebody, I don't remember who. We didn't make up all the dirty songs, neither. We heard 'em in the streets an' we sang 'em in the streets. Now they say we invented jazz. Ain't nobody invented that music.
>
> Later on I really became a musician. Played for a livin'! I never knew no music, but I worked playin' the guitar . . . We played for fun, y'see.

So Emile 'Stalebread' Lacoume may not have invented jazz, but it is obvious that he certainly played a form of skiffle on the streets of New Orleans one hundred years ago.

It was Bill Colyer who was credited with suggesting that the group featured inside the Colyer, Barber, Donegan set-up be called 'skiffle'. Bill worked in Collett's book shop. Being fairly left wing they catered for their customers by including records that had a folksy and radical association, and jazz came into this category. They also had a special allocation of foreign currency, particularly dollars, that enabled them to import records with ease. Consequently Bill had access to many recordings of the early bands, notably Dan Burley and his Skiffle Boys. Originally Bill and Ken had called the inner group the Breakdown Band.

Micky Ashman, who later played bass with Humphrey Lyttelton and Lonnie Donegan, had bought the Burley record in Switzerland in 1949 because it featured Pops Foster on bass. The Lyttelton band included Barrelhouse as part of their repertoire, so maybe Ashman can claim to have introduced the record over here, but there is no doubt that Colyer was the first to use the epithet commercially in the UK. Although when referring to Colyer, the word commercial doesn't readily spring to mind.

Collins English Dictionary defines skiffle as 'a drizzle', like 'a skiffle of rain', often used in the Ulster dialect, which in turn probably comes from the Scottish word 'skiff', to move lightly.

In Eric Partridge's *Dictionary of Slang* skiffle is defined as: 'A great hurry; among tailors, a job to be done in a hurry.' Not a musical expression, but very close to describing the treatment songs were given when 'skiffled' by the 1950s groups.

However, the actual musical influences were much more varied than the 1920s skiffle and jug bands. Something else must have provided the catalyst.

In the early 1950s, James C. Petrillo, the president of the American Federation of Musicians, was in dispute with the Musicians' Union in Britain. Consequently no American musicians were permitted to play in the UK if supported by British union bands. The British public was starved of American jazz and blues musicians. Getting round these restrictions would provide Lonnie Donegan with a springboard to success, but more of this later. In 1954, the *Melody Maker* organized an excursion to Dublin by rail to hear the Woody Herman Band. The cost was 17s. 6d. or in today's coinage, 87p. The boat-train was packed and the audience filled the Theatre Royal in Dublin, demonstrating their delight at being able to hear American musicians in the flesh.

Television was in its infancy and one seldom heard Afro-American music on the radio. With a bit of luck you might catch the Dukes of Dixieland or the drummer Preacher Rollo and the Five Saints on Radio Hilversum or the American Forces Network from Germany, being sure to mark the spot on the plastic dial of your bakelite 'wireless' with one of those newfangled biros. Only on rare occasions would you hear the blues. Soon it began to change. The BBC started to air programmes on American folk and blues, sanitized and acceptable to white audiences, but at least it was a breakthrough. Most of the skiffle groups acknowledge this source as inspiration for their interest in the music, and most cite Josh White and Burl Ives as being their initial influences. Both had developed a pleasing, refined, commercial style, and both were featured on the BBC and in concert and cabaret throughout the land.

Josh White

Born on 11 February 1908 in Greenville, South Carolina, Josh was already on the road before his tenth birthday, acting as the eyes for a local blind singer. Over the next decade, Josh acted in a similar capacity for such blues giants as Blind Lemon Jefferson,

Josh White, 1951.

Blind Blake, Blind Willie Johnson and many other itinerant musicians. He gradually picked up much of their guitar technique, eventually recording in his own right, sometimes using the pseudonyms Pinewood Tom or the Singing Christian, and specializing in spirituals and sacred songs.

In the 1930s he moved to New York and played the club circuit, almost becoming a fixture at the uptown night club, Café Society. He appeared in Broadway plays and concerts and as a result his style became very smooth and sophisticated. On 4 March 1941, Josh and Lead Belly were on Alan Lomax's radio show, 'American School of the Air'. On 4 June, he appeared in concert at the Town Hall in NYC with both Lead Belly and Burl Ives. In 1946 Brunswick issued Josh White's US Decca recordings in the UK, 'House of the Rising Sun' and 'Strange Fruit'. In 1951, he was in London, broadcasting for the BBC.

It was at this point that his music reached the ears of many a future skiffler. 'St James Infirmary Blues', 'Miss Otis Regrets' and his signature tune, 'Wanderin'', were all well aired. His more controversial 'Strange Fruit' didn't get the same exposure. 'Wanderin'' bears a marked similarity to 'I'll Never Fall In Love

Again' written by Lonnie Donegan for Tom Jones. It was during this visit that he was seen by Wally Whyton at the Shepherd's Bush Empire. Wally recalls the knack Josh had of intentionally breaking a string in mid-song, changing it, tuning it and discarding the old string, without missing a beat.

On 30 January 1956, Josh White recorded some tracks for Nixa with a jazz line-up and on 31 January he recorded such skiffle favourites as 'Careless Love', 'St Louis Blues' and 'Goodmornin' Blues'. Phil Seaman was on drums and on bass the ubiquitous Jack Fallon, later to be featured with Johnny Duncan's Bluegrass Boys, and more recently with the Chas McDevitt Skiffle Group.

Although Josh had recorded and broadcast prolifically in the UK in the early 1950s it was the arrival of Big Bill Broonzy in 1951 that was to introduce the public to the down-home blues of the Mississippi and the house-rent stomps of Chicago. Broonzy's style and delivery were to provide the bridge between the sophisticated offerings of Lonnie Johnson and Josh White and the earthier performances of Muddy Waters and Bo Diddley in the later years of the decade.

Big Bill Broonzy

William Lee Conley Broonzy was born 26 June 1893 in Scott, Mississippi. While still a child, he moved to Arkansas, where in the 1950s he was to have his own farm. He was born a twin, one of 21 children, of whom only 16 survived their childhood. At the age of 10 Bill had already made, for himself and his friend Louis Carter, a cigar-box fiddle and a guitar made from packing cases. They began playing at picnics and before too long they were given real instruments. For a while Bill became a preacher but after four years he realized that he could earn more money by playing the guitar.

From 1917 until 1919, Bill was in the army. On his discharge he concentrated more on his music and by 1923 had recorded 'House Rent Stomp' for Mayo Williams. He recorded this again for Lester Melrose in Chicago in 1928 and included it in his first session for Vogue Records in Paris on his European tour in 1951. Throughout the 1920s and 1930s Bill appeared with many a hokum or goodtime band. Never strictly bound by the Mississippi blues style of guitar playing, he can be truly classified as one of

Big Bill Broonzy, 1957.

the innovators of the Chicago style. His guitar licks can still be recognized in the playing of today's young lions of the blues guitar. In New York in 1932, as Big Bill and the Jug Busters, he recorded 'Long Tall Mama' and 'M and O Blues', the line-up including washboard and two jugs. The early 1940s saw him recording many tracks for Okeh Records that included, on washboard, his half brother Washboard Sam and, on piano, either Big Maceo Merriweather, Memphis Slim or Blind John Davis.

By day working as a yardman for the Pullman Company in Chicago, in the evenings Bill would play for parties, dances and occasionally the theatre. In December 1938 he was brought to New York to sing in the Carnegie Hall concert Spirituals to Swing, promoted by John Hammond. Big Bill had been booked to replace the legendary blues man, Robert Johnson, who had been poisoned by a jealous husband and who had died earlier that year in Greenswood, Mississippi. John Hammond recalls in his autobiography, *John Hammond on Record*:

> Big Bill Broonzy sang with the backing of Albert Ammons on piano, Jo Jones on drums and Walter Page on bass. Backstage, Bill happened to mention to the stage manager Goddard Lieberson that he'd always disliked Chicago. 'But you're not in Chicago,' Goddard explained soothingly, 'This is New York.' Bill, who farmed in Arkansas with a couple of mules, shuffled out and sang about a dream he'd had in which he sat in President Roosevelt's chair in the White House. The audience screamed. It had never heard anything like this.

After the success of this performance he appeared for over two years at New York's Café Society where he came into contact with both Josh White and Sonny Terry.

By 1951 Broonzy's reputation had reached this side of the Atlantic and the French jazz critic and record producer, Hugues Panassié brought him over for a European tour. On Saturday 22 September 1951, Bill made his first solo appearance at the Kingsway Hall in London, on some numbers being accompanied by Roy Sturgess on piano, George Hopkinson on drums and Brillo Ford on bass. He was back again on Sunday 2 January 1952 at the Cambridge Theatre, supported by the Crane River Jazz Band (without Ken Colyer) and on Sunday 2 November 1952, supported by the Christie Brothers Stompers. From these concerts he built up a firm following and his records sold well. He became a regular visitor to these shores coming over in 1955 and in 1957, at the height of the skiffle craze.

A measure of Bill's popularity can be gauged by the two benefit concerts held on his behalf when he was in poor health. On 9 March 1959, the first ever benefit concert for an American musician was held in England at the Coliseum Theatre in St Martin's Lane. Bill needed financial support to help with hospital bills and to pay for the treatment he was receiving for his lung cancer. 'Help Bill sing again!' was the cry.

As Alan Lomax had said, 'Bill had that rooster crow in his voice,' and it was sorely missed.

Broonzy's first UK concert. Note Robert Brown's (Washboard Sam) address.

Broonzy Benefit Poster

The leading jazz bands and four skiffle groups donated their services free and countless offers to appear were turned down because of limited time. All this was to no avail, Bill died shortly after these tributes, leaving a treasure chest of recordings that in its own way would shape the future.

Apart from Bill's recordings his charisma had a great influence on his popularity. Jack Hutton wrote in the *Melody Maker* of 16 March 1957:

> Bill, disdainful of the bounding energy and slick appearance gimmicks adopted by successful skifflers, stood there in his street clothes singing and playing and allowed his natural charm to work on the audience.

His obvious joy in delivering a song with both swing and feeling made him magic to behold. His choice of material was never limited to just the blues, incorporating as it did both guitar rags and pop tunes such as 'The Glory Of Love' and 'When Did You Leave Heaven'. The skiffle fan could not have wished for a better role model.

In his autobiography, *Big Bill Blues*, as told to Yannick Bruynoghe in 1955, Bill says:

> But when you write about me, please don't say I'm a jazz musician. Don't say I'm a musician or a guitar player – just write Big Bill was a well-known blues singer and player and has recorded 260 blues songs from 1925 up until 1952; he was a happy man when drunk and playing with women; he was liked by all the blues singers, some would get a little jealous sometimes but Bill would buy a bottle of whisky and they would start laughing and playing again; Big Bill would get drunk and slip off from the party and go home to sleep.

Lonnie Johnson

Big Bill Broonzy was not the only visiting blues guitarist to register with the British in the early 1950s. One cannot help acknowledging the influence exerted by Lonnie Johnson.

Born in New Orleans on 8 February 1889 into a large and musical family, Lonnie worked in a lumber yard but from a very

Lonnie Johnson

early age he was able to play a variety of instruments including guitar and violin. In 1917, he visited the UK in a revue to entertain the US troops. That same year the epidemic of influenza hit the USA and virtually wiped out his whole family. In New Orleans alone on some days there were as many as 100 deaths. Disillusioned he left the Crescent City and drifted on through Texas to St Louis and Chicago. In Texas, he provided the guitar accompaniment for Alger 'Texas' Alexander, a blues singer, straight from the hollering and moaning tradition of country blues that had been honed and shaped by many a penitentiary and chain gang. It was to Lonnie's credit that he was able to adapt his smooth guitar style to such rough and ready interpretations. Years later he was equally at home playing with the jazz guitarist Eddie Lang, a much more sophisticated musician. For a while Lonnie played on the river-boat *St Paul* out of St Louis with Charlie Creath's band.

In 1925, he was persuaded to enter a blues contest at the Booker T. Washington theatre in St Louis. The winner was guaranteed a recording contract for Okeh Records. Lonnie won and remained with Okeh for seven years; during the first two years Okeh issued a record every six weeks. He thrived not only as a performer but also as an accompanist. His diction was precise and his style very laid back and silky smooth. Although a blues singer he was not a blues shouter and brought a certain sophistication to the country blues style.

His second visit to the UK in 1952 was to have a profound effect on the music of the mid 1950s.

Starved of visiting American artists by the MU ban, the public eagerly sought out any concert that was able to bend the rules. One such show took place at the Royal Festival Hall on Saturday 28 June 1952. The promoters had hit on the idea of booking non-union bands as support thereby avoiding a head-on clash with the union. Happily one of the bands was the Tony Donegan jazz band and in the excitement of the moment Tony was introduced as Lonnie Donegan and the name stuck. In the audience that night was Chas McDevitt who remembers Donegan resplendent in his yellow band shirt, coming to the front mike with his banjo to sing the hymn 'Sweet Heart of Jesus'. But without doubt it was the genuine Lonnie Johnson that was the star of the show and he left a lasting impression on Donegan and the whole audience. Once again an American blues guitarist had made an impact and popularized the guitar at an important crossroads in time.

Following an accident and a stroke, Lonnie Johnson died in 1970 leaving a legacy of stylish guitar playing and a song bag of mellow, almost ballad style, blues.

Josh White, Big Bill Broonzy, Lonnie Johnson and to a lesser extent the records of Tampa Red, Hudson 'Tampa Red' Whittaker (1902–81), and those records by Muddy Waters (McKinley Morganfield) which one could obtain but with great difficulty – all these had their effect on the British musicians and opened up their minds and hearts to the earlier and more obscure artists. One man above all others had the most profound influence and strictly he was more of a folk singer than a blues singer. This giant of a man was the great Lead Belly.

Lead Belly

Lead Belly, arguably the greatest American folk singer, song collector and composer of the twentieth century, was born on 29 January 1889 in Mooringsport, Louisiana. Hudson (Huddie)

Leadbetter was the only son born to Sallie and Wesley Leadbetter.

Lead Belly was a colourful but violent man whose early years were in marked contrast to the life he found after being discovered in 1934 by John A. Lomax and his son Alan.

From an early age he was always on the move; from Mooringsport to Leigh in Texas, from his period in Angola prison to New York, Canada and France. From 1916 to 1918, as Walter Boyd, Lead Belly farmed and worked horses in north-east Texas. He was an enthusiastic horseman and often rode around on his ebony horse, Booker, which was reputed to have four white-stocking feet and a star on its forehead. Many of his songs had a cowboy feel about them. 'Western Plains' opens with, 'When I was a cowboy way out on the western plains.'

Lead Belly also acted as guide to Blind Lemon Jefferson. They travelled mainly by train, but it was difficult and dangerous for Blind Lemon to hop freight trains, so in 1914 they got a second-hand Ford. Years later, Studs Terkel recalls that Lead Belly drove a car, 'Like a tractor, zig zagging at 80mph with one hand on the wheel.'

In 1948, Lead Belly wrote 'Relax Your Mind', based on driving etiquette, hoping that a safe driving organization might adopt it as a theme.

A third of his life was spent in one jail or another: between the ages of 25 and 50 he was incarcerated in three separate prisons for a total of 13 years. On 29 June 1918 he was indicted for the murder of Will Stafford, who was married to his cousin Mary Pig Walker. He escaped but was recaptured after three days. Although he pleaded not guilty, after a speedy trial, in the name of Walter Boyd, he was sentenced to 20 years for murder. On 1 April he escaped again and running from the dogs he even tried to drown himself rather than surrender. Tried again for the escape, he was sentenced to a total of 35 years' hard labour.

On 7 January, escorted by Bud Russell, the legendary ('Midnight Special') Texas convict transporter, he was taken to Captain Francis at Shaw State Farm. On 16 January 1925, after serving six years, seven months and three days, he was pardoned by the Texas Governor Pat Neff. Between 1925 and 1928 he sang at nights in Houston's Third Ward bars and Oil City clubs and even at Sunday fish fries for the oil roustabouts. During the day he worked in Houston at the Buick agency and sometimes drove a truck for Gulf Gas.

In 1928, he killed a black man, shooting him five times; he

Bunk Johnson and Lead Belly, New York Town Hall Concert.
(Gottlieb/Redferns)

pleaded self-defence and was not charged. On 1 January 1930, he fought at a Salvation Army band concert held on a store porch in Mooringsport. He was alleged to have 'Resented the efforts of a white man to prevent his dancing on the streets of Mooringsport whilst a Salvation Army religious service was in progress.'

He was jailed on assault with intent to murder a certain Jack Elliott, who was, 'Severely cut on the arm.'

Elliott, was 'a splendid white citizen of Mooringsport', who was at home when attacked by 'the drink-crazed Negro'.

On 18 February 1930, he was sentenced by the Judge T. F. Bell to Angola State Farm for six to ten years.

John A. Lomax and his son Alan toured the American continent in 1933–4 collecting folk songs for the Archive of American Folksong in the Library of Congress. Rather than go into the barrelhouses and bars to record the blues, they toured the countryside using their primitive recording machine in work camps and prisons. They wanted to capture the pure unadulterated folk tune rather than the popular songs prevalent in the bars.

Many of their subjects used *noms de guerre* that were as colourful as their backgrounds – 'Iron Head', 'Bow Legs' and 'Clear Rock', to name a few. The Lomaxes recorded Lead Belly and were instrumental in persuading the governor to release him. Lead Belly claimed that it was because of a song he had written pleading with the governor to set him free. On his release he worked for the Lomaxes as a chauffeur and musical adviser. He recorded prolifically for the Library of Congress Archive. Over 900 songs were taped and he virtually established Folkways Records by his prodigious output.

Lead Belly travelled extensively, performing in 25 states. Through his concerts in the theatre and college campuses and his appearances in clubs, particularly the Village Vanguard in New York, he created a new and enthusiastic audience for his art. He broadcast and recorded with the famous Golden Gate Quartet and played concerts with Josh White, Burl Ives and, in Chicago, with Woody Guthrie, another profound influence on the skiffle groups of the 1950s. He was a friend of Big Bill Broonzy, who even dedicated a song he wrote and recorded to Lead Belly's wife, 'Martha'.

In May 1949 Lead Belly undertook a European tour, appearing in Paris with Bill Dillard who accompanied him on trumpet and vocal chorus. The tour had to be curtailed because a deadly paralysis was overtaking Lead Belly. He died of ALS (Lou Gehrig's Disease) on 6 December 1949 in New York and was laid to rest beneath a big oak tree in the graveyard of Shiloh Baptist Church, just south and west of Mooringsport where he was born. He died a poor man, his head and body scarred by his knife wounds. Yet within six months of his death his songs were selling by their millions.

His love of women and his fast and violent life may have lead him off the straight and narrow, but without doubt his experiences will have contributed to his legacy of song. He may not have composed all the songs attributed to him but he collected hundreds and recorded them for posterity. He was a master of the 12-string guitar, a Stella, and also played mandolin, concertina and piano.

His original compositions included 'Goodnight Irene', 'Cotton-fields', 'Bourgeois Blues' and 'Goodmornin' Blues'. Nevertheless he recorded other songs he had heard throughout his life and these too became popular with the skiffle groups. Here's a short list:

'Frankie and Albert' July 1933 'Frankie and Johnny', most likely an old minstrel song.
'Have a Whiff on Me' July 1933 'Take a Drink on Me', recorded on 27 July 1927 by the white string band, Charlie Poole and the North Carolina Ramblers.
'Midnight Special' July 1934, an old traditional song.
'Alabama Bound' 21 January 1935, written by Jelly Roll Morton in 1905.

'John Hardy' 23 August 1940, collected by the Carter Family and recorded in 1928.

'John Henry' 23 August 1940, was a traditional blues song.

'How Long Blues' 1940, one of the pianist, Le Roy Carr's, original compositions.

'Diggin' My Potatoes' June 1946, written and recorded by Washboard Sam, 1939.

'Careless Love' September 1948, an old blues that Lead Belly said was first recorded by Blind Lemon Jefferson.

Other songs recorded by Lead Belly that became skiffle anthems were:

'The Rock Island Line'	'On a Monday'
'Ol' Riley'	'Bring a Little Water Sylvie'
'Green Corn'	'Julie Ann Johnson'

According to the Lomaxes, Lead Belly learned 'Poor Howard' at the age of 14, from 'two young courting fellows'.

Some songs recorded by Lead Belly were notated from versions collected by the Lomaxes from other prisoners. 'Iron Head' (James Baker) in jail for life and not eligible for reprieve or pardon, as he was classed as an 'habitual criminal', contributed 'Grey Goose' and 'Yellow Girl'. He had learned the song from an older prisoner, also a lifer in the Texas State Penitentiary. The songs were obviously a product from the days of slavery and were kept alive by such lifers. The Lomaxes had heard 'Alabama Bound' sung by 'Bowlegs', a prisoner on Parchman's Farm, Mississippi, and they said that they had heard 'Pick a Bale of Cotton' shouted out by 'Clear Rock', a seventy-year-old water boy on the Central State Farm, near Sugarland, Texas.

In any event all these fascinating recordings by Lead Belly were accessible to all at the Library of Congress. Lonnie Donegan, Wally Whyton and Chas McDevitt all explored this source of material; Lonnie even confesses to having purloined a record from the archives, recorded in the field by Lomax featuring the country blues singer McKinley Morganfield. Morganfield had records released in the UK in 1955 using his childhood nickname Muddy Waters. He was soon to reach worldwide acclaim as the darling of the rhythm and blues aficionado.

Also readily available from the same source were the books written by the Lomaxes that covered the whole field of American indigenous music, from cowboy songs to jazz. Their prodigious works like *Best Loved American Folksongs* and other collections, such as *Negro Songs as sung by Lead Belly*, were like manna from heaven to the skiffler trying to increase his repertoire.

An amusing device that can be used to see just how much Lead Belly influenced skiffle, and Lonnie Donegan in particular, is to play a Lead Belly 33 rpm record at 45 rpm or a Lonnie Donegan 45 rpm at 33 rpm. They almost sound identical.

Lead Belly's impact on the twentieth century can also be gauged by the fact that nearly 50 years after his death there still thrives a Lead Belly Society with a large international membership which exists specifically to appreciate and celebrate the music of this colossus.

Burl Ives

Burl Icle Ivanhoe Ives was born 14 June 1909 in Hunt Township, Jasper County, Illinois. From a very early age he was singing professionally; even as a child he had quite a reputation as an evangelist and he and his sister often performed at revivalist meetings. In the middle of his studies at the Eastern Illinois State Teachers College in Charleston, Burl decided that, for a while at least, he'd had enough of the academic life. He took to the road, in the middle of a lecture. As he said in his autobiography *The Wayfaring Stranger*:

> I went to my room and packed a change of clothes, got my banjo, and started walking down the road. I became a 'wayfaring minstrel'.
>
> There's an old joke that says a tramp is a tramp, but a hobo is a tourist without funds. That's what I was.

For a couple of years he toured the logging camps and steel mills, all the time performing and collecting songs for his repertoire. He returned to his studies for a while but still carried on singing in local bars. In 1933 he went to New York to study at the university, still trying to make it as a folk singer. He began to get recognition as an actor and appeared in numerous plays. All the while his reputation as a singer was increasing and eventually he held down a prolonged residency at New York's Village Vanguard. It was around this time that he came across the other folk singers who were also to have such a profound influence on the skiffle craze.

I found myself in that first group of folk singers along with Lead Belly and Josh White and the rest. What stands out to me from that era is the emergence of, say, Josh White. He'd make the hair stand up on the back of your neck; he was so exciting and vital and new. Well, not new, but the interpretation was.

Soon I was playing benefits of various kinds with my colleagues in the renaissance of American folk music; Alan Lomax, Josh White, Lead Belly, Earl Robinson, Woody Guthrie, the Golden Gate Quartet, and others.

In 1940 Burl hosted his own radio show 'The Wayfaring Stranger', a major factor in popularizing his songs.

In 1944, after a spell in the army during the Second World War, from April 1942 till the end of 1943, he opened at the Café Society Uptown and later that year he received rave reviews for his performance on Broadway in *Sing Out Sweet Land*. His renditions of 'Big Rock Candy Mountain' and 'Blue Tail Fly' earned him an award as the best supporting actor of the season.

In 1948 and 1949 he had international hits with 'Blue Tail Fly', 'Lavender Blue', 'Riders in the Sky' and 'On Top of Old Smokey'. His worldwide appeal prompted him to travel, and in the early 1950s he was a regular visitor to the British Isles. At one point after his theatre and concert appearances he would play a late-night cabaret spot in the Royal Court Theatre Cabaret Club in Sloane Square, Chelsea, run by Clement Freud, long before his reincarnation as an MP or even as a TV cooking guru.

Back in 1944, with an all star folk group, the Union Boys, including Pete Seeger, Josh White, Alan Lomax, Brownie McGhee and Sonny Terry, he recorded some overtly political material. Such songs as 'All of You Fascists Bound to Lose', 'Jim Crow' and 'Solidarity Forever' became a stumbling block for him in later years. He was thought to be a communist in the days of the McCarthy witch-hunts and, to safeguard his career, he appeared voluntarily before a Senate subcommittee investigating the enter-tainment industry. He didn't endear himself to his fellow folk singers; many were political activists who resented this right-wing conspiracy. He even implicated other folk singers when disavowing his association with communism at the investigation in May 1952.

In the end, however, this did not affect his career and he went on to even greater success in the theatre and on record. His portrayal of Big Daddy in Elia Kazan's *Cat on a Hot Tin Roof* and his international hit record of 'Little Bitty Tear' alone would establish him as a major force in the field of entertainment.

Apart from his broadcasts in the UK and his many folk records, he also published collections of his own material that was eagerly sought by the newly created guitar-playing public. Rather than the songs he sang, it was the laid-back way he had of playing the guitar that influenced the skiffle fans. He made it look so easy and encouraged hundreds of youngsters to follow suit. He recognized that such people as Lead Belly and Woody Guthrie had the key to the art of writing folk material and said of Guthrie:

> Very few people can write as well as he did, adding to the tradition. What a great talent. It's too bad that he didn't live longer and continue to develop. He was an innately creative talent. Some of the other fellows could sing and perform, but Woody had the gift of being able to create.

Burl Ives (Bear Family coll.)

Woody Guthrie

MOTLEY 4,000 BEGIN H-BOMB PROCESSION – so read the rather derisive report in the *Daily Telegraph* on 5 April 1958. The newspaper was covering the 50-mile march by protesters from Trafalgar Square to the Atomic Research Establishment at Aldermaston in Berkshire. The report continued:

> From Trafalgar Square to the first halt, the Albert Memorial, marchers were supposed to remain silent. But they laughed, talked and 'skiffled' their way along.

The chances were 100 to one that they were singing a Woody Guthrie song. Woody Guthrie had a profound impact on the skiffle generation. His songs reflected the political ideals of many a left-wing intellectual and were gleaned from an almost bottomless song bag.

Woodrow Wilson Guthrie was born on 14 July 1912 in Okema, Oklahoma. The date, Bastille Day to the French, was a fitting debut for such a character. He took to his wanderings at a very early age, like so many others who were forced by the depression and the frequent dust storms to abandon their homes in Oklahoma. He became a dustbowl refugee and travelled extensively. While touring with a Texas magic show he learnt to play the guitar, touring the migrant labour camps and singing at political rallies and union meetings. He was a prolific writer and was able to express the injustices and inequalities he witnessed in a trenchant manner. Some of his songs have become anthems of our time and no doubt 'This Land Is Your Land' was one of his songs sung on that Aldermaston march.

He moved to Los Angeles where he broadcast regularly. Prior to 1940 he had already recorded titles for the Library of Congress. He met up with Pete Seeger and they formed the Almanac Singers. This in turn encouraged the foundation of the Almanac House, a co-operative in Greenwich Village that became the focal point for the East Coast folk scene.

He appeared for a while in 1942 with Lead Belly, Sonny Terry and Brownie McGhee. On one of these occasions he had allowed Lead Belly to drive his big Pontiac; obviously nobody had warned him about Lead Belly's erratic driving and, sure enough, this resulted in the inevitable crash, albeit a minor one.

In 1943, he published his autobiography *Bound for Glory*. With

Woody Guthrie (Bear Family coll.)

his buddy, Cisco Houston, he enlisted with the US Merchant Navy and stayed on until the end of the Second World War. His enthusiasm for writing continued unabated until the late 1940s when he began to suffer the effects of Huntingdon's Chorea, an hereditary disease of the nerves that is passed on through the female line.

He lingered on for a while but as his reputation grew his health deteriorated and he died on 3 October 1967. He had indeed become a legend in his own lifetime. His songs and vocal style have been passed on by many singers, notably his one-time acolyte, Ramblin' Jack Elliott and, in more recent times, by Bob Dylan, Bruce Springsteen and their disciples.

Jack Elliott, from New York, had befriended Woody in 1949 and often accompanied him on his travels. In the mid 1950s Jack came to Europe and influenced many an aspiring musician with his interpretations of Guthrie's songs. In 1956, four years before his first US album, Topic in the UK issued Jack's mini LP *Woodie [sic] Guthrie's Blues*, the tracks being:

'Talking Columbia Blues'	'Talking Dustbowl Blues'
'1913 Massacre'	'The Ludlow Massacre'
'Hard Travelling'	'Talking Sailor Blues'

It was at this time that he accompanied the City Ramblers on their European trip and recorded with them in Copenhagen. Jack and his wife, June, lived at the Yellow Door, behind Waterloo station. This was virtually an open house, a Mecca for young skifflers; it could almost have been London's answer to Guthrie's Almanac House in New York had it not been for the complete lack of discipline. At the rear of the property was an extension, a sort of outhouse where everyone seemed to meet for a brew and a jaw. Anthony Beauchamp Buquet (Tony Bucket) collected the rents for a while, illegally it now seems; Tony Tolhurst of the Vipers was an erstwhile resident, as was Morris Aggis, now a noted sculptor. Another guest was on permanent unemployment benefit; he had registered as a lion tamer and there was not a great demand for lion tamers . . . It was nothing out of the ordinary to see Jack and his buddy, Derroll Adams, ripping the slats off the plaster walls to kindle the open fire. Apart from such eccentricities, Jack was a master of the flat-picking style of guitar, the envy of many skifflers. A colourful and laid-back artist, his strength was in the performance of a song rather than in its creation.

Guthrie was essentially a lyrical poet although he was still capable of composing strong and memorable tunes. He would often add his lyrics to older folk songs, occasionally adding a chorus of his own. Here is just a short list of the songs he sang, which were favoured by the skiffle groups:

'This Land is Your Land'	'Dead or Alive'
'Gamblin' Man'	'Hard Travelling'

'The Grand Coulee Dam'	'New York Town'
'1913 Massacre'	'Pretty Boy Floyd'
'Talking Columbia Blues'	'Talking Dustbowl Blues'
'Union Maid'	'Times Are Getting Hard Boys'
'So Long It's Been Good To Know You' (his signature tune)	

He borrowed melodies freely: the popular 'This Land Is Your Land' is based on the Carter Family's 'When the World's on Fire'. The Carter Family also contributed a clutch of songs to the skiffler's repertoire: 'My Dixie Darlin', 'Worried Man Blues' and 'Wabash Cannonball'.

With this wealth of excellent material in the Library of Congress Archives, published in books and available on record; with the arrival in the UK of the visiting American artists and their exposure both on record and in broadcasts, the skiffle movement really had the ammunition to explode on to the music scene. And explode it did with thousands of groups taking advantage of its popularity.

However, only four leading groups achieved hit parade success and only two registered in the USA. Nevertheless, chart success was never the over-riding impetus. Many groups, both recording and non-recording, had an almost cult following. Skiffle was a way of letting loose; very often it released the performers from their shyness, it was a way of getting involved, of creating music and happiness for oneself and for anyone else who would care to listen or join in. It aroused an interest in music and the arts that might well have remained dormant in the average man in the street. It created the guitar-playing teenagers who would become the stars of 1960s beat-music scene. Without these beginnings there may never have been an Eric Clapton, a Pink Floyd or a Led Zeppelin.

PART TWO
The Explosion

3
Recording Groups

Avon Cities Skiffle Group
with Ray Bush

Ray Bush and the Avon Cities Skiffle Group were an integral part of the Avon Cities Jazz Band. The band was formed in 1949 when the jazz revival was just beginning to gather momentum. In London, trad bands were already playing regularly in a few West End clubs. The provinces were as yet uninterested in the jazz movement.

Until the Avon Cities band took shape, this was also the case in Bristol. After a few rehearsals, the band made its debut at the local arts ball.

In April 1950 they made their first visit to London to take part in the NFJO National Jazz Band Contest at the Empress Hall, surprising everybody, including themselves, by coming second out of 23 entrants. One outcome of this was that the band signed to Decca Records and soon made their first 10-inch LP for Tempo.

In 1956, they began to feature the skiffle group, which included four of the original founder members of the band plus Wayne Chandler on banjo and guitar. Wayne eventually left the band in September 1957 to join the Terry Lightfoot Jazz Band, replacing Hugh Raney who had been called up for National Service only two weeks after he himself had joined the band.

In April 1957, the skiffle group and jazz band were featured in the first big skiffle session at the Royal Festival Hall. In the massed finale, 'Mama Don't Allow', the jazz band supplied the anchor for all the wayward skiffle groups present. In the two renditions of the song they first featured trumpet and then trombone, making a pleasant contrast to the skiffle instruments. They were also on hand to play a stirring version of the National Anthem, something that would have been beyond the scope of the average skiffle group.

The four original members were Michael Hitchings on mandolin, trombone and soprano sax; Basil Wright on drums and washboard; Geoff Nichols on trumpet and double bass (trombone for a while after his demob in 1953) and Ray Bush, the lead singer with the skiffle group. Ray had taken up clarinet at the age of 18 and, when his National Service took him to London, he visited many jazz clubs, even sitting in with the young Ken Colyer before he had formed the Crane River Jazz Band in 1949. Ray joined the Avon Cities on his demob in 1949.

While on holiday in Spain in 1954, Ray had bought a guitar. Initially the skiffle group was formed for the band's own amusement, but it became an immediate success with the public.

The group's style and performance was slick and swinging, obviously a spin-off from the discipline found in the jazz band. A couple of their Tempo recordings have become classics of their genre: 'Green Corn' and 'This Little Light of Mine' stand out in the crowd. Possibly because Tempo was regarded as a minor label, Decca never really plugged their wares, consequently Ray Bush and the Avon Cities Skiffle Group never got the distribution and recognition their talent deserved.

Jan Ridd on piano and Malcolm Wright, Basil's brother, on bass, together with vocalist, Pam Coster, were the other members of the jazz band. Although Pam sang such skiffle titles as 'Long Gone, Lost John', 'Ace in the Hole' and 'Salty Dog', she never recorded with the skiffle group.

The new generation of the Avon Cities Jazz Band is still going strong to this day, though without the skiffle group. Ray Bush is living in the USA near Palm Springs and is still playing clarinet as well as a mean blues harmonica. With this instrument he causes considerable interest and argument. He does not play in the accepted blues inversion style but uses the natural style, i.e. he blows a tune in the key of G on a G harmonica. With this method he confounds all the pundits by still being able to blend

Avon Cities with Ray Bush. (M. Bevan)

First major Skiffle Concert.

the notes. Mike Bevan, the group's manager in their heyday, was described as 'the band's sternest critic and yet its most loyal supporter'. Today he is retired, but still retains his membership card (No. 134) to the Russell Quaye Skiffle Cellar. When Ray visited the UK in the spring of 1997, he teamed up with the original front-line musicians of Avon Cities Jazz Band for nostalgic shows. Together with Mike he was able to trace some obscure recordings by the skiffle group to be released on a Rollercoaster skiffle compilation.

Chris Barber Skiffle Group

Born in Welwyn Garden City, Herts, on 17 April 1930, Donald Christopher Barber originally played the violin and soprano saxophone. He later concentrated on the double bass and trombone when studying at the Guildhall School of Music. As a teenager he played in the bands of Doug Whitton and Cy Laurie, forming his own band in 1949.

In 1953, his current band, minus trumpeter, Pat Halcox, busy with his studies, was taken over by Ken Colyer on his return from his celebrated sojourn in New Orleans. Some skiffle tracks were recorded for the Danish Storyville label during this period, but they were not issued until 1993 by the Bear Family label in their monumental eight-CD boxed set of Lonnie Donegan's material, entitled *More than Pye in the Sky*. The band continued as the Chris Barber Band after Colyer had departed in a haze of musical discontent.

The policy of including skiffle in the programme started during Colyer's reign as leader and was carried on, with Lonnie Donegan, Chris and sometimes Ottilie Patterson, taking the vocals. Chris abandoned his trombone in favour of the double bass when playing with the skiffle group.

During the recording of the 10-inch Decca LP *New Orleans Joys*, two tracks, 'Rock Island Line' and 'John Henry' were devoted to skiffle; featuring Chris on bass, Beryl Bryden on washboard and Lonnie on guitar and vocals. As defined in the opening paragraphs, this became a worldwide hit and Lonnie left to promote the record in America. Dickie Bishop took over the empty banjo chair, and before long he was joined by Johnny Duncan. Together, as the Chris Barber Skiffle Group, they recorded four tracks for the Pye-Nixa label on 14 September 1956:

Chris Barber LP featuring 'Rock Island Line'.

'Can't You Line 'Em'	'Doin' My Time'
'Where Could I Go'	'Gypsy Davy'

Although not obvious hits, these four recordings are regarded as classics of their genre.

With the ever-increasing success of Donegan and the anticipated rewards of a solo career, both Bishop and Duncan left to form their own groups. Barber abandoned the skiffle format but continued to feature great American blues singers with his band. Over the years, Big Bill Broonzy, Sister Rosetta Sharpe, Sonny Terry and Brownie McGhee, Muddy Waters and Louis Jordan have all been a featured attraction.

In 1958, when Chris introduced Sonny and Brownie to British audiences he said: 'In our skiffle groups we tried to play the folk music of the American Negro. Here are two of the great blues and folk artists who actually created the music we were attempting.'

Chris Barber and Brownie Mcghee. (M. Sharratt/C. McD)

February 1959 saw Chris Barber with a worldwide million-selling record. The Sidney Bechet composition 'Petite Fleur' was a vehicle for Monty Sunshine's mellifluous clarinet; Chris was not even on the track.

Recent years have seen the Barber band combining, to their mutual benefit, with the legendary Dr John (Mac Rebennack), the New Orleans blues piano professor.

Recreating the original skiffle group, in 1995, Chris undertook a nostalgic nationwide tour with both Dickie Bishop and Lonnie Donegan as special guests. He still includes a small combo in contrast to the full New Orleans band, but this is usually much more in the R&B idiom than in any skiffle style.

Barnstormers Spasm Band

Jim Robinson and John Gunn decided to form the Barnstormers Spasm Band whilst recuperating in hospital in 1956. The group was augmented by the brothers John and Pete Wadley and, on 8 February 1957, the jazz record authority, Brian Rust, came in on washboard, being joined later that year by his brother-in-law, John Denning.

On 14 September 1957 they had the thrill of hearing one of their acetates played on Rex Harris's noted jazz broadcasts on the BBC.

Having failed an audition for Hughie Green's talent show, they spent the winter getting stuck into rehearsals. This eventually paid off, for guitarist Neville Skrimshire, acting again as talent scout (cf. Bob Cort and Jimmy Jackson), recommended them to George Martin at Parlophone Records.

The group was featured on the BBC's 'In Town To-Night', and in concert at the Queen Elizabeth Hall at the Royal Festival Hall. They also made guest appearances at the annual radio show, 'Radiolympia'. A couple of television shows followed, Brian Rust being replaced by J. R. T. Davies on the second of these, 28 December 1958. Brian's boss at the BBC's Gramophone Department had refused to give him permission to appear, not realizing that he had already been seen on the 28 September show.

On 3 February 1959, they laid down four tracks for Tempo at the Decca studios in Hampstead. This was released in October 1959. Two of the titles, 'Storming The Barn' and 'That's All There Is' appeared on one of the last 78s made in England.

Due to pressure of work Brian Rust left in October 1960, being replaced by John Fry.

For a semi-pro band the Barnstormers Spasm Band had enjoyed a fair degree of success, limited only by their regular jobs. By 1961 they had used up their 'fifteen minutes of fame' and were no more.

Dickie Bishop and his Sidekicks

Dickie 'Cisco' Bishop was a big fan of Woody Guthrie and adopted the 'Cisco' tag from Guthrie's sidekick, Cisco Houston – a fitting tribute to one of his heroes and, appropriately, he named his backing group the 'Sidekicks'.

He was born in West Ealing on 16 April 1935. His initial interest in the guitar and in western music was aroused while he was still at school, when he heard Big Bill Campbell who was regularly aired on the wireless. Big Bill Campbell and his Rocky Mountain Rhythm were the radio's equivalent of the movies' cliché camp-fire, singing cowboys. '*Howdy pard!*' and '*Mighty fine!*' were the programme's catchphrases. Nevertheless, in these musically austere times, Campbell inspired many a young guitar player, as did the other singing cowboy, Gene Autrey.

Dickie had learned the banjo and ukulele at school in Middlesex. After completing his National Service in the RAF he turned professional. He recalls:

> The first band I played with was the Brent Valley Jazzband which included Pat Halcox, Colin Kingwell and Don Wilson [a future Sidekick]. Then Pat and I both joined the Albemarle Jazz Band. Pat left to play with Chris and the band folded. Next came a spell with Charlie Connor's Jazzmen which also included Ian Wheeler. After that I did odd gigs on the banjo and solo country folk things with guitar; that was when Chris heard me and asked me to join the skiffle group.

With Chris Barber he shared the vocals with Lonnie Donegan, taking over the banjo chair when Lonnie left for the USA. He remained with the Barber Band for 18 months before briefly joining the Lonnie Donegan Group. He recorded an EP with the Chris Barber Skiffle Group, splitting the lead vocals with Johnny Duncan. His solo tracks were 'Gypsy Davy' and 'Can't You Line 'Em'. With Lonnie in January 1957, he recorded an album at the Conway Hall, *Donegan on Stage*.

Dissatisfied with the way his career was shaping up, on 17 March 1957 he formed his own group. On guitar he had another Guthrie fan, Bob Watson. In 1955, Bob, together with Cyril Davies, had opened the London Skiffle Centre at the Roundhouse, a pub in Wardour Street, just adjacent with what was to become the 2 I's Coffee Bar. The line-up also included Stan Belwood on drums, from Mick Mulligan's Jazz Band, Pete Korrison vocal and guitar and Don Wilson on bass. Don was one of the first British bass players to switch to bass-guitar; thereby giving the group a heavier rock feel.

Bob Watson and Dickie co-wrote their first recording, 'No Other Baby', released in the UK on Decca. London Records rushed released it in the USA but it was covered by Bobby Helms whose version entered the US country charts in 1957. Issued in the UK, the following year it peaked at number 30 in the hit parade, pushing Dickie's fine re-recording out of the ratings.

In April 1957, less than a month after their formation, Dickie Bishop and his skiffle group (not yet billed as his Sidekicks), appeared with their former stablemate, Johnny Duncan, together

Dickie Bishop, Pete Korrison, Don Wilson. (Flair)

with the Bob Cort Skiffle Group, Ray Bush and the Avon Cities Skiffle Group and the Chas McDevitt Skiffle Group at London's first Mammoth Skiffle Concert, held at the Royal Festival Hall. In the finale each combo featured one instrument in a massed skiffle group rendition of 'Mama Don't Allow'. It was quite pointed that Dickie's choice was Stan Belwood on drums; at that time they were more commercial than any of the other groups on the bill, Dickie's vocal sounding positively Presley in performance.

When the skiffle boom subsided, he carried on recording for the Society label, mainly covers of popular hits. He played banjo with the Kenny Ball Jazzmen and was on the session for their one-off skiffle recording, 'Wabash Cannonball', issued on Collector Records in 1957.

Since 1981 he has been playing with a jazz trio called Papa Humbser's Jazzmen. In June 1996 they undertook a tour promoted by Swatch, flying round Germany in an old Junkers propeller aircraft.

In 1995, Dickie Bishop was reunited with Lonnie Donegan when they were both featured guests on Chris Barber's nostalgic Reunion Tour. Only Johnny Duncan was missing; all efforts to find him having proved fruitless. Dickie is currently living in Elchingen/Thalfingen, Germany.

The City Ramblers

The City Ramblers were much closer to the ethos of the early jug and spasm bands than any of the other 1950s skiffle groups. They had a vast repertoire, over 300 songs, covering the whole spectrum of people's music: from blues to spirituals, from hokum to jazz and cockney songs to Victorian music-hall ditties. Their instrumentation was as varied as their repertoire. The statutory guitar was included, but even this was a variation; Russell Quaye usually favoured the quattro, a small four stringed guitar. A large collection of 'wind' instruments could be called on to provide a special effect: kazoos, jug spitting or blue-blowing, even a trumpet mouthpiece played through a paraffin funnel. This effect is still used by John Wall of the Leed's based group, the K.C. Moaners. Before they were joined by Vic Pitt on double bass they featured the tub bass.

The group's approach to the skiffle scene was well managed, perhaps influenced by Russell Quaye's background as an art teacher. When in concert they presented a dapper sight, the lads in striped trousers, dark sweaters and ties and Hylda Sims and Shirley Bland in matching colourful dresses. Most of the professional groups of that period would sport a uniform look, bowing to the standards of the showbiz Establishment; it tended to give an air of respectability. Lonnie Donegan even insisted on wearing dinner suit and black tie on the 'Six-Five Special'. This custom persisted right up to and including the Beatles, whose initial outfits were all uniform black leather: their sophisticated collar-less suits, tailored by Dougie Millings, were no less showbiz. It wasn't until the Rolling Stones came along that this convention was cast aside.

Russell Quaye was born in Beckenham, Kent on 6 December 1920. He served in the RAF during the Second World War and had many a hair-raising tale to tell.

At the age of 15, he and his brother David, who played harmonica and piano, ran away from home. They became wandering minstrels, playing in the streets and pubs of Yorkshire and Lancashire. Red-bearded Russell was often compared to a pirate, and that was not so far from the truth: his ancestors were pirates from the Isle of Man. Two of them were hanged at Tyburn.

In 1954 he married Hylda Sims. After a brief spell with Topic Records in 1956, they moved to Tempo and remained with them throughout their recording career.

George Melly singing 'Frankie and Johnny' with the City Ramblers. (T. Cryer)

The Princess Louise, a public house in Holborn, played host for a while to the City Ramblers. This venue was very popular with the groups, who each in their turn used to run their own club on the premises. Both Nancy Whiskey and Chas McDevitt ran separate nights there. Russell realized the benefit of having a club dedicated solely to this new music, and on 14 April 1957 he opened the Skiffle Cellar at 49 Greek Street, in the heart of Soho. This club acted as a magnet to skiffle groups and fans alike from all over the country. The policy was to feature a star group with support, often an amateur and unknown group; to have played the Skiffle Cellar was indeed an accolade for a newly formed band. They were one of the first clubs to promote all-night sessions, along the lines of Cy Laurie's all-night jazz sessions in Windmill Street. Guest spots were sometimes filled by solo names like Steve Benbow or Redd Sullivan, and occasionally by visiting Americans of the calibre of Derroll Adams and Jack Elliott. Ramblin' Jack Elliott even accompanied the City Ramblers on one of their European tours and, in Copenhagen in September 1956, was featured on their Storyville recording of

'Midnight Special'. Other name guests included Sonny Terry and Brownie McGhee and Jody Gibson. Jody was an American serviceman over here on his tour of duty. He played a mean bluegrass banjo and guitar, fronting a band that consisted entirely of GIs. He built up quite a cult following in this country.

The City Ramblers were regular visitors to Europe often appearing on Belgian television, and were even featured on Russian television. As part of the British jazz contingent they had been invited to play the Sixth Annual World Youth Festival in Moscow in July 1957. Back home they became regulars on BBC's 'Saturday Skiffle Club' and on television's new cult youth programme 'Six-Five Special'.

There had always been a shortage of female performers in skiffle but the City Ramblers tried to redress this imbalance by including two in their line-up: Hylda Sims, who sang and played guitar, and Shirley Bland, who sang and played a very fine washboard.

At that time Shirley was married to Jimmie MacGregor who had joined the group in early 1957. Prior to this Jimmie had played solo around the clubs and briefly joined the Chas McDevitt group as a replacement for Dennis Carter. He remained long enough to play on three recordings, using guitar and mandolin and left Chas just before the success of 'Freight Train'. After leaving the City Ramblers, Jimmie played with various groups including Steve Benbow's Folk Four before teaming up with Robin Hall. They gained an immense following appearing nearly every night of the week for 14 years on BBC's 'Tonight' television show. International acclaim followed their run on the White Heather Club, which they hosted for five years and resulted in regular tours of Canada and New Zealand. Jimmie still broadcasts regularly and hosts a TV series about the West Highland Way. Having become an authority on the Scottish countryside, he not only writes the script but also plays and composes all the music for the programme.

The Skiffle Cellar closed in 1960, the Ramblers carried on for a while, but the bubble had burst. In the 1960s and 1970s Russell still played his spasm music and in 1961 recorded an album for Elite Records in Frankfurt, Germany. Apart from Russell, none of the original Ramblers were on the session. They called themselves 'The London City Ramblers'.

During the 1970s and 1980s Russell was often to be found on the continent touring with Mimi Daniels. They appeared on several TV and radio shows as 'Ragtime Mimi and Washboard

Russell Quaye's City Ramblers.

Russell', and recorded two albums for Windmill Records and one for Mumpus.

While waiting for a heart bypass operation, Russell Quaye died of a heart attack in March 1984. He had shown great foresight in establishing the Skiffle Cellar and had provided a Mecca for all aspiring skifflers, leaving behind him a wealth of recorded goodtime music.

Coffee Bar Skifflers

The Coffee Bar Skifflers are a group made up from session musicians. Not all the tracks were recorded by the same group. Music publishers again seem to be heavily involved with this production; three of the six titles are by the same publisher, Pan Musik.

There is no record of the musicians involved in these tracks. At times it seems that Diz Disley is playing lead guitar and it has been suggested that the Sonny Stewart Skiffle Kings were used to accompany session singers. It has also been implied that because Nancy Whiskey and Chas McDevitt wrote some of the songs, Coffee Bar Skifflers is a pseudonym for the McDevitt Group. However, these sides were recorded after Nancy had left the group and she swears that although the female vocalist has her phrasing and accent, the heavily disguised voice is not hers. Obviously the singer had heard Nancy's Oriole recordings of 'Ella Speed' and 'He's Solid Gone'. Likewise, Chas McDevitt denies any connection with the record.

Ken Colyer Skiffle Group

Ken Colyer was born in 1928 in Great Yarmouth, Norfolk. He became the Godfather of British New-Orleans-style jazz and built up a dedicated and fanatical following. So much so that even today, years after his untimely death in March 1988 at the age of 59, there is a Ken Colyer Trust. The main aims of the Trust are:

> To preserve and protect the memory of Ken Colyer.
> To promote continuance of New Orleans Jazz in the principals and intentions of Ken Colyer so that his music and memory are not lost to future generations.
> To encourage young musicians whose prime interest is in New Orleans music as above.

It all began back in 1935 when Ken's brother, Bill, got interested in New Orleans jazz through, of all things, Bing Crosby movies and hearing a friend's Bix Biederbecke records. While Bill was serving in the Army, Ken absorbed the music in his older brother's record collection. When Ken joined the Merchant Navy he was able to acquire a collection of Lead Belly 78s in New York. From this early interest in music, he was to become the fountainhead of New Orleans jazz in Europe.

A hard taskmaster and a man of strict musical principles, he never really reaped his true rewards. He would not pander to popular tastes and kept his music pure until the end.

Returning from his historical visit to New Orleans in 1953, he fronted the band that was assembled to greet him; it included Chris Barber and Lonnie Donegan. When they were in Denmark

Ken Colyer. The Guv'nor. (M. Sharratt/C. McD)

some tracks were recorded clandestinely, notably 'Midnight Special', on which Ken and Lonnie duet.

When he left that band to form his own jazz band, he lost no time in getting together a skiffle group that would follow his principles. They began recording for Decca in 1954. The group featured Alexis Korner on guitar and mandolin, Johnny Parker on piano, Micky Ashman, bass and Bill Colyer on washboard. Never one to mince his words, in his unedited autobiography, *When Dreams Are in the Dust*, Ken says: 'This, to my knowledge, was the best skiffle group that England produced, though Russell

Quaye had a good group.' The last phrase is praise indeed, from such a highly critical source.

Ken's repertoire of songs was all embracing, from Cripple Clarence Lofton's 'Streamline Train' to Lead Belly's 'Grey Goose'; from Woody Guthrie's 'New York Town' to the traditional spiritual, 'Down by the Riverside', the latter being the signature tune of his original band, the legendary Crane River Jazz Band.

It was in the Crane River that Ken first featured the skiffle group. Playing guitar and singing, he was supported by Ben Marshall on banjo and guitar, Pat Hawes on piano and washboard and Julian Davies on bass. However, at that time in the early 1950s there was no demand for this kind of music. Nevertheless, Ken always included a skiffle set.

The Ken Colyer Skiffle Group, often including piano, was always nearer to the true skiffle and rent party music of the 1920s and 1930s than it was to the brash new skiffle of the 1950s. Instead of being at the forefront of the onslaught, adored by the masses, he was content to please those that revered him and his music. The music had to stand up by itself without too much adornment.

Lonnie Donegan, Bill Colyer, Ken Colyer, Chris Barber, Bristol New Orleans Jazz Club, 5 March 1954. (Alan Tucket/ Mike Bevan)

He carried on playing skiffle long past its commercial sell-by date, his last skiffle recordings being made in Hamburg in 1968. As late as 1987, featured as a guest along with Cy Laurie, on a nationwide tour with Max Collie's Jazz Aces, he could be heard playing his guitar, now a left-handed Ovation; a solitary figure on a large stage, seated at the microphone singing 'The Postman's Lament' with that soft lisping lilt in his voice and a wicked twinkle, as ever, in his eyes. As if to say, 'You may think that you are listening to a legend, but I'm no legend, I'm just enjoying myself.'

But legend he was and legend he will remain.

Upon hearing news of his death an Early Day Motion was signed by nine Members of Parliament and the House of Commons interrupted their business to honour Ken Colyer and praise his life's work: a fitting tribute to the Guv'nor, jazz giant and skiffle king.

Bob Cort Skiffle Group

Born in Loughborough in 1930, Bob Cort had developed an interest in music and particularly jazz at college. He learned to play guitar and sat in with local jazz and dance bands.

He moved to London and had a well-paid job in advertising; consequently, like many a prospective skiffler, he was reluctant to give up a lucrative career. He only ever worked as a semi-pro, taking a short leave of absence from work to play in pantomime in November 1957.

A suitably down-to-earth skiffle type, complete with beard, Bob was cast as the figurehead of the group. Mark White of Decca Records wanted a group to compete with and cover existing skiffle hits and potential hits and to this end surrounded Bob with a bevy of professional musicians. Prime examples of this process were the first few recordings by the group, 'Daddy O', 'Worried Man' and 'Freight Train'. For the latter they even brought in a female vocalist Liz Winters, a pseudonym that imitated the basic down-home feel of the name Nancy Whiskey, and near enough to cause confusion to the record-buying public. However, this practice rebounded on Decca when Bob recorded, at very short notice, the theme for the popular TV show, 'Six–Five Special'. Not long after it was used over the opening credits to the show; after

Bob Cort solo.

a few weeks it was superseded by the HMV recording by Don Lang. Nevertheless, neither had chart success.

Other musicians in the group were, George Jennings on bass, Neville Skrimshire on guitar and Bill Colyer on washboard, the only one with a skiffle pedigree.

When Bob was booked into the Prince of Wales theatre for a fortnight's engagement, supporting Dickie Henderson, Bill Colyer was working at Dobell's record shop:

On matinee days I was able to get off work a little early and I used to have a swift couple of pints with the bass player, George Jennings in Archer Street, before going on to the Prince of Wales. Not a very clever move, when the group's first entrance was made on a revolving stage!

With appearances on the 'Six–Five Special' and broadcasts on 'Saturday Skiffle Club', the group built up quite a considerable following, without ever having had a hit record. They played a regular weekly show at the recital room at the Royal Festival Hall, featuring guests and other groups. After a while Bill was replaced by Viv Carter on drums and washboard, and Ken Sykora and Neville on guitars were replaced by Diz Disley and Vic Flick.

For a while they toured in package shows but, by the beginning of May 1958, Bob had abandoned the life of a semi-pro and returned full time to his job in the advertising agency, only playing the odd Sunday concert.

Bob Cort went on to record a popular LP *Eskimo Nell* that featured 'Bawdy Barrack Room Ballads'. He eventually retired to Lincoln where he ran a public house but, sadly, he died in the 1980s.

The Cranes Skiffle Group

Embassy Records produced cheap covers of all the current hits and potential hits and was available only in Woolworth's Stores.

The label was a subsidiary of Maurice Levy's Oriole Company and he was not averse to even covering Oriole's hits. Oriole, although a small concern, had their own pressing facilities and even undertook work for other companies, at times neglecting their own artists to fulfil an urgent order. Instead of paying the artists a royalty, all the participants were given a one-off session fee. By keeping the cost of production, pressing and distribution to a minimum, Embassy records were able to be sold at a retail price well below the average.

The artists were often well-known recording names, sometimes even music publishers, like Paul Rich and Franklyn Boyd. Often a pseudonym was used, as in the case of the Chas McDevitt Skiffle Group, who assumed the name the Cranes Skiffle Group, an oblique reference to their recent association with the New Crane River Jazz Band.

The Cranes Skiffle Group.

Four tracks were originally recorded for Embassy: 'Freight Train', 'Worried Man', 'Banana Boat Song' and 'Don't You Rock Me Daddy O'. Jimmie MacGregor had joined the group on the last three tracks. However, it was decided that 'Worried Man' should be issued on Oriole to be replaced by 'Cumberland Gap' which was originally intended as an Oriole release. Consequently, Jimmie, though only with the group for three weeks, appears on both labels. All recording sessions took place in Levy's Sound Studios in New Bond Street, London, in 1957.

Lonnie Donegan

Anthony James Donegan was born in Glasgow on 29 April 1931. His family moved south in 1933 and settled in East Ham but, in 1939, during the war he was evacuated to Cheshire. By 1946, the young Tony Donegan was working in a stockbroker's office and was able to buy his first guitar. His father, Peter, was a violinist and there was no doubt that music was in Tony's blood; even his uncle played guitar. By the age of 16 he had already been introduced to the blossoming London jazz scene and in 1948 was playing in an amateur jazz band along with Chris Barber. For a while he also played drums with the Wolverines Jazz Band but this was to be interrupted by two years' National Service, when he was called up. Part of his time in the Forces was spent in Vienna where he was able to indulge his interest in jazz and blues by listening to the local American Forces Network radio station and by the easy access to jazz records afforded by his proximity to US servicemen.

On his demobilization Tony played banjo with Bill Brunskill's Jazz Band but, as he was the prime mover and virtually the band's manager, it was decided that henceforth the band should be called the Tony Donegan Jazz Band.

The Tony Donegan Jazz Band was approached by the National Jazz Federation to appear in a concert at the Royal Festival Hall, on Saturday 28 June 1952. Also booked were George Webb's Dixielanders, Ron Simpson's Commodores and guest singers George Melly and Neva Raphaello. The bands were non-union and this was a necessary prerequisite for inclusion in the show. Headlining the concert were two American stars: blues singer and guitarist, Lonnie Johnson and the jazz pianist, Ralph Sutton. The Musicians' Union was still in dispute with its counterpart in the USA and wanted to ban American musicians from working in this country, as the American Federation of Musicians had banned the British. (Years later both Donegan and the McDevitt Group would be affected by this very dispute when appearing in America.) To get round the union ban on professional support, which would have condoned the employment of American artists, the promoters enlisted the use of non-union bands.

It was at this concert that the compère confused Tony Donegan with Lonnie Johnson and Tony became for ever Lonnie Donegan, a happy reduplication that Donegan realized was pleasant on the ear and easily remembered. Henceforth he would for ever be Lonnie Donegan.

In 1953 Lonnie teamed up with Chris Barber and Monty Sunshine and they decided to go fully professional. At that stage the young trumpeter in the band was Pat Halcox, only 17 and still taking exams. He was reluctant to abandon his studies so the

Lonnie Donegan in pensive mood and (left) Festival Hall ticket for Lonnie's 'christening'.

band decided to contact Ken Colyer, returning from his legendary sojourn in New Orleans, to join this ready-made band. Almost immediately the band took an engagement in Denmark to get into shape and called themselves the Ken Colyer Jazzmen. Unbeknown to them they were taped by a local Danish enthusiast and what could legitimately be described as the first recording by a commercially formed skiffle group comes from this period: 'Midnight Special' with Colyer and Donegan on vocals and Barber on double bass.

In 1954 due to irreconcilable differences, Ken Colyer left and the band was rechristened the Chris Barber Jazz Band. The truth of what really occurred may never be known; accounts by Bill Colyer, Monty Sunshine, Jim Bray, Colin Bowden and Ken himself all differ considerably. What is known is that in 1953 at the height of the band's popularity, Ken was offered the opportunity of fronting the remaining members of Mutt Carey's New Yorkers on a European tour. This would have been a dream come true for Colyer but he told the American agent that there was no way he would let his own boys down and declined the offer. The break up of his band a few months later was an even more bitter pill to swallow, when one considers the loyalty Colyer had only recently expressed.

On 13 July 1954 the new Chris Barber Jazz Band recorded a 10-inch LP for Decca, called *New Orleans Joys*. Because on the live dates the band always featured a skiffle interlude, a legacy of the Colyer days, Chris decided that the LP should reflect this practice and consequently four skiffle tracks were recorded: 'Rock Island Line', 'John Henry', 'Nobody's Child' and 'Wabash Cannonball'. Only the first two tracks were issued. A few titles had already been taken off this collection and released as singles, when it was decided that 'Rock Island Line' and 'John Henry' should also be put out on the 78 rpm format. Released in 1955 and hitting the charts in 1956, it was an amazing success. The recording session included Chris Barber on bass and Beryl Bryden on washboard with Lonnie on lead vocals and guitar. Following this sudden success Lonnie was signed to a solo contract for Pye Record's Nixa label, captured from under the noses of the less than vigilant Decca Record Company. On 11 January 1956, he recorded 'The Ballad of Jesse James', 'Ol' Riley' and 'Railroad Bill' with Chris, Dickie Bishop on vocals and guitar and Ron Bowden on drums. Just before he left for a promotional trip to the USA on 20 February, he recorded 'Lost John' and 'Stewball'.

'Rock Island Line' reached number eight in the US charts and Lonnie proceeded to tour in support of this interest. He met with opposition from the American Federation of Musicians, who four years before he had connived in outwitting. He was classified as a variety performer and not as a musician, consequently he was unable to use his guitar when appearing on such programmes as 'The Perry Como Show'. While in America 'Lost John' and 'Stewball' reached number two in the British charts as a double-sided hit. Anxious to cash in on Lonnie's success and amend their lack of foresight, Decca issued the only other tracks they had title to, 'Diggin' My Potatoes' and 'I Don't Care Where They Bury My Body'. But the A side was banned by the BBC and consequently it was not broadcast. Performed originally by the great Lead Belly and written and recorded by Big Bill Broonzy's half brother, Washboard Sam (Robert Brown), the song featured rather earthy and suggestive lyrics, deemed to be unsuitable for the delicate ears of innocent record-buying public.

Although all hadn't gone well on this first American trip, Lonnie returned to find the skiffle fad in full swing. His recording manager Denis Preston was eager to get a follow up to 'Stewball' in the can. As Dickie Bishop was still with Chris Barber, a lead guitarist had to be found. Lonnie had been told about the Vipers, who were playing regularly at the Cat's Whiskers Coffee Bar in Kingly Street, and one evening he went along to poach one of

The Rock Island line-up – Chris Barber, Beryl Bryden and Lonnie Donegan. (Peter Hearn)

Dirndl skirts and stocking tops at 100 Oxford Street. (Peter Hearn)

their guitar players, Johnny Martyn (Booker). Lonnie instructed him to be at Denis Preston's Lansdowne Road Studios early the next morning. However, Johnny didn't show; he'd overslept, having sat up all night practising. Johnny questions this interpretation of these events. He said that he did in fact attend a preliminary rehearsal but this was for such titles as 'Stewball'. It was when Donegan annnounced that he intended to record and copyright 'Don't You Rock Me Daddy O' that he decided not to co-operate, particularly as this was in the pipeline for the Vipers to record. At the last minute, Denis Preston suggested that Denny Wright, a well-respected jazz guitarist, should do the session. Denny had to rush down to Charing Cross Road, borrow a guitar and join Micky Ashman on double bass and Nick Nicholls on drums. And so was born the swinging Lonnie Donegan Skiffle Group that eschewed the use of the washboard and was nearer to the new rock and roll and rockabilly bands. Denny Wright was to set the pattern for all Lonnie's lead guitar players, notably Jimmy Currie and Les Bennetts. The electric guitar was a powerful sound that most other skiffle groups had to include in their line-up to remain commercially viable.

Initially the skiffle groups had relied on numbers rather than amplification to reach the audience. Six acoustic guitars beating out the same rhythm was not an unusual sight in a monster-sized dance hall. When the fully acoustic Chas McDevitt Skiffle Group first appeared at the Metropolitan Theatre in London's Edgware Road, they were so spread out across the wide stage that they could hardly hear each other let alone project their sound into the auditorium.

Lonnie was now set to take his group to even greater success. He made a second trip to the USA and began to headline in variety. His American trip included an appearance in New York. When asked how had he reacted to this Lonnie replied, 'I was terrified. They put me on at Madison Square Garden and I was very aware of the fact that 17,000 people had come along to see the Harlem Globe Trotters. But don't be misled by the stories you've read. They yelled for more when we finished.'

On 30 April 1957 he opened at the famous London Palladium for two weeks co-starring with the Platters. That same week he was greeted with the news that 'Cumberland Gap' was number one in the Hit Parade. He appeared on numerous television shows, notably 'Sunday Night at the London Palladium', the top-rated TV programme, and it was not long before he had his own series, 'Putting on the Donegan'. While at the Palladium he made a live recording of 'Gamblin' Man' and 'Putting on the Style' and by 7 June 1957 this too was number one. Lonnie had already set new standards when in December 1956 his LP, *Lonnie Donegan Showcase*, was the first LP to enter the singles' chart. His EP *Skiffle Session* had already entered the chart in July 1956, another first.

In the *Musical Express* readers' poll, Lonnie far outstripped his nearest rivals, Chas McDevitt and the Vipers. In that paper's Hit List for the first half of 1957, Lonnie came fourth, only to be pipped at the post by Guy Mitchell, Pat Boone and Johnnie 'Cry' Ray, respectively placed at one, two, and three.

The *Melody Maker*'s review for Donegan's show at the Prince of Wales was glowing:

> His act? An agreeable surprise to one accustomed to the self-conscious posturing of so many pseudo-American singers. Lonnie is about the most uninhibited British singer I have yet seen. His dedicated intensity may be assumed; most important, it looks real. His wan face lends a touch of sincerity to his simple announce-ments, which are adroitly leavened with humour. In action, he shuts his eyes, rocks his body in frenzied abandon to the beat from his skiffle group.
>
> And make no mistake, the skifflers do generate a beat, far more beat than many more publicized and 'modern' outfits. A word here for the tasteful work of guitarist Denny Wright, who certainly does not let the fetish for amplification dominate him. In short, Lonnie Donegan is a natural.

Thus wrote Laurie Henshaw, the *MM* critic, in December 1956. Praise indeed from the musical Establishment!

Christmas 1957 saw the beginning of Lonnie's appearances in the seasonal pantomime productions, to be balanced by regular stints at the top coastal resorts in the summer season.

In the summer of 1958, Jimmy Currie, himself a replacement for Denny Wright, left the group. He in turn was replaced by Les Bennetts, formerly the leader of Les Hobeaux Skiffle Group and briefly, before joining Lonnie, with the McDevitt Group, with whom he broadcast and made one record, 'I Dig You Baby'.

Lonnie continued his chart success and in all had 30 hit records, including three in the number one position and 14 other top-ten entries. 'Does Your Chewing Gum Lose Its Flavour' reached number three in the UK in February 1959 but it did not enter the American charts until 1961, becoming a million-seller.

Bob Cort, Cy Laurie, Lonnie, Chas, Geoff Nichols, Royal Albert Hall, 9 June 1957.

In October 1961, Lonnie was presented with two gold discs by Bing Crosby: one on Decca, for 'Rock Island Line' and the other on Nixa, for 'Chewing Gum'.

Les Bennetts left the group in 1962 settling for a while in Las Vegas, playing banjo in the nighterie, My Father's Moustache. Lonnie charted again with 'The Party's Over', which proved to be rather prophetic; for by now the skiffle boom had really exhausted its popularity. He was to have one more hit with 'Pick a Bale of Cotton', back to the skiffle theme again with Denny Wright on guitar.

With the arrival of the Beatles and the complete change in the pop scene, Lonnie concentrated on all the other aspects of showbusiness. He recorded with his music hall idol, Max Miller; he visited Nashville and appeared on the Grand Ole Opry and he even recorded a George Formby song, 'Auntie Maggie's Remedy', reputedly, with Joe Brown on ukulele. In February 1984, he played the lead in the 1920s musical *Mr Cinders* at London's Fortune Theatre. Although throughout these years Lonnie appears to have abandoned his skiffle roots, on closer examination this is not true. He constantly paid homage to his past. In 1974 and 1975 he recorded with the German group,

Leinemann, and toured with Chris Barber and his original band, being featured in a skiffle set. In 1978 he was honoured by the rock and roll stars he had helped influence, when such 'faces' as Elton John, Brian May, Ringo Starr and Ronnie Wood helped Lonnie reinterpret his skiffle hits, prompting Lonnie to say, 'That's what I really meant in 1956!'

The record was the brainchild of one of Lonnie's early skiffle fans, Adam Faith.

Having had problems with a heart disorder, Lonnie had retired to Lake Tahoe in California and because of these problems and for tax purposes he limited his visits to the UK. However, in 1981, he recorded a skiffle EP with the Scottish group the Shakin' Pyramids and, in 1986 and 1988, he toured with Monty Sunshine in a joint venture, with both Acker Bilk and Kenny Ball. In April, May and June 1989, he undertook an extensive tour called *This Y'ere De Story*. Lonnie would open the show on his own seated at the microphone and with his guitar and the aid of pre-recorded tapes he would retrace his early years, culminating with the full skiffle group on stage to end the evening.

Recurring illness forced Lonnie to take it easy and he moved his family from Lake Tahoe to Fuengirola in Malaga, southern Spain. In spite of all these problems Lonnie continues to record and make public appearances. In 1991, he was honoured by television's 'This Is Your Life'. He recorded a new album with quite a few skiffle-style tracks in 1996 and continues to entertain and keep a full diary in spite of his illness, safe in the knowledge that his place in popular history is assured as the king of skiffle, the fountainhead of British pop music, the first real British pop superstar.

Shirley Douglas

Kathleen Barbara Marie Douglas was born 2 December 1939, in Athlone, Eire. Her parents, Charles Douglas Maber and Lillian McEvoy, were both musicians. Charlie played cello, guitar and banjo and led a small band playing the Bournemouth hotel circuit. In the 1930s, Charles Maber and his Star Artistes Dance

Band also played for Prunella Stack and her League of Health and Beauty when they went through their paces on the Bournemouth sands. Lily McEvoy was discovered playing the violin in the streets of Dublin by the famous concert violinist, Fritz Kreisler, and the ensuing publicity enabled her to tour in concert and variety. It also introduced her to Charlie – he read about her as he was eating his fish and chips from the newspaper that carried the report and he got in touch.

'Babs' Douglas, as she was originally known, learnt the guitar from her father and as soon as she was old enough toured with her parents: violin, cello and guitar, the Douglas–McEvoy Trio. They performed throughout the British Isles. For a short time she played the guitar in a dance band made up of musicians in the theatre where they were resident. At one gig in southern Ireland they were embarrassingly advertised as 'the greatest band in the world'.

When Chas McDevitt was auditioning for a replacement for Nancy Whiskey, a mutual friend who was working in the same show in Northern Ireland as Babs, suggested that on all accounts she should be heard. Consequently it was arranged that she should audition down the line from the BBC in Belfast. The group was so impressed that they flew her over for rehearsals while they were appearing at the Manchester Ardwick Green Hippodrome and also the following week at the Liverpool Empire.

Babs Douglas made her debut with the group as Shirley Douglas on a TV show 'Now, the Hop Fields' on 11 September 1957. It was a live show held in the open air and it rained 'cats and dogs'. She must have wondered what she had let herself in for, because after their next engagement in the Isle of Wight they were stranded without transport back to the mainland and had to sail back in an open fishing smack lashed by wind and rain. Their co-star at the two concerts on the Island, Michael Holliday, had conned them into going on last at the second venue, thereby causing them to miss the last ferry.

On another occasion, on a tour of Scottish dance halls, they were locked out of their digs at 1 am. Some of the group decided to sleep in the mini-bus. Shirley, Chas and manager, Bill Varley, went to the local police station where they were each given a cell. In the morning they were woken by a friendly bobby with a cup of tea in his hand. Shirley soon became inured to the ways of a band on the road.

Not having had sufficient time for proper rehearsals, Shirley at first had to sing some of Nancy's songs, learnt from the group's recordings. However, by the end of August she had released her first single 'Across the Bridge', the theme music to the film of that title. This was issued by Oriole at the same time as Nancy's last record with the group: 'Johnny Oh' which was featured in the film *The Golden Disc*. Oriole wanted to profit from this

Shirley Douglas.

exposure. As the group was busy plugging Shirley's record, it meant that they were in direct competition with themselves and neither disc got the attention it deserved.

Shirley's next single 'Real Love' was altogether different, more of a ballad, with hardly any trace of skiffle. It just failed to reach the charts, having been covered and copied, right down to the exact arrangement by a compatriot, Ruby Murray. Her next, 'Sad Little Girl', was in a similar mould, an original composition that revealed her talent for song-writing. With Chas, she was later to compose 'How Long is Forever' for Cliff Richard and 'Move Over Tiger', a hit for the leather-clad rocker, Vince Taylor.

She appeared in many TV shows with the group and starred alongside top comedian Dave King in his own spectacular. With Chas she toured with the Beatles, Cliff Richard and the Shadows, Chubby Checker, and the Fabulous Treniers. It was hearing the Treniers that persuaded Shirley to start playing the bass-guitar. At first she played a Framus but later switched to a Fender Precision Bass-Guitar. In late 1959, she published the first tutor available in this country for the bass-guitar: *The Shirley Douglas Easy Guide to Rhythm and Blues for Bass-Guitar*. This proved extremely popular and she had the field to herself for nearly two years. Many of the star rock bassists of the 1960s acknowledge their debt to the *Easy Guide to R&B*.

When the group disbanded in 1960, Shirley continued writing and recording with Chas, moving from Oriole to Top Rank, recording for Dick Rowe (later to be castigated, wrongly, for turning down the Beatles), to HMV for Denis Preston (the Svengali behind Donegan, Barber, Acker Bilk and Johnny Duncan), and Columbia, as well as Fontana Records, where they renewed their acquaintance with Jack Baverstock, the producer on the 'Freight Train' session. They finally settled down with President Records. Albums on Columbia and President featured considerable skiffle material and they both went on to release solo albums on President's Joy label. Shirley's album *Heart on the Loose* included six of her own compositions.

In the 1990s Shirley Douglas is still singing and playing 12-string guitar in both lounge and cabaret settings and is sometimes persuaded to dig out the bass-guitar when Chas reconstitutes the group. Their daughter, Kerry, often augments the line-up on vocals and washboard. In 1994, the whole clan played in New Orleans during the Jazz Fest.

Johnny Duncan and his Bluegrass Boys

John Franklin Duncan was born 7 September 1931. Originally it was claimed that Johnny came from Oliver Springs, Knoxville, Tennessee; but it is now readily accepted that he was born and brought up in Michigan. His brother, serving as a GI at Alconbury USAAF base, has confirmed this assumption.

Johnny didn't really need the fake pedigree; his appearance and falsetto country voice were convincing enough. They set him apart from all the other skifflers and gave him an air of authenticity. He was able to deliver the lyrics in true country style. His guitar and mandolin playing was also in tune with the idiom. He had been playing from the age of 16 and toured with various country trios.

In 1952 he was conscripted into the US Army and posted to Molesworth American Air Base, near Huntingdon, in Cambridgeshire.

While in England, in 1953 he met and married his first wife, Betty, and in 1954 on completion of his service as a GI they returned to the USA.

However, by 1955 they were both back in the UK. Betty had been taken ill. For a while Johnny worked on his father-in-law's clothing stall in Huntingdon market, but he was ever eager to put his talents to better use. To further this ambition one night he visited, at random, a London jazz club. That club happened to be the Humphrey Lyttelton Club at 100 Oxford Street. This is Johnny's account of what occurred that evening:

> Chris Barber was playing that night. The first thing he said to me was, 'Don't you look like Lonnie Donegan?'
>
> That was who the audience thought I was.
>
> I told Chris that I could sing and play guitar so he gave me an audition. That same weekend I joined the band.

Chris had him singing with the band the very next night, at the Royal Festival Hall.

While with the Barber band, Johnny recorded two tracks: 'Where Could I Go' and 'Doin' My Time', released on an EP with two other tracks featuring Dickie Bishop. Dickie had stepped in to fill the banjo chair vacated on Lonnie Donegan's departure.

It was Denis Preston who was instrumental in persuading Johnny to go solo. Already Denis had steered both Lonnie and Chris to recording success and he wasted no time in finding a suitable backing group for Johnny. To this end he had asked the doyen of bass players, Jack Fallon, to form a group. This choice could not have been better. Jack, from Ontario in Canada, had provided backing for numerous jazz greats and country stars, from Sarah Vaughan to Tex Ritter and Tennessee Ernie Ford; he was sympathetic to Johnny's style and chose the group for both musicianship and flair. The extrovert, legendary jazz drummer, Lennie Hastings (renowned for standing up in the middle of a drum solo, twirling his wig on the end of a drumstick and shouting 'oolyah, oolyah!') added a certain colour to the group, which was completed with Danny Levan on fiddle and Bryan Daly on guitar. Bryan was later replaced by Lonnie's original guitarist, Denny Wright.

Johnny Duncan's first single drew on another skiffle roots influence, Hank Williams. Hank's composition 'Kaw Liga' was backed with Lead Belly's 'Ella Speed'. This record failed to make an impression. His next release 'Last Train to San Fernando' was a classic. This song had in fact previously been offered to the McDevitt Group, as a follow-up to their train record 'Freight Train' but although Chas was attracted to the lyrics, he did not think the calypso arrangement on the demo record was suitable for skiffle. He hadn't seen the possibilities, exploited by Jack and Denny's arrangement. Denny Wright's tearaway Latin-American guitar solo will for ever remain a classic of its time.

'Last Train to San Fernando' was a runaway success and assured Johnny of a fruitful career. In October 1957 he had a minor hit with 'Blue Blue Heartaches' and, in November 1957 and January 1958, his Christmas offering, 'Footprints in the Snow', made a brief appearance in the top 30.

He continued over the years playing more country-style music. Changing the group from time to time, at one stage including Joe Moretti, an excellent Scot's guitarist, and in November 1959, on drums, Red Reece a refugee from Les Hobeaux and the Chas McDevitt groups. Red was eventually to join Georgie Fame and the Blue Flames.

Johnny Duncan's music, although labelled skiffle, never really came under that umbrella, being too country and too ambitious musically for the true skiffle fan. He himself had no intent to deceive, calling his group 'The Bluegrass Boys', right from the

Johnny Duncan and his Bluegrass Boys – Denny Wright, Jack Fallon, Danny Levan, Johnny Duncan and Lennie Hastings. (Flair)

beginning. He had said way back in 1957, 'Don't get me wrong. I like skiffle – but I aim to introduce a broader pattern of music. After all country and western is really nothing but a modification of skiffle. I think British audiences will like it.'

For a while Johnny hosted his popular radio series 'Tennessee Song Bag' and had an album released to coincide with its airing. He undertook many one-night stand tours, appearing all over the UK. He was a regular on the radio programmes like 'Saturday

Club' and 'Guitar Club'; television and concert appearances filled his date sheet. Nevertheless, his star began to wane when the horse to which he had hitched his buggy began to falter. Although strictly country, Johnny Duncan suffered the same fate as all the skifflers who would not or could not adapt to the ever increasing demand for rock and roll and the emergent folk rock of Dylan and his acolytes. His dilemma was manifest in his switching back and forth between Pye and Columbia, yet still turning out records of high quality.

Having remarried and settled for a while in Sunderland, in 1976 he emigrated to Australia. From that moment onwards his 'Footprints in the Snow' become decidedly faint. His present whereabouts were unknown until recently when he was heard of in Harrington, N.S.W. Australia.

All one is left with is his quite comprehensive catalogue of over 30 records, singles, EPs and LPs, recorded between 1956 and 1970 with Chris Barber but mainly in his own right, and the endearing memory of him standing out front, holding his Martin guitar chest high, soundhole to the microphone, hillbilly style, flat-picking a solo. He would at times repeat this process with the Gibson flatback curly-top mandolin; hoisting it behind his head and confounding the audience with his dexterity and virtuosity.

Eden Street Skiffle Group

In late 1957 Headquarters & General Supplies Ltd, a mail order company of Coldharbour Lane, London, ran an advertisement in the national press for a set of ten polythene flexi-records, by the Eden Street Skiffle Group. They promoted the gatefold album of 10 records for only 10s. including postage as, 'Brand New, Red Hot, Skiffle Records, by 6–5 Special Stars, the Eden Street Skiffle Group.'

Playing instructions said that these records were intended to be played on modern machines with light pick-up heads. 'Should your needle jump, it is suggested you tape a coin to the player arm for extra weight.'

The group appeared on the 'Six–Five Special' and broadcast six times on the 'Saturday Skiffle Club', the last few dates being billed as Leonard Hill's Eden Street Skiffle Group.

Named after the street where three of the group worked, they had an extensive repertoire and featured a wide variety of material including calypsos and country and western. For a while they were resident at the Skiffle Cellar appearing also in concert at both the Royal Albert and Royal Festival Halls. In December 1957, they were part of the Skiffle Jamboree Concert tour, presented by James Laurie. The show played Lewisham, Bexhill, Southampton, Tunbridge Wells, Margate, Leicester and Bristol and included Russell Quaye's City Ramblers, Les Hobeaux, Don Lang and his Frantic Five and the Chas McDevitt Skiffle Group with Shirley Douglas. Programme notes pointed out that,

> As yet this group has not been snapped up by any recording company, but indication has it that it will not be long before they have a disc on the market.

Prophetic words for, although they only made ten titles, these have become collectors' rarities.

Flexi-discs

Apart from the flexi-discs issued by the Eden Street Skiffle Group as a set of ten transparent records in a gatefold format, other companies followed a similar marketing system using session musicians.

For the price of 1s. 6d. and three wrappers from Nestlé's chocolate, a 7-inch cardboard 78 rpm, single-sided flexi-disc was available of the Tin Pan Skiffle Group singing 'Poor Howard'. It was produced by the Hardy Record Manufacturing Co. for Nestlé's *New Star* series and recorded in the heart of Tin Pan Alley (Denmark Street) at Star Sound Studios. This disc was numbered NR 06. The only other skiffle type release was NR 08 'Last Train to San Fernando', Benny Lee and the Jackson Boys.

Previous releases were:

NR 01 'Bye, Bye Love'   Franklyn Boyd
NR 02 'Rockin' Shoes'   George Doree
NR 03 'In the middle of an Island'   Margaret Rose
NR 04 'I'd Give You the World'   Roy Edwards
NR 05 'Teddy Bear'   Franklyn Boyd

Another oddity was *The Washboard Birthday Special.* A 7-inch flexi 78 rpm record set into a gatefold birthday card and produced by Melody Cards of London. The trite lyrics rang out thus:

Happy, happy birthday (2)
On this anniversary of the day that you were born,
Let's get goin' down the track,
Once I'se there ain't comin' back.
Git those presents on the rack, of the
Washboard Birthday Special.

This release was numbered MC 101. A previous record *Rock-a-Boogie Birthday Rock*, was number MC 100. Other cards featured opera and jazz.

The Washboard Birthday Special flexi-disc.

Frog Island Skiffle Group

Jazz record shop proprietor Doug Dobell and his 77 label accounted for many an obscure recording. Released in limited editions to avoid purchase tax, they often featured little-known artists. The Frog Island Skiffle Group recorded one EP for the label. They had taken part in the Soho Fair of July 1957 and were regulars in Jimmy Tate's Modern Music Club at 5 Gerrard Street, but little else is known about the group.

Brian Harvey, who was in charge of their record production, wrote in his sleeve notes,

> Yes, skiffle has become a major industry and, at the same time, a musical monster, for most of the practitioners know nothing of its folk origins and only succeed in producing a hopped up kind of hillbilly music. But there are people around to whom the art of making money is of secondary importance, and the art of music foremost. The Frog Island Skiffle Group come into that category. These are a group of talented and enthusiastic young amateurs who make no claim other than to entertain and they really enjoy doing just that . . .

Hallelujah Skiffle Group
featuring Clinton Ford

Clinton Ford came into showbusiness in the 1950s, as a wandering troubadour, singing and playing guitar at private parties, jazz clubs, theatres and holiday camps. It was while he was at Butlin's, where he was a Red Coat for three years, that his link with skiffle was established: he fronted a skiffle group for a Butlin's TV commercial.

This was perhaps the episode that was influential in his recording for Oriole. They'd recently had a million-selling hit with a former Butlin's Red Coat, Russ Hamilton. Hamilton's record of 'We Will Make Love' went Gold. This was swiftly followed by Oriole's only other million-seller, the skiffle hit 'Freight Train'. They were possibly trying to combine two winning formulas.

The Rev. Geoffrey Beaumont was producing a TV show that was recorded at the Hackney Empire and featured Clinton singing

Clinton Ford, 1996.

with a skiffle group. The Hallelujah Skiffle Group was an off-shoot from the interest this programme aroused. Never an authentic skiffle group, it was made up of session musicians: Ernie Shear on guitar and members of the Mike Sammes singers. All four tracks were spirituals. Clinton Ford has said:

The Hallelujah Skiffle Group was just a commercial idea thought up by the powers that know nothing! Although I did play skiffle back in the 1950s, I never recorded anything remotely authentic.

It is a pity that he had not delved more into the skiffle idiom; his remarkable voice would surely have resulted in some classic records. The truth is that he cannot be typecast; he is as at home singing with a dixieland band, and a country band, as he is with the massed bands of HM Guards division.

While singing with the Merseysippi Jazz Band at Liverpool's Cavern Club, he was offered a job with Kenny Ball's Jazzmen, which led to a residency on Brian Matthew's BBC radio show 'Easy Beat'. He then starred in the very successful ITV series, 'Stars and Garters'.

Over the years he has travelled the globe, entertaining all with such songs as Charlie Chester's 'The Old Bazaar in Cairo' and his major chart successes, 'Old Shep' in 1959 and 'Fanlight Fanny' in 1962.

Just a point or two of interest regarding the Rev. Geoffrey Beaumont. In the *Radio Times* of 11 October 1957, a photo was printed of the 'Rev.' jamming on piano with a skiffle group. He was the vicar of St George's in Camberwell, south London and was publicizing a folk mass he had written, which featured jazz, skiffle and calypso and which was to be televised from St Augustine's Church in Highgate. This was long before the charismatic movement and the vogue for religious pop and it caused quite a stir, even prompting vehement discussion on BBC's 'Any Questions' and 'Any Answers'. The Church of England 'jazzuit', as he was dubbed, had already in 1957 held a harvest festival in his own church accompanied by a skiffle group.

The Salvation Army also contributed to the craze with their own group the 'Joy Strings', as ever insisting, 'Why should the devil have all the best songs?'

Les Hobeaux Skiffle Group

In August 1957 the original members of this group were still students at the Polytechnic in Regent Street, London. In the space of five months they went from being just a group of busking students to a top-of-the-bill attraction.

Alan Jones, David Russell on washboard and Winky

Wimbledon on box-bass left before the group took up professional status as Les Hobeaux. The other three founder members of the group – Les Bennetts, guitar; Keith Larner and Roger Smith, both on vocals – recruited Darrell Lyte on piano and guitar, Roy Tobin on guitar and Brian Gregg on tea-chest bass. The tea-chest was Les Bennetts's idea. Brian soon dispensed with the use of this and reverted to the double bass in double quick time. Brian Gregg would later change to electric bass-guitar and go on to play with Colin Hicks, Terry Dene, Johnny Kidd and the

Les Hobeaux in 2 I's gear.

Pirates and the instrumental sensation of the 1960s, the Tornados. His place in Les Hobeaux was taken by Rex Rehak (Dabinett) and Red Reece came in on drums.

Initially the group busked around Soho and at the Gyre and Gimble as well as under the arches behind Charing Cross Station in Villiers Street. Paul Lincoln asked them to support the Vipers at the 2 Is and when the Vipers left to go on tour, Les Hobeaux took up their position as resident group. They had already won the international skiffle competition at the 1957 Soho Fair and followed this with appearances at the famous Stork Club and the Côte d'Azur.

While playing a Sunday concert at the Commodore Theatre on the Isle of Wight, they were seen by Norman Newell of HMV Records who came back stage and immediately offered them a recording contract. It's not difficult to see why he was so impressed. They were a lively multi-racial group with a colourful and universal appeal. It was a curious fact that, although the original skiffle music was essentially a black man's music, Keith Larner was the only black member in any of the leading skiffle groups (he was reputed to be a direct descendant of the African Chief, Kawaikasaaba).

They did the usual rounds of radio broadcasts, TV and concerts, on one occasion deputizing for the Lonnie Donegan Group at the Regal, Gloucester, when Lonnie was confined to his bed with Asian flu. Les realized that all the other leading skiffle groups were already working and that the promoters were desperate, so he insisted that they were to be paid the same fee as Donegan. He must have clinched the deal, because that week Les rowed in his two brothers as additions to the group.

At the peak of their career, Les Hobeaux had a guest spot in Terry Dene's film *The Golden Disc*, along with Nancy Whiskey and Sonny Stewart's Skiffle Kings.

At the tender age of 17, Les was the youngest band leader in the UK with a recording contract. This didn't make for an easy life, the group were constantly arguing; on one occasion they all banded together and sacked Les. Still Les had the last laugh, it was he who had signed the contract with the agent Hymie Zahl, and the group had to take him back or be replaced themselves.

Once, while travelling on the underground to a recording session, Les announced to the group in a high-handed way that some of them might be replaced by session men in the studio. They didn't mind just as long as they were paid. However, on this occasion, the lads had the last laugh for when they arrived at the studio, it was Les who had been demoted to rhythm guitar in favour of Roy Plummer the session man. It had been decided that Roy should play Les's guitar solo in 'Mama Don't Allow'. Naturally Les was severely 'pissed off'.

When the group normally performed this song on stage they would shout out 'Take it fags' (Les smoked heavily), when it came to Les's guitar solo. Even though Les wasn't playing the solo on the session, they still shouted out 'Take it fags' and Les retorted with 'Fuck off'! It went unnoticed at the time by the recording engineer and is now enshrined for posterity, surely the first example of the expletive on a pop record.

Les was always involved in some prank or other. On one occasion a party had been arranged that included Wally Whyton and Johnny Booker of the Vipers, Les Hobeaux as well as their assorted girlfriends, dancers from the Windmill and Murray's Cabaret Club. The girls wanted to leave as the atmosphere was getting a little tense – there were a few West End villains in attendance. After some altercation, involving Johnny Booker, Les had fizzed up a bottle of beer and began pouring it over the hard men. An almighty punch-up ensued. Les and Wally positioned themselves at the door and kicked one of the gang into a dustbin, another they threw on top of a car, the rest of Les's group, already on the lam, turned back when they saw that they were winning the battle. All mayhem broke loose: it was absolute pandemonium, aggravated by Fraser White, the Scottish newspaper-man, publicity agent to many of the skiffle groups. Fraser had a weekly skiffle column in the bizarrely named *Weekly Sporting Revue and Showbusiness*, and was often privy to many of the goings on. On this occasion Fraser didn't help things by running around frantically blowing a police whistle that he kept on his person for self-protection.

The following night when Les Hobeaux showed up for their regular spot at the 2 I's; Big Roy, the doorman, waved them off. The Curly King Gang, for that's who their adversaries had been, were waiting for them with axes, baseball bats and a shotgun. Les and Brian Gregg disappeared for a couple of weeks, hiding out in a wooden hut that they had been smuggled into, on a US airbase in St Neots. They remained there until Paul Lincoln had organized his professional wrestling buddies into bodyguards for the wayward skifflers. Wally was not so fortunate; he and the Vipers were appearing that week at the Met, Edgware Road. They felt themselves to be decidedly vulnerable, so Wally went along to Savile Row Police

Early Les Hobeaux at the Poly.

Station to complain that they were being threatened by these villains with shotguns. The police sergeant said,

> Now listen, son, you keep well away from this, we don't want you getting involved in any retaliation; if we find any of your lot carrying illegal weapons then it's you who will be nicked.

Wally came out in a cold sweat; at that precise moment, wrapped in a newspaper, concealed down his trouserleg, was an 18-inch heavy sash weight.

When Les Hobeaux finally disbanded, Les, together with their drummer Red Reece, joined Chas McDevitt. Soon he was to join the Lonnie Donegan group where his fast single-string guitar work and vocal harmonies added a new dimension to their arrangements. He was in his element banging the dustbin when they played 'My Old Man's a Dustman'.

On leaving Donegan he went to the USA and ran banjo parlours in the My Father's Moustache chain in New Orleans, Boston, St Louis and New York. He worked in Las Vegas for three years before returning to England and opening a hotel in Margate. Eventually he returned to Redcar where he had been born in

1940. There he drove a taxi before spending three years down the coal mines as a face worker.

Les Bennetts was truly a renaissance man, a man for all seasons. In his time he had been a boxer, a silkscreen printer, an insurance salesman, a tractor driver, a scriptwriter, a dry-stone waller in Cleveland, a tour manager for Diana Dors in Australia, a researcher-writer for the English Tourist Board and he'd even bought fresh eggs from farmhouses, touring the south coast in a small van, selling them on to private hotels. Transcending all these peripheral attributes was his guitar virtuosity and his love of music, in particular, skiffle music. In 1995, just before his untimely death from lung cancer, he was rehearsing a revival skiffle group to take out on the road. 'Days of Skiffle' were to have played all the old skiffle classics and were shortly due to embark on a tour with the Chas McDevitt Skiffle Group.

Together with Denny Wright, Jimmy Currie and Bill Bramwell, Les Bennetts left a diverse collection of skilful skiffle guitar solos that can be enjoyed to this day.

The Imps

Carrol Levis discovery, the Imps, was a group of five 12-year-olds. Accompanied by the father of one of the Imps on guitar, they made a couple of television appearances: on the 'Discoveries' Show and on the 'Six–Five Special', as contestants in the National Skiffle Competition. They came from Miles Platting in Lancashire.

George Martin and orchestra director, Ron Goodwin, produced the Imps' first and only record for Parlophone: 'Dim Dumb Blonde' and a cover of the Sonny Stewart recording of 'Let Me Lie'. The group disappeared from the scene as swiftly as they had arrived. The *Record Mirror* review of their record, on Columbia DB 4074, just about sums up their career:

IMPS LEAVE ME LIMP

The youngsters from the north have had a lot of advance publicity, some of it very smart. Now they emerge on disc – presumably with their tiny plastic guitars.

This gets my nomination for the week's worst record! 'Dim Dumb Blonde' is not a bad song, but the five 12-year-olds do their best to alter that belief. From skiffle contest to recording studio the Imps bring an air of confidence that is quite shattering. To my mind their place at the moment should remain in amateur contests where local audiences can go wild with glee at the sight of the tots behaving with such precocity. The music business becomes more difficult to understand each time it deliberately puts out items like this with such solemnity. Youth's having its fling all right at the moment; and in many cases I'm all for it; but this one wasn't flung far enough.

On the turnover they chant the strummer, 'Let Me Lie'. There's a whistler and a deal of flat singing which should never have passed the man in the box. I've no wish to sound unkind but the disc is aimed at the market in adult competition and must be assessed on that level. The only buyers can be the Imps' relatives and friends.

So wrote Don Player on 15 February 1958, illustrating just one of the trends that Tin Pan Alley had created, thereby providing another nail in the coffin being prepared by the musical establishment for this irreverent skiffle craze.

The description of the group's line-up was suitably twee:

David McGee with his granny's washboard; Don Ainsworth with his father's fishing line attached to an old soap box and his mother's broom handle; Geoff Wood, Jeff Tranter and Howard Tonge each playing a miniature thirty-shilling plastic guitar.

Jimmy Jackson and his Rock 'n' Skiffle

Jimmy Jackson – yet another skiffler with Glasgow roots – by the age of 15 was already singing and playing drums with local bands, taking up the guitar two years later when he joined the RAF.

When the Mick Mulligan Jazz Band was playing an RAF base near Liverpool in October 1956, Mick heard Jimmy singing with the station band and was sufficiently impressed to invite him to appear in concert with the Mulligan band the following Sunday in Liverpool. Jimmy also sat in at various clubs in London and on one occasion was heard by guitarist Neville Skrimshire, a representative of Columbia Records, who arranged for him to have a record test. The result was his first offering for Columbia, 'California Zephyr' and 'I Shall Not Be Moved'.

By now Jimmy was a corporal drill instructor at an RAF base near Bedford. In 1953 he had signed on for 12 years but, with work now piling up, including concerts in Denmark backed by the orchestra of Norrie Paramour, the Columbia A & R director (later to produce Cliff Richard's sessions) and the possibility of recording success, he was bought out of the RAF. He signed for a variety agent, touring and broadcasting regularly, including four appearances on 'Saturday Skiffle Club'.

Billed as 'skiffle with a jazz beat', on record his backing was provided mainly by the rhythm section of the Mick Mulligan Band, augmented by Neville Skrimshire on guitar and various session musicians. However, he showed a preference for country and western, along with Johnny Duncan and Dickie Bishop and, with the demise of skiffle as a commercial proposition, he recorded one or two pop songs before throwing in the towel.

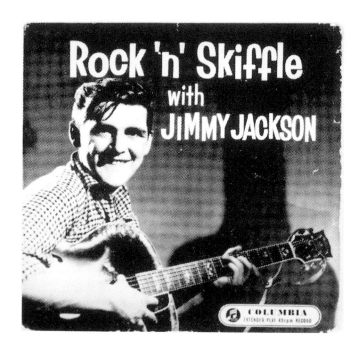

Alexis Korner and Cyril Davies

Alexis Korner was the kingpin of the British R&B explosion in the 1960s. He had the conviction and the unshakeable ambition to play the blues American style, when many of his contemporaries thought that this was impossible and solely the domain of the black performer. In Cyril Davies he found a kindred spirit and together they prepared the British public for the arrival of the rhythm and blues bands of the early 1960s.

Alexis Korner was born in Paris in 1928. Having been brought up in France, Switzerland and North Africa, he came to England with his family, at the outbreak of the Second World War, in 1939.

When Chris Barber formed his first band around 1949, Alex occasionally played in the line-up. In 1954, when Ken Colyer had split from the Barber, Sunshine and Donegan set-up, Alex joined the Colyer Skiffle Group on guitar and mandolin. This was the group that Colyer claimed was 'the best skiffle group that England produced'.

With this group, Alexis recorded seven titles. By November 1956 he and Cyril Davies had recorded four tracks with Beryl Bryden's Backroom Skiffle. Only two were issued because of a faulty balance in the mix. It suffered from an echo surge, as if the engineer couldn't make up his mind, or perhaps he kept knocking the controls with his elbow each time he raised his glass.

Cyril Davies and Bob Watson had opened the London Skiffle Centre at the end of 1955. The club met on the first floor of the Roundhouse pub, situated on the corner of Brewer Street and Wardour Street. Every Thursday night one could be sure to hear Cyril belting out his favourite Lead Belly songs, eyes firmly closed, ruddy faced, his features looking fit to bust. He played a custom-built Emile Grimshaw 12-string guitar and occasionally the harmonica. He was later to abandon the guitar and concentrate on amplified harmonica. Bob Watson, a Woody Guthrie enthusiast, balanced the proceedings with his selection of material, and floor singers were encouraged.

At first the audiences were quite thin and, more likely than not, would probably be made up of other musicians and skifflers anxious to pick up a few pointers and maybe a new song or two. When Alex became a regular and visiting American artists

Cyril Davies watched closely by Chris Farlowe. (M. Sharratt/C. McD)

Alexis Korner playing mandolin with Sonny Terry and Brownie McGhee.
(Terry Cryer)

Cyril Davies, Frank Cash, Alexis Korner, Beryl Bryden and Dave Stevens.
(H. Lührig coll.)

dropped in, the venue became a Mecca for skiffle and blues fans. Jack Elliott, Sonny Terry and Brownie McGhee, as well as Big Bill Broonzy, all called by.

In December 1956, the venue was still being advertised as a blues and skiffle club, but Alex, always uncomfortable with the skiffle tag, especially when it became associated with the more commercial and popular style, renamed it the Blues and Barrelhouse Club. However it was still affectionately referred to as the Roundhouse. Cyril and Alex gradually introduced more electric blues and the club attracted such artists as Long John Baldry, no mean 12-string player himself, and the great Muddy Waters and Otis Spann. By 1960 the landlord said the music was too loud and replaced them with an accordionist . . .

In a way this propelled them to find larger premises in Ealing which became the spiritual home of British R&B and fostered the interest of a new generation of blues enthusiasts.

On 13 February 1957, at the Roundhouse they had recorded an 8-track album for Doug Dobell's 77 label. This was released in a limited edition of only 99 copies to avoid the purchase tax due on pressings of 100 and over. It was often suspected that once the initial 99 had sold a further 99 were pressed. This was released as the 'Alexis Korner Skiffle Group', but a further recording in April 1958 was issued as 'Alex Korner's Blues Incorporated' even though the musicians were identical except for Chris Capon, who was replaced by Jim Bray. Nevertheless, their choice of material echoed their skiffle heritage: three songs associated with Lead Belly and the inclusion of the piano played in the style of Big Maceo Merriweather, the doyen of Chicago skiffle in the 1920s and 1930s.

It has been argued that, as Alexis never had a great singing voice, he was able to concentrate and develop his guitar technique. What is certain is that he befriended many a blues great, often inviting them to stay at his home in Notting Hill Gate, no doubt acquiring many guitar licks in the process. His husky deep voice was ideal for broadcasting and he hosted many specialist blues programmes. His Blues Incorporated gradually developed into a jumping rocking combo with a saxophone lead and he moved back to the West End and the Marquee Club.

Cyril Davies went on to form his All Stars and recorded a rocking instrumental on harmonica, 'Country Line Special'. Cyril died prematurely of leukaemia at the age of 32, on 7 January 1964. Alexis died almost exactly 20 years later, on 1 January 1984.

Always maintaining that they were never a skiffle group, they still left a small catalogue of authentic-sounding skiffle sung and played with conviction and style and between them sowed the seeds for the blues fever that has lasted through until the 1990s and still shows no signs of abating.

Alan Lomax and the Ramblers

A form of pseudo skiffle came from the folk purists. It is difficult to ascertain their motives: were they trying to set the record straight or did they merely want to dip their bread in the gravy? Alan Lomax regarded the British skiffle scene as a musical entity in itself, essentially a British phenomenon. Anything that encouraged the young to play an instrument and perhaps discover folk music could only be a bonus; so perhaps their reasons were altruistic.

Alan Lomax who, with his father John A. Lomax, had contributed so much to the American folk-song heritage, and through their recordings of Lead Belly directly to the skiffle song bag, decided to form a group called Alan Lomax and the Ramblers. This group included Ewan MacColl (Jimmy Miller), who was known for his wealth of British folk material; Ewan's wife, Peggy Seeger, the sister of Pete Seeger, on banjo and vocals, and Shirley Collins on vocals. The rest of the group included Allan 'Little Bear' Sutton on washboard, from the City Ramblers; John Cole on harmonica; Jim Bray on bass; Bryan Daly, guitar and, at times on clarinet, Bruce Turner. With such a complement and such pedigree, it was a great pity that they did not record more than four titles for Decca.

As individuals the members of the group contributed hugely to the later folk boom in the early sixties. Ewan MacColl wrote 'Dirty

Alan Lomax and the Ramblers. (M. Sharratt/C. McD)

Old Town' based on his childhood memories of Salford, in Manchester, and later saw the song he wrote as a love song for his wife, Peggy, reach worldwide acclaim when in 1972 'The First Time Ever I Saw Your Face' became a million-seller for Roberta Flack. Peggy Seeger herself toured throughout the world singing her folk songs and recorded several skiffle songs on an album, notably 'Freight Train', 'Cumberland Gap' as well as 'Sail Away Lady' (Don't You Rock Me Daddy O) and 'Bring a Little Water Sylvie'.

Chas McDevitt Skiffle Group

One of the few groups to have come through both the jazz-club and coffee-bar environment, the Chas McDevitt Skiffle Group was the only other British skiffle group, along with Lonnie Donegan, to achieve success in the USA.

Charles James McDevitt was born in Glasgow on 4 December 1934. Glasgow seemed to be a catchment area for future skifflers; Lonnie Donegan, Nancy Whiskey, Jimmie MacGregor and Jimmy Jackson were also born there. After moving south to Hampstead, the McDevitt family decamped at the beginning of the war to Camberley in Surrey. Chas's father was a master tailor and business, in the shape of the troop concentrations at Aldershot and Sandhurst, was close at hand.

During a prolonged illness in 1950–51, Chas started playing the banjo, a gift from the local baker. His interest in jazz and the blues developed during this period and he was corresponding regularly with such blues artists as Josh White and Lizzie Miles who was singing with Sharkey Bonano's Dixielanders at the Mardi Gras Lounge in New Orleans. As soon as Chas returned to college, he began playing with the local dixieland band, the High Curley Stompers, often featuring within the band a small ensemble: piano, bass, banjo or guitar and drums or washboard. Then it wasn't called skiffle, just barrelhouse music. They played songs like 'Down by the Riverside', 'It's Tight Like That' and 'Trouble in Mind'.

At the end of 1954, Chas had moved back to London and in 1955 he was playing banjo with the re-formed Crane River Jazz Band. The only link with the seminal band of 1949 was Sonny Morris, the original second trumpet to Ken Colyer. Sonny occasionally fronted the band together with the regular leaders, Neil Millett and Mole Benn.

By day Chas was working at Unilever House in Blackfriars and during his lunch break would rehearse the skiffle group in the basement archives. Marc Sharratt, a pal from the early High Curley days, played washboard and various guitar-wielding mates would augment the floating personnel: John Summers on guitar, Ken Aggus on mandolin, Reg Linay on guitar and piano and Ken Lovett vocals.

Chas could often be found in Soho during this period, busking with the mighty Redd Sullivan, a real eccentric and Lead Belly freak. At a brisk pace, marching through Soho, Redd would start singing in his powerful bluesy voice and Chas and Marc would scramble along behind trying to keep up with the giant's stride. Zom, another Soho 'face', would bring up the rear. When Redd found a suitable pitch or doorway, and if sufficient punters had tagged along Pied-Piper like, he would stop and they'd sing two more songs. Then it was up to Adam, the bottler; he would pounce on the more affluent-looking spectator, hold out his collecting bag and they'd bottle and go before the law could move them on. This always proved to be a fairly lucrative gig, especially during the Soho fair. Redd Sullivan and Zom would later join John Hasted's Skiffle and Folk Group, resident at the 44 Club in Gerrard Street.

The Cy Laurie Jazz Club in Windmill Street was almost as well known as the Windmill Theatre, the home of striptease. It was a venue that had a cult following and Chas featured a trio here during the interval sessions, the St Louis Trio, a name bestowed on them without their knowledge by Cy Laurie. Marc Sharratt was on washboard and Pete Timlett on piano. Pete was the piano player with the Crane River and Chas's skiffle group had a regular spot with the band. The group now included Dennis Carter and Alex Whitehouse on guitars; Alex had joined the group while Chas was playing at the Fantasie Coffee Bar in the King's Road, Chelsea. John Paul came in on bass, having taken over from Ron Ward who had left to join the Ken Colyer Jazzmen and skiffle group.

For a while the group played the usual jazz clubs, such as the Kingsbury Baths, often the scene of Teddy-boy punch-ups, and at the jazz club over Burton's in Kingston and the Weyman's Hall in Addlestone in Surrey. At the same time they played regularly in the Breadbasket, the Gyre and Gimble, the Cat's Whiskers and the 2 I's coffee bars.

Dennis Carter, a beardless Chas and Ron Ward, Kingsbury Baths, 1956.

In November and December 1956, for four consecutive weeks, they entered and won a talent contest promoted by Pye on Radio Luxembourg. On the last week they lost to a Noël Coward style pianist, their choice of song – 'Freight Train', sung by Chas.

The group had already recorded 'Freight Train' for Oriole Records, thanks to the demo discs produced by their new manager, Bill Varley. Bill ran Trio Recordings, a small studio in Tin Pan Alley. It was Varley who suggested that to get an edge over the other skiffle groups they should include a girl in their line-up. Folk singer, Nancy Whiskey, who had also appeared on the Radio Luxembourg talent competition, was invited to join the group. At first reluctant to give up her folk singing, she joined the boys at the end of December 1956. They re-recorded 'Freight Train' with Nancy taking the vocals. On the same session they recorded 'Cotton Song', 'New Orleans' and 'Don't You Rock Me Daddy O'. The last track was released on Embassy Records, Oriole Records' cheap subsidiary that sold in Woolworth's. They used the pseudonym the 'Cranes Skiffle Group'. 'Worried Man', originally recorded for Embassy while Jimmie MacGregor was with the group, was substituted on their second Oriole release.

About that time they also won other talent shows at the Hammersmith Palais which resulted in their making guest

Handout publicity for 'Greenback Dollar' (top) and poster for a first week in variety, January 1957.

Dickie Bishop, Johnny Duncan, Geoff Nichols, Chas and (seated) Bob Cort, Ray Bush, Nancy Whiskey.

appearances with Lou Preager's Band, Freddy Randall's Jazz Band and in concert with the Eric Delaney Band, with whom Chas was sometimes featured as skiffle singer, with Eric Delaney playing washboard.

The group made their first major appearance at the Metropolitan Theatre, Edgware Road. The show's promoters were Bert Ambrose, the celebrated band leader, and Joe Collins, the impresario, father of the then starlets, Joan and Jackie Collins.

On Easter Monday, 22 April 1957, the group played the Royal Festival Hall in London's first big skiffle session which included: Johnny Duncan; Ray Bush and the Avon Cities Jazz Band and Skiffle Group; Bob Cort and Dickie Bishop. Rollercoaster Records recently released a mini-album of the McDevitt group's contribution to this epic show, using tapes that had lain dormant until 1994. The excitement of this event is captured faithfully and demonstrates that audience hysteria didn't only start with the Beatles. There are existing tapes of two renditions of 'Mama Don't Allow' by the whole ensemble; maybe one day they too will be released.

In June 1957 the group appeared on the first 'Rock across the Channel' on SS *Royal Daffodil*. The 2 Is had chosen a day trip to

McDevitt group in Calais serenading bewildered bridegroom, watched by Freddy Irani (in striped jacket), one of the original 2 I's.

invade France with rock and skiffle. It never really caught hold at the time but nowadays there is a cult following for this music in France, Holland and Germany, which puts the British fans to shame. Chas regularly takes the current group over and remembers vividly a show the McDevitt group and the Donegan group played in Nantes in 1988. The audience were all either rockabilly or black leather rockers yet they were so knowledge-able about the music and its origins, it was a sell-out show.

May 1957 saw the major change in the group's personnel. Alex, Dennis and John left and formed the Old Timers Skiffle Group. They were reluctant to abandon their successful careers for the precarious life on the road. For a while Jimmie MacGregor was with the group, but left to join the City Ramblers just before 'Freight Train' hit the charts. He was replaced by Tony Kohn,

The new group, from September 1957.

Terry Dene, Chas, Paul Lincoln and Fraser White 'Rock Across the Channel' on SS Royal Daffodil.

formerly with the Ghouls and the Cottonpickers. Bass player, Bill Bramwell, was recruited on guitar and on bass, Lennie Harrison, the daddy of the group. Before the war, Lennie had played in Paris with Benny Carter and Django Reinhardt and even before that with some early jug bands. He had also accompanied Big Bill Broonzy on one of his visits to the UK. Lennie was a much loved 'character' often seen around Archer Street on a Monday morning, regaling everyone with his outlandish stories about his experiences; all so unbelievable yet always proved to be absolutely true.

With promotion on radio and such television programmes as the popular 'Six–Five Special', 'Freight Train' zoomed into the hit parade on both sides of the Atlantic. Gerry Myers, a disc jockey in Canada, had plugged the record regularly; this was picked up by the nearby New York jocks and in no time it was a hit throughout the USA. It peaked at number four in the Variety Disc Jockey Charts but was overtaken by Rusty Draper's version in the Billboard Chart. Nevertheless, by the end of July, it had become a million-seller. No doubt this was achieved with the impetus provided by the trip the group made to New York at the end of June 1957. They were booked to appear on Ed Sullivan's show, on the same day that the Everly Bros. first sang 'Bye, Bye Love'. On this occasion Marc Sharratt's washboard was classified as a musical instrument and at first it was thought that the group would suffer the same fate as Lonnie Donegan and not be allowed to play their instruments. The American Federation of Musicians relented a little and gave them the nod, providing they use three American musicians. Consequently, the group was augmented by such noted session musicians as Hank Garland and Billy Mure on guitars and Sandy Block on bass. One more performance took place at the famous Palisades Park (as featured in Freddie Cannon's hit song). It was held al fresco and the show included the blues singer Jimmy Witherspoon singing his hit 'Who, Baby, Who' and the doo-wop group, the Heartbeats, singing 'Everybody's Somebody's Fool'. Chas recalls having to follow an act that jumped off an 80-foot tower on horseback, into a tank of flaming water . . .

It had been very difficult to get working visas for the group, so Chic Records, their American label, employed Lauri Ames as sponsor to facilitate their entry into the USA. Unfortunately, they were only cleared for one day's work. Chas still has the entry in his passport and when he showed this recently to immigration

officials at the customs in the USA they were absolutely amazed that such an arrangement could have been made. Another arrangement that was made at the time was that their proposed appearance on the Ed Sullivan show should be brought forward by two weeks to counterbalance the recent appearance by Rusty Draper. When Chas naively inquired how this had been managed he was informed, 'By bedroom diplomacy!'

The group was scheduled to appear on Alan Freed's 'Big Beat' TV show on their last day in New York. However, this had to be cancelled as any later flight would have caused them to miss their opening night at London's Finsbury Park Empire, and this was the beginning of what proved to be a record-breaking tour of the Moss Empire circuit.

While in America, Nancy had agreed to sign representation forms with Lauri Ames. When Chic Thompson, the head of Chic Records, heard of this, fearing Nancy might leave the group and thereby endanger his investment, he pulled the plug on the venture, and any negotiations for extending the trip were cancelled, both with the AFM and with the agencies back in the UK. Arguments over expenses between Ames and Chic Records swallowed up any payments due to the group; even the fee from the Ed Sullivan show was absorbed by the squabbling parties. This, together with pending litigation over the copyright of 'Freight Train', caused even more mayhem. Eventually the

Marc, Nancy and Chas with Ed Sullivan.

copyright argument was settled amicably out of court; all interested parties receiving an equal share of the performing rights. Chic Records then disappeared into the blue beyond and no record royalties were ever paid out from the US sales.

On their return from America, Nancy had given notice that she did not want to renew her agreement. She had never been happy as part of a group. Her much-publicized outbursts made headlines, like: 'I hate skiffle', 'I'm sick and tired of skiffle' and 'Miss Whiskey sloshes skiffle'.

She went on to say, 'The public likes it frantic and frenzied. I don't like that kind of music. But I sing it for the money. I'm going to make all the money I can before the kids get tired of the craze.'

All this did not endear her to the skiffle fans nor did it help the atmosphere in the group. Part of the reason for Nancy's disquiet could also have been the result of turmoil in her personal life. In August, just before she left, the publicity broke: 'My boyfriend is married sobs Nancy Whiskey.'

Nancy had announced to the press that she was engaged to Bobby Kelly, prompting Kelly's wife to announce that this couldn't be. The ensuing publicity might have helped boost the figures for the last few days of the Moss Empire tour, but as far as the group was concerned it was publicity that they could have done without. Nancy stayed until the end of the tour, enabling Chas to audition for a replacement in every major city they played. Hundreds of hopefuls were auditioned before it was decided that Shirley Douglas (whom they had heard down the line over a BBC link-up with Belfast) should join the group. She made her first appearance with them on a television show, 'Now, the Hop Fields'.

'Greenback Dollar' was the second record with Nancy to enter the charts, but 'Face in the Rain' and 'Johnny Oh', technically better records, failed to register. The skiffle group had made a guest appearance in the movie *The Tommy Steele Story* and on its release in September 1957, it prompted a brief re-entry for 'Freight Train'.

When Shirley Douglas made her first record with the group, 'Across the Bridge', it was released at the same time as Nancy's last record with the group, 'Johnny Oh'; consequently they were in competition with each other, neither getting its fair share of promotion. However, Shirley quickly established herself as a firm favourite with the skiffle fans. Her folksy soprano voice added another dimension to the group's repertoire.

Already there was Chas specializing in the skiffle standards and folk beat songs; Tony Kohn, he of the rich brown voice, covering the blues-flavoured titles like 'Everyday' and 'I Want a Little Girl' and Bill Bramwell featuring the scat/jazz songs such as 'My Old Man', once recorded in the 1930s by the Five Spirits of Rhythm.

Maurice Burman, reviewing a broadcast by the Chas McDevitt Skiffle Group, on 'Saturday Skiffle Club' 1 July 1957 in the *Melody Maker*, picked up on this reference to the 1930s group. He reported:

In fact the line-up of this group was similar to the 50s skiffle groups; two guitars, a tipple guitar, bass and suitcase played with two clothes whisks. Substitute a washboard for the valise and you have the forerunner of skiffle.

You could have knocked me down with a feather when one of the McDevitt guitarists came forward and sang the ancient and honourable jazzer 'My Old Man' with a good beat and style.

The Chas McDevitt group, unlike nearly all skiffle outfits, contains good musicians. And because of that the players show taste and sensibility in their music.

Maurice Burman was so impressed that on this occasion he awarded his weekly 'Burman's Bauble' to Bill Bramwell.

He might not have been so generous with his plaudits had he been aware of another one of Bill's talents. Bill would always succeed in commandeering the front passenger seat in the mini-bus. He would jump in quickly, nursing his little hip-flask, while the rest of the boys loaded his guitar and amplifier; then he would remove his shoes and place his feet over the hot air duct, filling the vehicle with a nauseating malodorous funk.

The McDevitt group undertook numerous nationwide tours with Slim Whitman, Frankie Lymon and the Teenagers, Freddie Bell and the Bellboys and with the fabulous Treniers, replacing Jerry Lee Lewis, who had been withdrawn from that particular tour because of the scandal surrounding his marriage to his 13-year-old cousin.

By the end of 1958, Tony Kohn was called up for National Service, reducing the group to a quintet for a while. Eventually Chas disbanded the skiffle group bringing in Les Bennetts and Red Reece, both from Les Hobeaux Skiffle Group, Les on guitar and Red on drums. Shirley Douglas was now playing electric bass-guitar. When Les left to join Lonnie Donegan, Roy Powell came in on piano. The Freight Train Boys, as the backing was now called, had metamorphosed into a skiffle/rock band; their last record for Oriole being 'Teenage Letter', a song recorded by Big Joe Turner to be covered later by Jerry Lee Lewis. This was an out and out rock number and featured a tearaway trombone solo.

When the group finally disbanded, Chas and Shirley continued as a duo in concert and cabaret. As well as supporting such acts as the Beatles and Chubby Checker, they toured the world from Helsinki to Bangkok, and from New York to New Zealand. They occasionally reverted to playing skiffle on record. In 1965, they made an album for Columbia Records, with various skiffle tracks, which included Marc Sharratt on washboard, Wizz Jones on guitar and Pete Stanley on banjo as well as Red Reece on drums. Further albums were recorded for President Records in the 1970s that featured some skiffle tracks; they even re-recorded 'Freight Train' as a single. They split up finally in 1975.

In the 1980s, Chas was reunited with Marc Sharratt and John Paul. With Nick Lawrence on guitar, they toured on the continent and appeared in rock festivals throughout the UK. Returning from one such engagement in Holland, Marc Sharratt was killed in a head-on collision; it was his fifty-eighth birthday, 16 May 1991. A bitter blow to his many friends who held him in esteem not only as a washboard wizard but as a great raconteur and truly eccentric character. His technique was unique, both beating and scrubbing the board. At the height of the craze he had a standing order with Timothy White's, the hardware store, for the metal-ridged inserts to the washboard, as he'd beat one flat in a week. As a publicity stunt, he had his fingers insured with Lloyds for £5,000. Had they realized the potential danger and seen how his knuckles were pitted with zinc chips, often covered in blood, they never would have taken the risk. John Paul, no less a personality, played on with Chas for a while but on 8 December 1994 he died, having unfortunately succumbed to cancer.

The Chas McDevitt Group still survives, usually with Steve Benbow on lead guitar, Jack Fallon on bass and Chas's daughter, Kerry, on vocals and washboard. Shirley Douglas occasionally plays with the group on both guitar and bass-guitar. In 1994, they appeared in New Orleans during the Jazz Fest together with the K.C. Moaners Skiffle Group from Leeds.

So the Chas McDevitt Freight Train still rolls on, fired by the re-issue on Rollercoaster and Bear Family Records of all the early material.

The Old Timers Skiffle Group

Half the original Chas McDevitt Skiffle Group had been fully professional since mid-1956; the remainder had retained their day jobs. When it came to the crunch in June 1957, after the initial success of 'Freight Train' and the touring became too much, they resigned from the group.

Alex Whitehouse, a rubber broker, Dennis Carter, a travel

Old Timers in Skiffle Cellar. (D. Carter)

executive and John Paul, a civil servant at the Scottish Office, were all reluctant to abandon secure and profitable careers for the vagaries of an itinerant skiffler. Consequently they left and formed a semi-pro group, playing at a pub in Hampton Court, adopting the appropriate name, the Court Jesters. They recruited 'Little Joey' Jonkler on washboard and began doing the rounds of the coffee bars and clubs, almost becoming a fixture at the Skiffle Cellar.

Jack Baverstock, the A&R man on the original Oriole session of 'Freight Train', was now with Philips Records. Realizing their potential he gave the group a contract on Philips' subsidiary label, Fontana. By now they had become The Old Timers, possibly a reflection on their rapidly maturing years. With Hymie Zahl as agent, they secured many a broadcast and TV spot, in particular, 'The Max Wall Show'.

However, the group's true potential was never fully exploited, restricted by their semi-pro status. They had the ideal combination for success. Dennis Carter had once played trombone in a jazz band and had the phrasing and timbre of a true blues man. He probably had the best yet least broadcast voice on the skiffle circuit. Not surprisingly his idols were Jimmy Rushing, Big Joe

Turner and Joe Williams. Apart from the Fontana single, 'The Woman Who Loved a Swine', the only other example of his singing solo is on the Rollercoaster mini-album *Nancy and Chas*, where he performs to a live audience a spirited version of Lead Belly's 'Titanic'. On the same album is 'I Saw the Light', sung by Alex Whitehouse. Alex also sings 'Don't You Rock Me Daddy O' on the Embassy recording by the Cranes Skiffle Group, alias the Chas McDevitt Group. Alex played the nylon-strung Spanish guitar with great force and enthusiasm; in the film *The Tommy Steele Story* he can be seen thrashing away like a wild thing, contributing to the shuffle train-like effect. He was the glamour boy of the group; his Marlon Brando image played havoc with the ladies' emotions. Had he taken the plunge and gone solo in the rock field, he would have pre-empted the success of both Terry Dene and Cliff Richard. The only obvious drawback to his sex appeal was that it appealed to both sexes. Even in those relatively trouble-free days, Alex needed the benefit of a good right-hand punch to keep the more licentious agents, and the temptations of their casting couch, at arm's length. John Paul, the daddy of the group, provided a solid backing both physical and musical and Joey Jonkler laid down a swinging beat on washboard.

They had the sound and the essential pop appeal but not the enthusiasm to take it any further and disbanded in 1958. Both John and Dennis carried on guesting with various jazz bands. After a prolonged illness, John Paul died on 8 December 1994. For the previous seven years he had often been reunited with Marc Sharratt and Chas McDevitt to recreate the core of the original group. They appeared in rock festivals throughout the UK and on the continent, notably in Aalst, Alphen-am-Rijn and in Nantes at a memorable show with the Lonnie Donegan Skiffle Group.

Soho Skiffle Group

A few groups had a relatively short span of life in the limelight, although they recorded.

The Soho Skiffle Group appeared three times on 'Saturday Skiffle Club' and regularly toured in package shows, notably the *Stars of the Six–Five Special*.

When founder member, John Audrey, left the group he changed his name to John Leeman. He then led a very successful R&B band, the Marc Leeman Five, until in 1965 he died in a car crash.

At the time he left, his replacement in the group was Jim Sullivan, who later was with Marty Wilde's Wildcats before joining the James Last Orchestra, accompanying Tom Jones and establishing himself as a very popular session musician and solo performer.

Soho Skiffle Group.

Sonny Stewart Skiffle Kings

Originally from the Croydon area, this group was an offshoot of Jim Wella's Jazz Band. As was the current practice with many a jazz band, Pete Stewart, the banjo player, formed a group within a group, the Pete Stewart Skiffle Group, in late 1956. He was soon joined by Arthur Chamberlain (Sonny to his friends), on guitar and vocals. Shortly after, they amalgamated their names, and became the Sonny Stewart Skiffle Kings.

One of the few recording groups not to have been featured on 'Saturday Skiffle Club', they nevertheless had to turn professional to accommodate the dates lined up for them by the MCA agency.

For a while the group included Steve Benbow on guitar and vocals, later to make his name with his own Folk Four. He was to have a series on both radio and television, as well as a memorable guitar partnership with Denny Wright. Steve left the Skiffle Kings after being tipped off by Dave Keir that Ewan MacColl was looking for a guitarist to record and broadcast with his newly formed group.

Sonny's group had a residency at the 2 Is and occasionally played the Skiffle Cellar. In 1958 they landed themselves a part in the film, *The Golden Disc*. Terry Dene was the star of this film, which had musical interludes from Les Hobeaux and Nancy Whiskey as well as the Sonny Stewart group. They accompanied Nancy on her rendition of 'Johnny O'; she had already left the Chas McDevitt Group, with whom she had originally recorded the song. By now Nancy was heavily pregnant and was compelled by the producers to perform her entire sequence from behind a music stand.

The Sonny Stewart Skiffle Kings featured their last recording for Philips in the film, *Let Me Lie*, but it had little chance of success. Unfortunately for all concerned, the film was a disaster. Even viewed by today's standards, it lacks the naive charm of the earlier *Tommy Steele Story*. Terry Dene had by now accumulated a series of bad press reports concerning the break up of his marriage, public disorder and his clash with the authorities over his National Service. The film didn't stand a chance.

When the skiffle craze began to wane, Sonny recorded for Top Rank. The record, due for release in August 1960, remained unissued as by then the record company had collapsed.

Later Sonny played with various groups in Germany and even

recorded a couple of tracks for the Bellaphon label. Sadly, beset by problems in the early 1960s, Sonny took his own life.

The Vipers Skiffle Group

Like so many skiffle groups the Vipers had a fluctuating personnel but throughout their career the linchpin and founder of the group was Wally Whyton. Wallace Victor Whyton was born 23 September 1929, the day of the Wall Street crash. During the war he was evacuated to Minehead to escape from the bombing raids on London. As a youngster he developed a taste for jazz from listening to the radio and the ubiquitous 78 rpm gramophone records. He was brought up just outside London's West End, on the outer fringes of Soho, a fact which in later life would prove to be propitious. On completion of his education he began work in a commercial art studio, but between 1948 and 1950 he was called up and did his National Service in the RAF.

On his demobilization he further developed his musical interests and began borrowing records and folk song albums from the American Library of Congress. He discovered Muddy Waters, Lead Belly, Woody Guthrie and Burl Ives. Wally was also captivated by the music of Josh White and remembers the time he went to hear Josh at the Shepherd's Bush Empire, he had the gall to 'lift' Josh's photo from the display board and ask Josh to sign it. That same week a 16-year-old Chas McDevitt, confined to hospital, struck up a correspondence with Josh and he too became the proud owner of a signed photo, perhaps obtained a little more legitimately.

Wally bought his first guitar for £1; it had been left behind in his local pub and the landlord was glad to get rid of it. He wasted no time and immediately enrolled for lessons at the Kentish Town Institute. However, it was not long before he acquired his cherished Martin guitar, found in a Charing Cross Road music shop.

Virtually on Wally's doorstep, in Cleveland Street, was the Breadbasket coffee bar, a Mecca for many a young guitar player, the attraction being the amply proportioned waitresses rather than the coffee. Wally insists it was the music that drew him there and to another coffee bar in John Adam St, Charing Cross, the Gyre and Gimble. Here he began playing with a nucleus of musicians, at one stage including the young Tommy Hicks (Tommy Steele), Lionel Bart, and Mike Pratt who later gained stardom in the TV series 'Randall and Hopkirk Deceased'; they were known as the Cavemen. Lionel Bart and Mike Pratt went on to write Tommy Steele's first hit 'Rock with the Caveman' which reached number 13 in the hit parade in early October 1956. Lionel became a very successful song-writer, with hits for Adam Faith, a number one for Cliff Richard, 'Livin' Doll', and not forgetting of course his immensely popular musical *Oliver*. Regrettably, Mike Pratt died from lung cancer at the height of his career, on 10 July 1976. During the Cavemen's spasmodic sessions in the coffee bars, Tommy was travelling back and forth to the USA in the Merchant Navy and indeed was soon to be discovered. Consequently Wally decided to recruit a more stable ensemble in the form of Johnny Martyn (Booker), Jean van den Bosch, John Pilgrim and Tony Tolhurst. Over the next couple of years the personnel was fairly fluid, at one time including Freddie Lloyd from the Worried Men, and eventually such future luminaries of the Shadows as Hank Marvin and Jet Harris.

In 1956 the group was to be found playing around the West End and during the Soho Fair held to coincide with Bastille Day on 14 July, they joined the procession pausing at one stage outside a coffee bar in Old Compton Street, the Two Is, or to be more precise, The 2 I's.

The 2 I's got its name from the original owners, the Irani Brothers, who later owned the Tropicana, which in its turn became the Establishment, the cradle of British satirical comedy. It was currently owned by two professional wrestlers: Paul (Dr Death) Lincoln and Ray Hunter. Ray eventually had an interest in the Cromwellian Club in the Cromwell Road, where many a young rocker would jam the night away, notably Georgie Fame, Eric Burdon, Alan Price, Zoot Money and even the occasional visiting American act like 'Little' Stevie Wonder.

Wally and the group, having stopped for a coffee, began to play and drew a large crowd and Paul Lincoln, realizing their potential, asked them to play his venue on a regular basis. During the day Wally was still working in his office job and the freelance work brought him again into contact with Lionel Bart and this friendship became useful when Paul wanted the premises redecorated. Lionel had been a student at the St Martin's School of Art and was a natural choice for this task. He created a distinctive and decadent aura in this basement: black ceiling, large stylized eyes on the walls

The Vipers – Johnny Booker, Wally Whyton and (front) Tony Tolhurst, John Pilgrim, Jean van den Bosch. (Flair)

Wally sitting-in with City Ramblers – Russell Quaye, Hylda Sims and Jimmie MacGregor. (W. Whyton)

and cubist shapes on the wall behind the small stage platform. Small was the operative word, for the basement could hold only about 80 people crammed in tight. The skiffle groups hardly had room to set up when it was in full swing.

At first the groups would play for cokes and spaghetti but with their increasing popularity they were allowed to bottle for tips. After a while Wally decided that the group deserved a rise on the small salary he had eventually negotiated. He came up with a bizarre idea – he offered to wrestle Paul Lincoln for double or nothing. Wally must have been inspired, because he beat Dr Death hands down.

Two retired air stewards, Roy Tuvey and Bill Varley, had a small recording studio in Denmark Street, London's Tin Pan Alley. Trio Recordings was used by music publishers to produce demonstration records of the songs they were promoting. Roy and Bill decided to take their portable machine, a cumbersome EMI TR 50A, into the coffee bars and, in the Gyre and Gimble, recorded Jim Dale, the Vipers and the Chas McDevitt Skiffle Group. Bill Varley and Wally were credited as the authors of 'Don't You Rock Me Daddy O', released simultaneously by the Vipers and Lonnie Donegan. Bill Varley went on to manage the Chas McDevitt Group and Roy Tuvey to produce independent radio shows.

The 2 I's became a must for the talent scouts; Hugh Mendl signed up Tommy Steele for Decca Records and George Martin signed up the Vipers for Parlophone, acquiescing in Wally's request to be released on their Rhythm Series, the jazz-flavoured version of Parlophone that featured such legends as Louis Armstrong, Benny Goodman and Bessie Smith. Wally said,

> They offered us a $2\frac{1}{2}$ per cent royalty, less an allowance of 10 per cent for breakages of those old 78s. [Today 12 per cent isn't an excessive royalty.]
>
> So I worked by day at Dorland's Advertising Agency in Lower Regent Street, played at the 2 I's from 7–11pm, and recorded our first songs at Abbey Road, Studio 2 through from midnight. I had no thought of turning professional as I had a great job, earning twice the national average. The other lads though were keen to taste life on the road.

But having decided to turn fully professional and give it a go for six months, they accepted a two-week engagement at London's prestigious Prince of Wales Theatre. During the complete run of the show they came back each night to play at the 2 I's, much to Paul Lincoln's delight; the theatrical barring clause concerning proximity of venues was obviously ignored, the 2 I's being a mere two blocks from the theatre.

Amongst the Vipers' many fans was Iris Orton. Iris was dubbed the Poetic Queen of the Coffee Bars, and the Vipers, or more precisely Wally Whyton, was the source of her inspiration. In mid-February 1958, Iris achieved a first:

> I went on a platform before the distinguished Ben Uri literary society in Portman Square, and succeeded to do what neither skiffle fans nor members of literary societies would expect; I read my poetry to a guitar played by Wally Whyton of the Vipers. This was for me the logical result of 18 months of listening to spontaneous and creative music.
>
> I first heard the Vipers in November 1956. This group never rehearsed. After 14 years in the literary world I was seeing creative activity at its moment of creation for the first time. (I know I may have seen this in instrumental jazz sessions but certainly not elsewhere.) I did not miss a session of this group from that time and I made a rewarding study of their creative methods.

With the popularity of their records and their TV and radio broadcasts, their workload rapidly increased. A nationwide tour promoted by the impresario, Stanley Dale, starred both Jim Dale and the Vipers. This was the National Skiffle Competition where groups were featured every night of the week with the finals on Friday and Saturday. This was a great moneyspinner, the groups filling the theatre with friends and relations banking on their favourable applause to see them through to the next round. The tour covered most of the available variety theatres but no grand final was ever held.

In those days life on the road was fairly gruelling; this was before the so called advantages of the M1 and M25 motorways. However, the groups certainly enjoyed themselves; their behaviour was as ribald if not as publicized as that of the 1960s rock bands. At one time the Vipers Skiffle Group travelled the land accompanied by a virtual menagerie. Their transport reeked of monkeys, skunks, and coati-mundi. The flat in Victoria used by Johnny Booker and Jet Harris was about as savoury as a lion's den.

Touring had its pitfalls and there was a constant barrage of sniping from the Establishment. On 4 May 1957 the *Melody Maker* ran a headline: 'Vipers Ban, Sabrina Concert Cancelled'. The

Manchester magistrates had refused the Vipers a permit to appear in a concert at Belle Vue on Sunday 6 May. All the other acts received their permits but not the Vipers. Presumably they encountered the same opposition from the Sunday Watch Committee as did the Chas McDevitt Skiffle Group when they appeared in a Sunday charity show. Section 5 of the Sunday Entertainment Act of 1932: 'Allowed entertainment to be presented with or without singing.'

Cross talk between comedians was not permitted, so double acts could not perform and the groups were informed that they were not allowed to use any theatrical props, only their musical instruments, the washboard being classed as a prop. The irony was that this was pointless, for when the McDevitt Group later appeared in America on the Ed Sullivan TV show, the American Federation of Musicians defined the washboard as being a musical instrument. To mollify the Watch Committee the McDevitt Group agreed that on this occasion Marc Sharratt would play drums, and all was well. All was well until they saw the group's photo reproduced in the souvenir brochure – the authorities had gone to the considerable expense of airbrushing out the washboard in Marc's arms, and replacing it with drumsticks.

After a couple of years on the road the Vipers gradually wound down and came to a fairly dignified end when the popular taste changed to the more exciting and teenage-orientated fad of British rock and roll. Once Jet Harris and Hank Marvin had left to team up with Bruce Welch and Tony Meehan to form the Drifters and go on tour with Cliff Richard, Wally again turned to Johnny Booker and the eccentric Zom. But by now the enthusiasm of the early days had faded and soon Wally was left on his own. He went on to explore the folk field, and later to become one of Britain's foremost authorities on country and western music, with his own radio programmes. Parallel to this new career he appeared regularly on television with the children's favourite characters, Olly Beak and Pussy Cat Willum. He continued to record prolifically, but his material was aimed more at the folk field and often featured collections of children's songs, a legacy of his enthusiasm for Woody Guthrie.

At Bernard Miles's Mermaid Theatre in Blackfriars, Wally briefly re-formed the Vipers in 1960 to appear in a play with Sally Miles, *Mr Burke MP*.

When Wally was asked in an interview how long the Vipers had been a going concern, he replied,

Exactly two years. I can say that with some precision. I remember receiving a tax bill for the £20,000 the group had earned over two years! The authorities had a record of all the engagements we had played. When I protested that most of this money had been paid to the group, they wanted to see signed receipts, the wages book was not sufficient. It was a real nightmare.

One is left to surmise what might have been, had the Vipers not been covered by Lonnie Donegan on 'Daddy O' and 'Cumberland Gap'. In the space of five months the Vipers had seen three of their records in the hit parade, including two top-ten entries. They left a legacy of party music, played with excitement and verve, which was the hallmark of the British skiffle craze.

After an 18-month struggle with cancer, Wally died on the night of 22 January 1997. His funeral at Golders Green, on 31 January, was attended by hundreds of friends and fans from all fields of music; skiffle, country, jazz and folk and included many of his associates from both radio and television. It was a moving farewell to one much admired by his peers.

Nancy Whiskey

Anne Alexandra Young Wilson was born to Robert and Elizabeth Wilson in Bridgeton, Glasgow, 4 March 1935. She was the youngest of six children. Her father played the piano and it was he who taught her the guitar.

She acquired her stage name from a song she sang, 'The Carlton Weaver'. The chorus goes,

'Whisky, whisky, Nancy whisky, whisky, whisky, Nancy Oh.'

When asked why it was the Irish spelling of whiskey she used, she replied,

I must be absolutely honest about it. The fact is that I am an atrocious speller. Before I knew what I was doing I was signing my name Nancy Whiskey. And there I was, stuck with the Irish spelling!

After working in a pottery studio and going to art school in the evenings, Nancy decided to move south. Consequently, at the end

Nancy Whiskey, 1957.

of 1955, she and a group of friends which was to include Bobby Kelly, 'Broken' John (so named because of his usual financial status), Jimmie MacGregor and Bob's brother, Lex, all caught a bus down to the Big Smoke.

For about a year she worked in a coffee bar opposite Foyle's book shop in the Charing Cross Road, and in the evenings did the rounds of the music venues such as the Roundhouse in Wardour Street. At about this time Bobby Kelly was beginning to be the featured pianist with the Ken Colyer band. Nancy was well known on the folk scene and in 1956 cut a mini-album for Topic Records, not released until after the success of 'Freight Train' in late 1957.

On Sunday 14 October 1956, Nancy appeared at a concert at the Unity Theatre in Mornington Crescent. On the same bill were Nick Thatcher, Lionel Bart and Mike Pratt, the Satyrs, with Judith Goldbloom and Chas McDevitt's St Louis Trio. The trio received 30s. for the show. Hyam Morris, who organized the show, wrote to Chas on 21 October 1956.

Dear Chas,

I feel rather ashamed that I can only send you 30s. for you and the boys that did the Unity show.

However I think you will understand if I tell you that out of the gross takings of £9 (we actually had just over 50 real people there!!), £4 went to what advertising there was and to entertainment tax. The remaining £5 was split between us and Unity.

The concert itself was a hit, and Unity promise that the next one (?) will have the full publicity treatment. After getting 'sweet F.A.' out of this 'do', we sincerely hope so.

Anyway, thanks again for lending me your guitar, and for coming.

Within nine months of this engagement Nancy and Chas would be appearing on American Television contracted for a fee of $3,000.

At this point it may be of interest to know exactly what types of songs were being performed by such a melange of artists. The theatres in those days often included a complete rundown of the items used in their programme. Happily the Unity programme, a typewritten photostat, still exists. It reads:

A selection from the following items will be performed:

'Weary and Lonesome Traveller'	'If I Had a Hammer'
'Drinkin' Gourd'	'Gay Caballero'
'Bella Ciao'	'Gizratech'
'Walk and Talk with Jesus'	'No Hidin' Place'
'Black Eyed Susie'	'West Virginny Snows'
'Meeting in the Building'	'Ain't You Glad'

'Rock Island Line'	'Streamline Train'
'Crawdad'	'K.C. Moan'
'Midnight Special'	'Venezuela'
'Darlin''	'Union Maid'
'Ain't it a Shame'	'Rothsay'
'Siboney'	'Old Time Religion'
'Hen Reel'	'Liza O'
'We Shall Not Be Moved'	'Old Joe Clark'
'Easy Rider'	'900 Miles'
'Momma Don't Allow'	'Bring a Little Water Sylvie'
'Pick a Bale of Cotton'	'Chain Gang Blues'
'Dust Bowl Refugee'	'Freight Train'

Quite a varied programme, ranging from blues to folk song, spirituals to work songs, typical of any concert or club performance one might hear at that time.

Nancy and Chas would next play together on a talent show organized by Radio Luxembourg and Pye Radio. Nancy performed at one of the heats at the Chelsea Palace Theatre, singing 'The Fireman's Not For Me'. Bill Varley, Chas McDevitt's manager, suggested that Nancy be asked to join the group. He felt that the inclusion of a female in the group would make it a more commercial proposition. At first Nancy was reluctant to give up her folk singing, but in the end the decision to re-record 'Freight Train' with Nancy taking the lead vocal persuaded her to join the group. Another reason for her hesitation was that she had been approached by Pye-Nixa Records to do a recording test.

'Freight Train' was a slow starter; released in January, it did not reach the hit parade until March. But from that moment on it became a classic of its genre.

On 20 May 1957 Nancy and Bill Varley were rushed to the USA for a whistle-stop personal appearance, at the Seventh Big Annual Convention of the Music Operators of America – record companies, disc jockeys and artists, all meeting in Chicago to push their merchandise. It was a chaotic trip organized at the last minute and Nancy wasn't able to get on stage to perform 'Freight Train' until 2.30 am.

This set the scene for a return visit by the group, at the end of June, to appear on the Ed Sullivan show. Maurice Levy, the head of Oriole records, Chas's recording company, had done a deal with Chic Thompson of Chic Records from Thomasville, Georgia, for the group to go over and promote the single. However, he had neglected to organize work permits for the full group. Nancy,

George Jennings, Nancy Whiskey, Bob Kelly and Bryan Daly, 1958 (N. Whiskey)

Chas and Marc Sharratt, on washboard, went over for two weeks. They appeared on the Sullivan show which had a viewing audience of 45,000,000 and later in concert at the Palisades Park, in New Jersey. The trip was fraught with problems; Nancy had been approached by an American agency, prompting Chic Records to get cold feet. The various agents and sub-agents argued amongst themselves and the projected return tour of the whole group never materialized, for by then Nancy had decided she would branch out on her own.

On their return to the UK, the group undertook a five-week tour of the Moss Empire circuit supported by Terry Dene and the Dene Aces. At the end of this run Nancy left the group. Towards the end of 1957 she made a guest appearance in the Terry Dene film *The Golden Disc*, singing her last recording with the McDevitt Group, 'Johnny Oh'. In the film she was accompanied by the Sonny Stewart Skiffle Group. Appearing in the same film were Les Hobeaux Skiffle Group.

For a while Nancy took time off for the birth of her daughter, Yancey, named after an idol of both Nancy and her new husband Bobby Kelly. Jimmy Yancey was an exceptionally talented blues and boogie player from the Chicago scene of the 1920s and 1930s and had performed with many of the original skiffle bands of the period.

In February 1958, Nancy resumed touring with her skiffle group, the Teetotallers, with Bobby Kelly on washboard and also on piano. Diz Disley and Bryan Daly played guitar in various manifestations of the group.

Before leaving Oriole Records she recorded three more singles and then nothing further was released, until on 24 November 1967 when she re-recorded 'Freight Train' on CBS Records, with orchestral direction by Johnny Harris and production by Tony Reeves.

Nancy toured for a while in cabaret and on various cruises but eventually she settled down in Leicester. Occasionally she is tempted to make a foray into the world of showbiz. She appeared in the 'Arena TV Skiffle Special', and with the Chas McDevitt Skiffle Group on Noel Edmonds's 'Time of Your Life' in 1987. She also joined Chas for a one-off show at the Shaw Theatre and in the big reunion skiffle party, 'Kings and Queens of Skiffle', which included Lonnie Donegan and his group, Chas and his group and Beryl Bryden, plus washboard, at the Fairfield Hall in Croydon on 28 April 1991.

Worried Men Skiffle Group

When Les Hobeaux left their residency at the 2 Is, their place was taken by the Worried Men. They soon secured a recording contract with Decca Records but, within weeks of their first release, the group had virtually fragmented. It carried on for over a year, but the impact and unique style of the original group had been dissipated. As ever, a constant flow of changing musicians didn't contribute to a long-lasting career. They did, however, appear on 'Six–Five Special' and tour with Terry Dene and Chas McDevitt.

One of the first to leave was Terry Denver (Nelhams), later re-reincarnated as Adam Faith. When he first left the group he made a couple of singles, with little success: one for HMV and one for Top Rank Records. After appearing on BBC's pop TV show, 'Drumbeat', George Martin signed him to HMV. This resulted in the first of many hit records, the number one song 'What Do You Want'. Terry's place in the group was taken by Freddy Lloyd, but before long he too had left, to join the Vipers. Other members of the original group included Dennis Nelhams, Terry's brother, Chas Beaumont on lead guitar, and Hurgy (Roger Van Engel), Terry's best pal, on drums and washboard.

The Worried Men served as a proving ground for many of the young 2 Is musicians. Tony Meehan, later of the Shadows, and his replacement in the Shadows, Brian Bennett, both did a stint with this group.

Rick Richards (Hardy) came in for a while on guitar and vocals. It was Rick who had recommended Hank Marvin for the lead guitar job with the Drifters, later to become the Shadows. Rick too would soon leave the group. Together with Tony Sheridan, another stalwart of the 2 Is, he formed a rock and roll group, the Jets. Bruno Koschmider, of the Kaiserkellar in Hamburg, was looking for groups to replace the German bands, who naturally all sang with German accents. Rick Richards and Ian Hines persuaded him that the Jets were the answer to his dreams and consequently the first British group to play Hamburg was:

Rick Richards, guitar, voc.   Tony Sheridan, guitar voc.
Colin Millander, guitar   Del Ward, drums
Pete Wharton, bass

They were later joined by Ian Hines on piano and Chas Beaumont on guitar.

Rick Richards and Chas Beaumont, two of the Worried Men who, as the Jets, were in the vanguard of the British invasion of the German rock scene. (R. Hardy)

4
Non-recording Groups

Bill Bailey Skiffle Group

Many groups without a recording contract generated a loyal and sometimes fanatical following. Their club, concert and occasional broadcasting sessions aroused considerable interest among the skiffle fraternity. The Cottonpickers, the Ghouls, the Eastsiders, Pete Curtis, Brian Newey, Al Meek and his Rio Ranch Boys, the Westcott Skiffle Group, the Hi-Fi Skiffle Group, all had a dedicated fan following but never recorded commercially. The Brett Bros, although regulars at the Skiffle Cellar, and on 'Saturday Skiffle Club', didn't record until a few years later, as a country and western group.

The Bill Bailey Skiffle Group was one such group. They had made seven appearances on 'Saturday Skiffle Club' (only Johnny Duncan and Chas McDevitt had more slots on the show), yet no record company had signed them up.

They lay claim to have been the first British skiffle group for, in 1945, Bill Bailey on guitar, vocal and kazoo, Freddy Legon on guitar, vocal and blue blowing and Johnny Jones on washboard, formed the Original London Blue Blowers. They were featured in jazz broadcasts and as guests in the rhythm clubs that flourished on the fringes of the music scene. Playing mainly spasm and jug music, this jazz-related combo broke up in 1948 when the two guitar players began playing in various Dixieland bands.

While Freddy Legon was playing guitar and banjo with the Humphrey Lyttelton Band in 1951, he advised a 16-year-old Charles McDevitt on the type of banjo he should take up. Freddy suggested,

> A Clifford Essex G banjo. Listen to any early King Oliver and in particular to Fats Waller's 'Minor Drag' on HMV, with just the piano and Eddie Condon's G banjo as a rhythm section.

To this day Chas still plays that G banjo.

With the arrival of the skiffle craze the Blue Blowers re-formed and called themselves the Bill Bailey Skiffle Group.

Acetates of the group do exist, and a complete broadcast of one of their 'Saturday Skiffle Club' sessions may soon see the light of day.

Members of the group

Bill Bailey, guitar, kazoo, voc.
Dave Coward, bass
Stan Jayne, guitar, washboard, voc.

Bill Powell, guitar, banjo
Freddy Legon, guitar, comb and paper, voc.
John Beauchamp, drums

Cottonpickers

The Cottonpickers, originally founded by Mike Pratt and Dave Llewellyn, were as susceptible as all the other skiffle groups when it came down to keeping a regular line-up of musicians. This more than anything may have contributed to their lack of a recording contract.

Even so the Cottonpickers had their champions; they became a regular guest band at the Cy Laurie Jazz Club in Windmill Street as well as playing dates at the 2 Is and the Skiffle Cellar. They also starred in the Second Skiffle Jamboree at the Royal Albert Hall on Monday 14 October 1957, which included Johnny Duncan and the Bluegrass Boys, Cy Laurie's Jazz Band, pop singer Vera Day and the Eden Street and Bob Cort Skiffle Groups.

Dave Llewelyn and his group featuring a young Steve Benbow. (S. Benbow)

The function itself was a bit of a disaster, the Albert Hall, a little bleak at the best of times, was even more dreary when only half full. Clashing dates hit the box office, for in town were Count Basie, Jack Teagarden and Judy Garland. The choice of a Monday night for such a promotion was also a little less than inspiring.

The Cottonpickers appeared in many touring package shows and on one memorable occasion provide the support at a concert in Belfast to the legendary New Orleans soprano sax player, Sidney Bechet.

Members of the group

Mike Pratt, guitar, piano
Bill Moore, guitar
Alan (Little Bear) Sutton,
    washboard

Dave Llewellyn, banjo, guitar
Eric (Wally) Wallace, bass

In July 1957 'Little Bear' was replaced on washboard by Garry Winkler. Tony Kohn had left in May 1957 to join the Chas McDevitt Group. By early December 1957 Dave Llewellyn had left to form the Brady Boys, which at one time featured Steve Benbow. Mike Pratt got more involved in his song writing and acting and so the group gradually came to an end.

Pete Curtis

The Pete Curtis Group was formed in June 1957. Although they never recorded commercially, their standard of musicianship made them very popular and resulted in six sessions on 'Saturday Skiffle Club' between January and September 1958.

Pete Curtis had originally played with the Graham Stewart Band and the Waterfront Jazz Band; Frank Willett with the River City Jazzmen and the Cy Laurie Jazz Band.

The jazz pedigree of the founder members reflected their ability and their choice of material. One of their most requested songs was their interpretation of 'If You's a Viper', recorded by Rosetta Howard and the Harlem Hamfats.

> Dreamed about a reefer five feet long
> Mighty Mezz but not too strong,
> Light a 'T' and let it be,
> If you's a viper.

Members of the group

Pete Curtis, guitar
Roy Spalding, elect. guitar
Don Roome, bass

Frank Willett, guitar
Ted Crockett, guitar

John Hasted Skiffle and Folk Song Group

John Hasted was a professor of physics at London University. He yearned for a revival in folk singing and strived to promote its popularity. In a way his dream came true for, by helping create the interest in skiffle, he nurtured the interest for folk music in many a 'three-chord skiffler'.

He performed with various groups and choirs at political rallies and festivals. In order to promote any new political songs, he and Eric Winter produced the popular magazine *Sing*. British and American songs were collected and annotated.

The professor had said that he could never have much success as a solo singer of the material he collected, because his 'pleasant and patronizing Oxford accent precluded anything except play acting and mimicry'.

Consequently he surrounded himself with other singers, originally the London Youth Choir (to which Hylda Sims, later of the City Ramblers, belonged), and then with the mighty voices featured in his group, resident at 44 Gerrard Street in Soho. John would play banjo and 12-string guitar, leading the choruses and hosting a fine evening of song and laughter. His secret weapon was the selection of powerful voices he had at his side.

Colin 'Redd' Sullivan was born in London on 13 December 1930. He was a huge, intimidating, red-headed giant of a man, with a voice to match. A former artillery man, he had also worked as a stoker on the coal-fired ships. He had an amusing style as raconteur often debunking the more pretentious on the music scene. He was a true eccentric; once he was arrested for feeding stray cats from a milk machine, at other times he would assist Goon Spike Milligan to restore life to the blighted tree in Kensington Gardens by massaging it with linseed oil. His speciality, however, was the singing, often unaccompanied, of the songs by Lead Belly, of sea shanties and even of music hall ditties. He was arguably one of the best blues shouters around. He would dominate any room, head held high with his goateed chin jutting out at the audience like Don Quixote's lance, his arms swinging in unison by his side as he punched out his current favourite. In 1967 he was invited by Pete Seeger to be a guest at the Newport Folk Festival. In the 1960s he was a founder member of the seminal folk group, the Thamesiders. Few examples of his work can be found on record. In 1964, together with Martin Carthy, he recorded on a 'Hootenaney' album for Decca Records, produced by Wally Whyton. In 1969 he sang three blues tracks on the Saga album *Blues at Sunrise*. And again in 1971 he recorded an album for Deacon Records, together with Martin Winsor. Martin was to become the co-host with Redd at the renowned Troubadour coffee bar in Brompton Road. Redd died on 26 May 1992, while waiting for a heart bypass. His singing partner during all those years, Martin Winsor, died six months later.

Martin had provided an amazing deep rich baritone voice to the Hasted ensemble, which he would sometimes distort to produce a guttural trumpet effect. He also played washboard and guitar. The rest of the group included Frank Ogrodnovitch, John Cole on harmonica, Hyam Morris, who played bass and wrote some excellent lyrics, and on vocals and guitar the contrasting styles of Judith Goldbloom (Silver), and Marion Amiss (Gray). Completing this formidable line-up was the lugubrious Zom, later to feature with both Chas McDevitt and the Vipers Skiffle Groups, before launching himself on a solo career. His pallid hang dog expression, from which he got his name, was ideal for delivering his deadpan line in humour.

The 44 also presented visiting overseas artists: Jack Elliott, specializing in Woody Guthrie material; Peggy Seeger, playing 5-string banjo and the enigmatic Nick Thatcher on 12-string guitar. Nick was another mystery man who came and departed like a wisp of smoke. He had a great blues delivery and sang of the 'Boll Weevil' and 'Cocaine' and many other songs he had picked up in the clubs around Chicago. Though he was only on the scene a short while he had quite an influence on the aspiring musicians, especially those who were new to the 12-string guitar.

John Brunner, later to make his name as a top science fiction

Martin Winsor, Marion Amiss, Redd Sullivan, Frank Ogrodnovitch, Zom and John Hasted at the 44 Club. (M. Sharratt/C. McD)

Nick Thatcher with his 12-string. (M. Sharratt/C. McD)

writer, approached John Hasted when the first Aldermaston March was being planned. It was to be held over the Easter Bank Holiday in April 1958. Ken Colyer was to organize a trad band at Shepherd's Bush and the musicians and a choir would lead the march. What songs should they sing? It would be another five years before 'We Shall Overcome' would be adopted as their anthem. John Brunner came up with a verse beginning,

Don't you hear the H-bombs thunder, echo like the crack of doom?

Eric Winter and Hasted wrote some more lyrics and 'Ban the Bomb For Ever More' was sung with gusto to the tune 'The Miners' Lifeguard', a Pete Seeger, Woody Guthrie favourite.

The report in the *Daily Telegraph* on 5 April said that the marchers 'skiffled their way along'.

Apparently in deference to the God-fearers in the march organization, there was to be no singing on Good Friday, on religious grounds. That was why the jazz and singing would not begin until they reached Shepherd's Bush the following day. However, the City Ramblers, ignorant of this decision, turned up at Trafalgar Square and, after the launching speech by Canon Collins, broke into a rip-roaring rendition of 'Ain't Gonna Study War No More'.

The 44 Skiffle and Folk Song Club had exerted a profound influence on the material used and the way it was presented. In his *Alternative Memoirs*, John Hasted writes:

> Very seldom was there any complaint that our folk revival was part of a Communist plot, despite the strong political convictions of many of the prominent singers.
> We had three years of real excitement and inspiration with skiffle music. And when in due course the craze was superseded, the washboards returned to the cupboard under the sink and the tea-chests to the dump, those of us who had started it at least felt the satisfaction of having changed the face of British popular music, with a public revival of harmony, rhythm, counterpoint, and a celebration of laughter, love, drama, fame and money.

Original Riverside Skiffle Group

Karl Dallas, through his regular contributions to the *Melody Maker*, fostered an interest in the roots of skiffle and in particular the folk music of the British Isles. As many of his contemporaries, he was greatly influenced by Josh White and Woody Guthrie.

He formed the Original Riversiders to promote his principles. He shunned the more commercial side of skiffle, maintaining that the 2 Is style had sold out. Perhaps it was this attitude that prevented him from recording for a commercial label. His own preferences were coloured by his political leanings, decidedly to the left. He was not alone in his views, the 44 Skiffle Group, led by Professor John Hasted and the City Ramblers were fellow travellers. Indeed most skiffle groups, whether consciously or not, favoured the politics of the left and songs like 'Union Maid', 'The Miner's Lifeguard', 'We Shall Not Be Moved', and 'Joe Hill' were great favourites.

Members of the group

Fred (Karl) Dallas,
guitar, banjo, voc.
Betty Davis (Dallas),
washboard, voc.

Roy Mills, bass
Chris Ridley, banjo, voc.

WHERE TO SKIFFLE
IN LONDON

EVERY NIGHT:	Skiffle Cellar, 49 Greek-street, W.1. "Two I's," Old Compton-street, W.1.
MOST NIGHTS:	Cat's Whisker, Kingly-street, W.1. Nucleus, Monmouth-street, W.C.2. Gyre & Gimble, 31 John Adam-street, W.C.2. Troubadour, Old Brompton-road, S.W.
MONDAY:	Ken Colyer at "51" Club, Gt. Newport-street, W.C.2.
TUESDAY:	John Hasted Group at 44 Gerrard-street, W.1.
WEDNESDAY:	Chas. McDevitt at the Princess Louise, High Holborn. Chris Barber at the Harringay Jazz Club. Dickie Bishop at the White Hart, Southall, Middlesex.
THURSDAY:	Jack Elliott at the Roundhouse, Wardour-street, W.1. Johnny Makins at the Manor House Jazz Club, N.4 (near the Tube Station).
FRIDAY:	Johnny Duncan at the Skiffle Cellar.
SATURDAY:	Modern Music Club, 5 Gerrard-street, W.1.
SUNDAY:	Cy Laurie Club, Gt. Windmill-street, W.1.

PART THREE
The Nebula

5

Pseudo Skiffle and Parodies

The musical Establishment was quick to realize the commercial potential of skiffle. Those of the fraternity who did not continually put down the genre soon adopted the name if not the style and in so doing created a wider market for their products. They were never really accepted as genuine skifflers by the fans, but many used the exposure as a springboard to success.

Don Lang, Lorrae Desmond, Betty Smith and a few others all assumed the skiffle epithet. They played what was termed 'pseudo skiffle', very often without even trying to disguise their obvious dance-band background.

Of all these band-wagoners, Don Lang was by far the most successful. GorDON LANGhorn, was born in Halifax, Yorkshire. He played both piano and trombone and had been a sidesman with various dance bands, notably Teddy Foster and Vic Lewis. In 1953, he had played trombone on the Ken Mackintosh record of 'The Creep', which reached number ten in the hit parade of January 1954. He was also a solo singer with the band and due to the interest aroused when he was featured on their many broadcasts, he decided to break away and form his Frantic Five. A born showman, he delighted in the tear-away trombone solo and in his own speciality, 'vocalese', a form of singing lyrics to fit instrumental choruses, in the manner of the songs set to classic Charlie Parker saxophone solos.

In November 1955, he had a minor hit with 'Cloudburst' and, in July 1957, with his Frantic Five, he reached 26 with his rendition of Chuck Berry's 'School Day'. A year later, in May 1958, he peaked at five with his greatest success 'Witch Doctor'. By September 1957, he had released his *Skiffle Special* LP renaming his Frantic Five, his Skiffle Group, and using washboard on some tracks. He re-recorded the signature tune of the 'Six–Five Special' television show, replacing the Bob Cort version.

Don and his group were included in many skiffle package shows and promotions, but as Dave McAleer noted in his *Hit Parade Heroes*, 'Don Lang was essentially a square peg trying to force himself into a round hole.'

As late as May 1991, he was touring in 'The Six–Five Special Road Show', which included Terry Dene, Jet Harris, Tommy Bruce, the Avons and Pete Murray. The show, which was promoted by Robbie Mac, was beset with difficulties but nevertheless aroused a great deal of interest. Tragically, not long after the tour, Don Lang died.

Another refugee from the straight dance-band tradition was Lorrae Desmond, an attractive pin-up Australian singer who, years later, was to find fame in the TV soap opera, 'A Country Practice'. She made a series of singles for Parlophone Records as Lorrae Desmond and her Rebels. Although the songs were written to reflect the musical construction and arrangements of such skiffle hits as 'Freight Train' and 'Don't You Rock Me Daddy O', they lacked the conviction and enthusiasm of the original groups, and suffered from being too polished.

Betty Smith also was guilty of a similar misunderstanding of the idiom. A well-respected tenor sax player, formerly with Ivy Benson's All Girl Band and Freddy Randall's Dixieland Jazz Band, she formed her own quintet featuring herself on both tenor and vocals. She played a residency at Jack Isow's Doric Ballroom in Brewer Street, a favourite haunt of London's underworld, notably Jack Spot. About this time she recorded some tracks for Tempo, calling her band a skiffle group, but the content had little or nothing to do with skiffle. The review of the record in the *Jazz News* of September 1958 says it all:

> I can be led to believe a lot of things at times, but the latest thing from Tempo Records stretches things a little too far. I am asked to believe that a 78 rpm recording featuring Betty Smith is skiffle music. Now if you don't already know, Miss Smith is the gal who up to a short time ago could be found playing rather booting tenor with the Freddy Randall band.

Now Betty has a small group of her own, but she has not switched to guitar or washboard as you may think, she still plays tenor, and it is on this very un-skiffle-like instrument that she cut two sides for Tempo entitled 'Double Shuffle' and 'There's A Blue Ridge Round My Heart Virginia'. These two numbers are being advertised as 'A terrific new skiffle recording'.

I can only say that I am now prepared to receive an LP from Count Basie and his Skiffle Orchestra.

However, Betty was still featured on such programmes as 'Saturday Skiffle Club' and, with the reasonable success of her Tempo recording, Decca, the parent label, took over her future releases.

Benny Lee, comedian and jazz singer, a stalwart of the Bernard Braden Radio series covered 'Last Train to San Fernando' backed by the Jackson Boys on a 78 rpm flexi-disc put out as a promotion for Nestlé's Chocolate. The Beverley Sisters covered 'Freight Train' and Bill Maynard, comedian and jazz fan, recorded 'Hey Liley Lo'.

Bill 'Wakey, Wakey' Cotton even recorded 'Don't You Rock Me Daddy O'. It was quite a spectacle to see him fronting his big show band, dressed as a Teddy Boy, playing a tea-chest bass.

'Wakey, Wakey' Billy Cotton and tea-chest bass.

Dick James, with the Skiffle Sound, recorded what was termed a 'skiffle sing song', but which in reality was a cockney knees up medley, more in keeping with the early party records of Chas and Dave in the 1980s. Dick James later became a music publisher and for a while owned Northern Songs, the company that had most of the early Beatles' hits.

The Stargazers, a typical close-harmony vocal group, had a little success with their parody, 'Skiffling Dogs'.

Even in America, the 'swinging' Buddy Greco tried to cash in as Buddy Greco and the B.G. Skiffle Gang, singing 'Game of Love' and 'With All My Heart'. However he fooled nobody, as was evident by the review in the *Liverpool Evening Express* of 3 August 1957:

> Not bad efforts, but they are no more like skiffle than I'm like Abe Lincoln!

A sure measure of success is imitation and parody. Satirical versions of skiffle songs provided another source of pseudo skiffle. The American comedian and satirist Stan Freberg probably experienced the greatest success in this idiom. His parody of Lonnie Donegan's 'Rock Island Line' remains a classic to this day, capped only by his spoof of Harry Belafonte's 'Banana Boat Song'.

Comedian Jim Dale, originally a skiffler, later to achieve international acclaim through a series of projects including the 'Carry On' films, his appearances in 'Barnum' and more recently at the London Palladium in *Oliver*, recorded another parody on the Donegan song, 'The Piccadilly Line'.

Not to be outdone, arch Goon, Peter Sellers, recorded 'Putting in the Smile' later amended to 'Putting on the Style' on the LP. With his 'Mates Spoffle Group', reputedly Bob Cort's backing group, supervised by Wally Whyton, he did a version of 'Any Old Iron' which included a memorable solo on the spoons.

Morris and Mitch 'took the Micky' out of 'Cumberland Gap' and delivered a monologue on 'What Is a Skiffler?' They recorded an EP called *Six–Five Nothing Special*. Nothing special was the verdict on all their efforts. Having no appeal to the skiffle fans, the records failed to have the impact of their American counterparts.

As Morris, Marty and Mitch they had entertained as comedian scriptwriters. Marty Feldman left and established himself as the goggle-eyed star of his own television series as well as being one of the famous Monty Python team.

Morris Sellars and Mitch Revely later diversified into script writing and broadcasting. Mitch was an incorrigible 'chancer'. He ran up a huge bill telephoning the USA from the machine in the McDevitt Group's office in Tin Pan Alley. For months Bill Varley, the group's manager, chased after Mitch for the cash, eventually accepting payment in Russian roubles. These of course turned out to be absolutely worthless.

The pseudo skifflers had little impact on the music at the time of their release, but can now be enjoyed as examples of 1950s humour and parody.

Jim Dale, backed by Garry Winkler, Nucleus Coffee Bar, 1956.

Skiffle Cellar entrance. (Terry Cryer)

6

Soho Coffee Bars

Throughout the late 1950s coffee bars proliferated and every town could boast of a least half a dozen. But it was in London that they originated and promoted the growth of skiffle and beat groups. In particular, the square mile of Soho, ever the centre for innovation and experimentation, was at the heart of coffee-bar society.

After the first Gaggia espresso coffee machine was installed at the Moka, in Frith Street in 1953, the hitherto popular cafés and milk bars were gradually superseded. The new coffee bars had more mystique; they were a little more exotic.

Though many of these new bars encouraged music, many did not have a stage for any formal presentation of the groups. Consequently the audience felt really involved with the music, as it was being performed all around them, often at the very table at which they were sipping their coffee. Few charged an entrance fee as at first the groups would play free or maybe for a plate of spaghetti each. It was not until the groups had begun to realize their pulling power that they insisted on a fee.

Before even the 2 I's became established, other venues had provided a home for the new skiffle groups. The Breadbasket in Cleveland Street was where the Vipers, Johnny Yorke's Alleycats and even Alexis Korner first began to play. Being just beyond the fringe of Soho it was a little too off the beaten track to prosper from the West End crowds. More accessible was the Cat's Whiskers in Kingly Street. This was one of the more popular environments with the groups as it was quite spacious and afforded plenty of space for them to set up.

Right next to the 2 I's was Heaven and Hell. Upstairs on the

A busy night at the Gyre and Gimble (left) and (below) Johnny Booker leads the chorus. (F.W. Varley coll.)

2 I's Coffee Bar – Chas, Vince Taylor and Tony Sheridan.

ground floor, all was white and bright but downstairs, where the music was played, it was black and full of atmosphere. Appropriately enough one of the resident groups to perform here was the Ghouls. The group consisted of Tony Kohn and Ken Johnson on guitars, Colin Stroud on tea-chest bass and Pfaf Maitland on washboard. Tony was later to join the Cottonpickers before becoming a leading light in the Chas McDevitt Group.

Even weirder than Heaven and Hell was the Macabre, just around the corner in Meard Street, almost opposite the Roundhouse, where Alexis Korner and Cyril Davies would have a regular weekly session. The Macabre had coffins for tables and candles glowing inside repro skulls.

One of the least publicized yet most favoured among the musicians themselves was the Nucleus, in Monmouth Street at the top of Shaftesbury Avenue. Run by Garry Winkler, later to take over from 'Little Bear' Sutton, playing washboard with the Cottonpickers, this provided a refuge for skifflers and jazzers alike. Its unorthodox opening hours encouraged a weird mixture of regulars, from far left to far out. In one evening you could rub shoulders with such characters as Ironfoot Jack; Dirty Dave; Angel, a transvestite years before his time; George, an astrologer with a flowing white beard who would tell your horoscope by referring to his ageing charts and musical giants like Big Bill Broonzy, Jack Elliott and a host of jazz musicians both trad and modern. Jam sessions would often start up at the most unearthly hours. Another late-night venue was the A & A (Authors and Actors), upstairs in an alley, just off Charing Cross Road. This was patronized by just as colourful a clientele – taxi drivers, prostitutes, and musicians, all seeking some wholesome Greek food after a hard night's work. Banjo George would hold sway accompanied by Gypsy Larry on guitar and should Diz Disley happen to call by one could be sure of a fine session, albeit more Django Reinhardt than 'Django' Donegan.

However, it was the Gyre and Gimble, in John Adam Street just off Villiers Street in Charing Cross, that can lay claim to have been the first skiffle coffee bar. Run by John St John Crewe, it attracted a selection of musicians and singers who would later achieve stardom in their chosen field. It was here that Tommy Hicks (Steele) would spend most of his leave when home from the Merchant Navy.

When the G & G would close in the early morning, if the weather was fine, a mixed group would hire a taxi to take them

Jack Elliott and Derrol Adams.

to London Bridge where they would catch the 4.40 am milk train to Brighton. When the sun came up they would busk on the beach. Their record bottle was £7 in 40 minutes, not bad in 1956.

The Brighton Buskers were John St John Crewe, guitar; Johnny Martyn, guitar; Jean Van Den Bosch, guitar; Tommy Hicks, guitar; Hans on tea-chest and Martin Winsor and Redd Sullivan on vocals. All destined one way or another to climb the ladder of success.

It was at the Gyre and Gimble rather than the 2 I's that Tommy Steele was really discovered. After Roy Tuvey and Bill Varley had taken their portable recording machine to the G & G, and had realized the potential of many of the habitués, Roy and another business partner, Geoff Wright, signed up Tommy Hicks to a personal management contract. With the assistance of another business associate, Larry Parnes, and publicist John Kennedy, they promoted Tommy at various venues like Al Burnett's Stork Room. On one occasion royalty was present and the resulting publicity catapulted Tommy to stardom. Suddenly Tommy found himself with a new management team in Parnes and Kennedy. It was reported at the time realizing that Tommy was under legal age when he originally signed with Tuvey and Wright, the new team had signed a five-year personal management contract for Tommy with his parents. Thereby proving that it is not only the artists that get screwed but agents too have little love for each other.

Another venue to come along, a little later, was the Freight Train Coffee Bar in Berwick Street. Opened in early 1958 by Chas McDevitt, at first it encouraged music on the ground-floor site. Impromptu sessions often occurred with guitarists like Diz Disley and Les Bennetts jamming with maybe a trumpet player or a clarinettist. In June 1958, Cliff Richard and the Drifters played a session there en route to stardom. However, the basement was never developed, and the jukebox took over. Instead of being a live-music venue, it became a rendezvous for many of the London-based groups, a point where they could assemble to leave for a gig or unwind in the early hours returning from work. It was on one such occasion that ex-skiffler, Fred Heath of the Nutters, and Brian Gregg, ex-Hobeaux Skiffle Group, wrote 'Shakin' All Over' in the basement, surrounded by empty Coca-Cola crates and broken furniture. Fred, of course, was Johnny Kidd of the soon to be chart-topping Pirates.

In spite of the competition from all the other coffee bars, it was the 2 I's that became synonymous with success in terms of skiffle

Chas at the controls of the Freight Train Coffee Bar.

and rock and roll. All the acts that played there – Tommy Steele, the Vipers, Chas McDevitt, Les Hobeaux, Adam Faith, Terry Dene, Wee Willie Harris, Vince Taylor, Tony Sheridan – together with the televising of the 'Six–Five Special' from the premises, all helped to place the 2 I's in an unassailable position.

Shrewd promotion by Paul Lincoln and Ray Hunter, the two wrestlers who had taken over the property from the Irani brothers, ensured that package shows, LP's like *Rockin' at the 2 I's* and television made the venue a must for any aspiring pop star to include in their CV.

Paul Lincoln even went into management and looked after Terry Dene and Wee Willie Harris. His assistant at the 2 Is, Tom Littlewood, managed Vince Taylor, who later became a cult figure in France.

It was Tom Littlewood who played the judo instructor in the film of *The Tommy Steele Story*. Tom had connections in the cinema world. When Otto Preminger was making *Joan of Arc* with Jean Seberg at Shepperton Studios, it was Tom who supplied many of the 300 extras culled from both customers and layabouts at the 2 I's, including Terry Dene, Chas McDevitt and Wee Willie Harris; after all £3 per day was not to be sneezed at.

In spite of the commercial success of the coffee bars, skiffle gradually succumbed to the onslaught of the musical Establishment and the ever-increasing popularity of rock and roll. The rock clubs, pubs and specialist music venues, like the Marquee, became a substitute for the coffee bar and these either reverted to serving meals, or became sandwich bars, before eventually closing down, heralding the end of an era.

Soho Fair, July 1957. Freight Train float viewed from 2 I's, (note still empty bombed site).

Chas McDevitt group in 2 I's with typical audience.

Les Bennetts. (R. Hardy)

7

Guitar Kings

The lead guitar players of the skiffle era were a breed apart. They had the technique and the musical ability to convert an average-sounding group into hit-parade potential.

None of the skiffle groups used a lead guitar on their first recordings. Colyer, Barber, Donegan, McDevitt and the Vipers all used acoustic instruments, and rarely featured a guitar solo. When Lonnie Donegan called on the services of Denny Wright the die was cast. Skiffle became more jazzy and the guitar solos owed a great deal to the new style of rock and roll.

Only Les Bennetts had come through the ranks, having started with Les Hobeaux and Chas McDevitt before joining Lonnie Donegan. He played on Lonnie's monster hit, 'Does Your Chewing Gum Lose Its Flavour' and on such records as 'Have a Drink on Me'.

Most of the other lead guitar players were either well-established session or jazz musicians.

Jimmy Currie had been on the music scene quite a while before joining Lonnie. His fast single-string work can be heard on Lonnie's twin number one recording of 'Gamblin' Man' and 'Putting on the Style'.

Ken Sykora, often winning the guitar section of the *Melody Maker* poll, contributed the intricate guitar solos on Bob Cort's records. He has said that he was particularly peeved when, each week during the opening credits to the 'Six–Five Special', the music was faded just as he was about to take off on a flying guitar solo. The Bob Cort group had recorded the original signature tune to the programme.

Neville Skrimshire was a recording executive with EMI Records. He could be found on countless sessions, often in conjunction with Vic Flick (later of the John Barry 7). It is a little confusing, because sometimes Neville used a pseudonym, Nigel Sinclair, presumably because of his association with EMI. He toured and recorded with Bob Cort, Nancy Whiskey and Jimmy Jackson. Bryan Daly also graced many a skiffle group with his playing, including Alan Lomax and the Ramblers. In recent years he has become known as the writer of 'Postman Pat', the song featured in the popular children's television show.

But it was the Big Three – Denny Wright, Bill Bramwell and Diz Disley – who were the masters of the art.

Diz Disley

Diz Disley had played the guitar since he was 14, having heard a record by Django Reinhardt and the Quintet of the Hot Club of France. While studying at the Leeds College of Art he also played

Diz Disley in Freight Train.

banjo and guitar with Bob Barclay's Yorkshire Jazz Band, 'a baptism of fire' if ever there was. After his National Service and a season in a show on the end of the pier, he came to London in Coronation Year, 1953. He met Bill Colyer in Chiswick and as a result played with the Ken Colyer Band on Ken's return from New Orleans. He recalls:

> They did Friday nights at the 100 Club [then Humph's] in Oxford Street and halfway through the session came the 'breakdown group'. This consisted of Ken Colyer (guitar), Lonnie Donegan (guitar), Bill Colyer (washboard), Chris Barber (bass), Alexis Korner (mandolin) and myself (guitar). Bill paid me half-a-crown for this half-hour session, which went a long way at the time. I did this job for about 2 months till Mick Mulligan offered me a job with the Magnolia Jazz Band. The Colyer Band made an LP for Decca, *Back to the Delta*, one side of which was the skiffle group, Ken, Bill, Dick Smith, Alexis and myself.
>
> In 1954, when Ken had left the others, I played banjo with his new band and while in Dusseldorf the skiffle group was Ken and Bill, Ian Wheeler (guitar), Stan Grieg (drums) and myself (guitar).
>
> So I played in the first and second skiffle groups, a little known fact.
>
> Later in 1957, I did nine months with Bob Cort, loads of fun; we were once in pantomime with Winifred Atwell. Then in 1958 with Nancy Whiskey, with her beautiful throaty voice until her bun in the oven precluded further operations.

Disley was an accomplished cartoonist; his drawings often featured in the musical papers. In 1958, he decided to concentrate more on his art studies and formed a Django-style quintet to play part time. This included Dick Powell, violin; Timmy Mahn, bass; Neville Skrimshire and Denny Purssord, guitars. In 1959, Diz was placed second in the guitar section of the *MM* Poll. The quintet broadcast regularly and often accompanied the noted French jazz violinist Stephan Grappelli.

Denny Wright

The second member of the triumvirate, Denny Wright, is remembered fondly by Diz:

> I first heard Denny playing in a Wardour Street clip joint called the Torch Room, at the end of 1953. Bob Clarke, the fiddle player, took

Denny Wright and Steve Benbow. (S. Benbow)

me there. That was also my first meeting with Spike Mackintosh.

Denny's playing was highly exciting; tremendous swing and attack, real jazz, and as he was also a fine pianist and arranger, he had a unique approach to chords. Wonderful music. Impossible to praise him too highly. I was one of his foremost admirers.

However, Denny was a heavy drinker and this was to lose him his jobs with both Donegan and Duncan. For a while he was playing as a duo with Steve Benbow, who assured Disley that Denny was now on the wagon. In 1973, Disley booked Denny for the Cambridge Folk Festival but Denny was soon back to his old habits. Diz is convinced that the difficulties of working with Grappelli, with his frequent tantrums and insulting behaviour, contributed to his lapses. In his final tribute to Denny, Diz says:

> I think that his playing on the recordings of my group is the only indication of his real jazz ability, as all the other records are in the realm of pop. He was just as capable a musician as Grappelli, and a better pianist.

Bill Bramwell in full flight.

Bill Bramwell

The demon drink also had a detrimental effect on the third member of the triumvirate, Bill Bramwell. Bill was a natural-born guitar player who could swing like a gate. But on the odd occasion he would fall short of his high standards. If he stumbled backwards and fell over his guitar amplifier on stage, he would still come off convinced he had played a storm. Many such statements as 'I was bloody great tonight' would be followed by a punch-up, prompted by someone, usually Marc Sharratt, saying, 'Bill, you played like shit.'

It was a regular chore, prising Bill's ample body off Marc's and preventing his use of Marc's head as a door knocker.

When listening to a playback of one of his recordings, Bill would pace back and forth across the room, head bowed, cigarette in hand, listening intently and mouthing the lyrics, finally saying how good he was, much to the delight of all assembled. And he was good.

Bill Bramwell had been playing guitar and bass from the mid 1940s. His talent was recognized in 1947 when, on 17 December at the Birmingham Town Hall, he was chosen to be part of a quartet that was to represent the four most outstanding musicians to have played the venue that year. The other three were Humphrey Lyttelton, trumpet; Derek Franklin, bass, later of the Hedley Ward Trio, and Ray Foxley, piano, who was to record with many jazz bands, including Ken Colyer's Skiffle Group.

He toured abroad, both cruising and in cabaret. He was even a disc jockey in Honolulu. A complex character, both intense and at times flippant, he was into psychoanalysis and Zen Buddhism. His black side took over when he was feeling the pressure of just playing skiffle and he tended to drink away his troubles. When fully alert, none could surpass him.

On leaving the Chas McDevitt Skiffle Group, he toured for a while with Mick Mulligan playing banjo and guitar. He also broadcast with George Melly as part of his 'Bubbling Over 5'.

His guitar solos swung like mad and his punchy guitar chords complemented his unique style of scat singing. Bill will for ever be remembered for his recordings of 'My Old Man', on Starlite Records, in 1948, accompanied by just Bernie Woods on bass, and the four versions he recorded with the skiffle group, on Oriole and Rollercoaster Records. His scat singing became familiar to millions when he provided the theme music to the popular television series 'Candid Camera'.

8

Washboard Wizards

In 1933, the Duke Ellington Orchestra had undertaken a sensational tour of the UK. They were so awesome that the Musicians' Union put pressure on the Ministry of Labour to refuse working permits to any more American bands. Only bands that were classed as variety acts were allowed entry, a precursor to the similar ban in the 1950s. One of the bands to take advantage of this loophole was the Washboard Serenaders.

However, it is unlikely that very few, if any, aspiring skifflers had heard any of these American bands. The nearest they could have hoped for would be to hear some of the classic jazz releases by Johnny Dodds, with his brother Baby Dodds on washboard, issued by HMV in the early 1950s. There were also some records made with Jimmy Bertrand on washboard with the various combos assembled by Jimmy Blythe, such as Blythe's Blue Boys, released on the Champion label in 1927, as the State Street Ramblers. This music, however, was not readily available to the skifflers until its re-release, in the late 1950s, on the London label as Roy Palmer and the State Street Ramblers. It was promoted as a Chicago skiffle session. One extremely sought-after record was by the mighty 'Tiny' Parham and his musicians – 'Sudbuster's Dream' – on which the washboard playing is so precise and syncopated that it sounds like the sensational Nicholas Brothers going through their tap dancing routine.

When it was released in the UK in April 1932, on the back of 'One Hour', by the Mound City Blue Blowers, one review of the record in

Gramophone mistook Ernie Marrero's washboard playing for 'syncopated tap dancing, to help sell the record to the public'.

The jazz critic, Edgar Jackson must have been a little confused as he also referred to the pianist as 'Tiny Parham, well known as

Washboard Sam (Robert Brown) circa 1931.

a sound typical Negro musician, himself plays the solo trumpet.'

The only readily available record of one of the authentic maestros was 'Diggin' My Potatoes' by Washboard Sam (Robert Brown), reputedly the half brother of Big Bill Broonzy.

Consequently the locally bred washboard enthusiast had to base his interpretation on the local washboard professors. Either that or play by trial and error; anyway half the fun of skiffle was finding it out for yourself.

The notable experts of the skiffle era could be chosen from quite a short list: Bill Colyer, Beryl Bryden, Johnny Pilgrim, Shirley Bland, 'Little Bear' Sutton and Marc Sharratt.

There were others, such as Colin Bowden and Stan Grieg, but these were essentially musicians whose main instrument was either drums or piano.

The washboard itself was a bit of an anachronism and so too were its players. They acquired the sort of aura afforded these days to the trad banjo player: 'a few sandwiches short of a picnic'.

Except for Beryl Bryden, who was essentially a blues and jazz band singer, very few of the fraternity sang solo; occasionally they could be persuaded to contribute to the odd chorus. As for their set-up, most shunned the trappings of the novelty bands like Spike Jones and his City Slickers, maybe they would sport a cymbal or a wood block, but hooters and whistles were out. It was essential to lay down a solid beat to keep all the guitars in check; any fancy interpolation tended to interrupt the flow. The variety of playing styles was as diverse as the players themselves.

Bill Colyer, Shirley Bland of the City Ramblers, and Johnny Pilgrim of the Vipers usually played with both hands, laying the washboard flat on their lap. Beryl Bryden held it upright, between her thighs, enabling her to beat and scrub both sides at once. When singing from a standing position at the mike, she held it across her breast, playing with one hand. Marc Sharratt, apart from having a specially made washboard-shaped case, played from a standing position, clamping the washboard into a small frame; this way he had the freedom and flexibility to really 'give it some welly'. Many a night after a long session, his knuckles would be dripping with blood. Few, if any, used the style favoured today by the cajun and zydeco bands, hanging flat across the chest. In the current McDevitt group, Kerry uses this method, as it leaves her free to move around, and play with both hands, while singing at the mike.

"The idea is for you to keep the rhythm going when he stops to change the chord."

Scored for washboard

FRANCIS AND DAY'S "Album of music for skiffle groups," published at 2s. 6d., contains 11 numbers. Three of them might conceivably be adapted to skiffle—"Frankie And Johnny," "Steamboat Bill" and "Turkey In The Straw."

But it is hardly likely that the most impoverished library will be enhanced by "I'm Knee Deep In Daisies" and "My Bonnie Lies Over The Ocean"—though it might be interesting to hear what a washboard would make of a three/four rhythm.

The album advertises "full words and music for piano, guitar, ukelele, bass, drums and washboard rhythm," and explains how to adapt these from the normal sheet music it contains.

A new feature, however, is the washboard part with hints on loud and heavy "hits" and "strokes" across the corrugated surface.

This alone might commend the book to would-be skifflers anxious to wrestle with the complexities of this most basic of all instruments.

At this stage perhaps a few details about the various exponents of this basic yet popular instrument will not go amiss.

Bill Colyer

In July 1951 Bill Colyer had played washboard with the Crane River Jazz Band on their Festival Hall recording of 'I'm Travellin''. He had also played on what must surely have been the first British skiffle record, made in 1950, 'Muddy Old River', with Ken Colyer on vocal and guitar, Bill on vocal and washboard and John R. T. Davies on guitar. J. R. T. Davies played trombone with the original Crane River Jazz Band as well as saxophone with the Temperance Seven. Today he has a recording studio in Burnham, Bucks, and is in great demand, being one of the finest recording technicians around, able to convert an almost inaudible, mangled 78 rpm record into an impeccable CD. 'Muddy Old River' was released by 77 Records on the album *The Original Crane River Jazz Band*.

Bill had started playing with Ken back in the 1940s. He recalls,

> In the early days, when Ken and I were seamen together, we had our daily two-hour session in Ken's cabin, he on cornet or guitar, and myself using brushes on an upturned bucket or suitcase, with the ship's baker, Les, faking madly on another guitar along with the 'chippie'.

The chippie, the baker, Ken the second cook, and Bill, the trimmer (coal shoveller), even played a gig in far-off Montevideo.

Bill had gone ashore to the First and Last, the name usually given by merchant seamen to the nearest watering hole to their moorings, which often proved to be the only view many of them had of far-off exotic countries. He discovered that this particular venue in Montevideo, frequented by the usual ladies of the night, required some music, so he returned to the ship, rounded up the group and they played to the assembled ladies, in much the same way as Emile 'Stalebread' Charlie Lacoume had in Storyville, half a century earlier.

Bill Colyer played a great part in creating the legend that is Ken Colyer. While Bill was doing his patriotic bit with the British Army, Ken was turned on to New Orleans music by listening to his big brother's record collection. In 1953, when Ken was incarcerated in

Bill Colyer beating it out at Skiffle Party, 100 Club, 5 March 1997.

New Orleans' Parish Prison for 38 days, it was Bill who arranged for his letters home to be published in the *Melody Maker*, and for his experiences to be aired over the BBC, thus ensuring that on his return to the UK Ken was hailed as a folk hero. From that moment his place in the New Orleans hall of fame was secure.

The last letter written by Ken Colyer just before he left New Orleans was published in the *Melody Maker* on 14 March 1953. Ken gave a vivid description of the New Orleans Mardi Gras, which had taken place on Tuesday 17 March. He described his trip around the clubs and taverns, which were going at full blast:

> Dick Allen and I played at various places. We met up with Noone (Kid Sheik's guitar man) and a fellow guitarist named Sam, at a large patioed tavern, the Court of Two Sisters.
>
> Noone had his bazooka, a homemade instrument built out of two brass bedposts and a paraffin funnel, which he slides like a trombone to produce a bass tone not unlike Cyrus St Clair's tuba.
>
> With this, and a guitar, and Allen playing a galvanized washtub fitted with a broomstick and a length of clothes line, we had some real skiffle music.

This was probably one of the first occasions on which Colyer referred to skiffle as such in print. It was certainly the first time he had mentioned it in the context of his trip to New Orleans. It was published a month before recording 'Midnight Special' in Copenhagen in April 1953 and a year and a half before Lonnie Donegan's 'Rock Island Line' was recorded, in June 1954.

Bill is often credited with having suggested the word 'skiffle' to describe their own music. He used to work at Colletts International Bookshop and had access to all their imported jazz records. He had noticed the word skiffle applied to Dan Burley's small combo, and thought this would be appropriate for their group.

When Bill left the Ken Colyer band, he played washboard with the group that was formed to accompany Bob Cort.

Not long ago, when Ralph Sutton, the great American virtuoso of the stride piano, was in the UK, he phoned Bill and insisted that he bring his washboard over for a blow. Bill tried to cry off, but Ralph insisted, saying that he was tired of the serious stuff and wanted to have some fun for a change.

Most Saturday mornings Bill can be found occupying his favourite seat at the Moon and Sixpence, in Wardour Street, a couple of blocks from his pad in Soho and just round the corner from the site of the old Freight Train Coffee Bar and within shouting distance from the 100 Club. Surrounded by kindred spirits, he is delighted to expound on the origins of skiffle and the whys and wherefores of New Orleans Jazz.

Today if you go to the 100 Club in Oxford Street, as you enter the basement, on your right there is a plaque dedicated to the memory of Ken Colyer, and invariably, seated beneath this, with a constant flow of pints from well-wishers, is Bill Colyer holding court, reminiscing with one and all. If the truth be known, Billco is somewhat of a legend himself.

Beryl Bryden

Beryl Bryden, from Norwich, was an established blues and jazz vocalist long before the skiffle era. She had moved to London in 1945 and worked in music shops and later for both Esquire and Melodisc Records. Since the late 1940s she had been on the scene, playing her washboard and singing with many a jazz name.

She was encouraged to take up the washboard by Graeme Bell when he was touring the UK for the first time in 1948. He often featured the washboard in his own jazz line-up. She has remained in contact with the Australian band leader and in 1971–2 played many engagements with him down under.

Beryl recalls buying her first washboard in a hardware shop in Soho's Brewer Street; they had just returned a batch as faulty, and she had great difficulty in convincing them that she was not concerned about its condition, as long as it sounded right. It cost 4s. 6d. She still owns this very washboard, using one of two she has kept all these years. She also owns a mini collapsible wash-board 6″ × 4″, with an ornamental marquetry design which, on assembly, is capable of producing the sound of a regular board. It was made by Peter Hearn, a washboard freak, who has even fabricated a mini electric model.

In the 1950s, she had her own group, Beryl's Backroom Boys, looking very natty in their uniform with an intertwined logo of three Bs, designed by Beryl on their shirts. During the skiffle era this group included Alexis Korner on guitar, Cyril Davies on 12-string and harmonica, Frank Cash on bass and Dave Stevens on piano. Recording as Beryl Bryden's Backroom Skiffle they made four tracks for Decca, but only two were released, 'Kansas City Blues' and 'Casey Jones'. The other tracks were 'Rock Me' which had an echo surge on the master, a fault evident on other Decca skiffle releases, and 'This Train' which includes a fine harmonica solo from Cyril Davies. Beryl certainly chose her musicians well:

Beryl Bryden with Cy Laurie on her 75th birthday.

Alex and Cyril went on to be the inspiration and chief propagators of the R&B explosion of the early 1960s.

She is acknowledged to be one of Britain's foremost jazz singers. She has performed with Lionel Hampton, Mary Lou Williams (with whom she recorded), the Dutch Swing College Band as well as most of the British jazz combinations. In 1953, she was resident in Sydney Bechet's Paris haunt, the Vieux Colombier. Ten years later she was the artist chosen to star in the opening show at Hong Kong's luxurious Mandarin Hotel. With the New Orleans Syncopators she recorded for CBS and, with Bud Freeman and Lennie Felix, an album for Riff Records, *Bluesy Ballads*. In all, she has recorded over 100 different titles with 40 different bands in 12 countries.

Today she is still performing on the jazz scene, recently having celebrated her seventy-sixth birthday at the 100 Club, in the company of many of the friends and musicians she has worked with over the years. Her current recordings include many jazz standards, but the titles featuring the washboard inevitably have a skiffle flavour.

One of Beryl's more obscure claims to fame is that she is probably the only person ever to have been recorded and televised playing the washboard under water. She is a keen scuba diver, a hobby she picked up in Australia, consequently when the idea was proposed to her she had no hesitation in accepting the challenge.

Her niche in the hierarchy of skiffle is assured by the fact that she provided the washboard accompaniment to the first skiffle hit, 'Rock Island Line'. Lonnie Donegan has always complained about the paltry session fee he earned on that occasion; it could not have been less than Beryl's – she received the princely sum of £3.10s. Still with that amount in old money she could have bought 17 washboards back in 1948.

Marc Sharratt

Marc Sharratt had played both washboard and drums while training as an RAF navigator at Cranwell. During his service in the RAF he was posted to Canada and there he played with a small group, as well as acquiring some of the highly prized Library of Congress recordings of New Orleans jazz and Lead Belly. In 1952, he joined Chas McDevitt in his local jazz band, the High Curley Stompers. When Chas later joined the New Crane River Jazz Band in 1955–6, Marc was featured in the skiffle interludes.

He had an impish and at times withering sense of humour and was a keen practical joker, which one could never guess from the persona he displayed on stage. His serious intense demeanour never cracked into a smile; he relied solely on his technique to register, and register he did. One has only to listen to the audience reaction to his solo, captured by Rollercoaster Records on the live recording at the first Big Skiffle Concert at the Royal Festival Hall in 1957. He truly deserved the title 'washboard wizard'.

There is one incident in the group's career for which he never

Marc Sharratt and his £5,000 fingers.

forgave Chas. In 1956, when the Crane River Jazz Band was playing at the Kingsbury Baths, Marc was seated close to the band
waiting to go on at the interval. Chas was on stage with the band,
playing banjo. Suddenly all hell broke loose; the club had been
raided by a gang of Teddy Boys. In the true Chicago tradition the
band carried on playing. Chas could see that Marc was being set
upon by two Teds so, tradition or not, he put his banjo down and
went to the assistance of his mate. However, much to Marc's
annoyance, when Chas saw the bottles and chairs flying through

the air and landing very close to his precious Regal banjo, he returned to the bandstand and put his banjo back in its case before returning to Marc's assistance. After all a mate's a mate, but a banjo is for ever. Well, what was one to do? Marc left Chas in no doubt . . .

Apart from providing the unique on-beat rhythm on the hit version of 'Freight Train', Marc accompanied Chas and Nancy on the Ed Sullivan show in June 1957. In recent years Marc recorded and toured with the McDevitt group but, on returning from one of their appearances at a rock festival in Holland, he was killed in a head-on crash. It was his fifty-eighth birthday, 16 May 1991.

Shirley Bland

Shirley Bland was the exception that proved the rule. Not only did she occasionally take the lead vocal but her washboard was equipped with a variety of accoutrements. The traps included woodblock, cowbell, cymbal and hooter. As the City Ramblers were essentially a spasm band, this was ideal as a fill in to the various jugs, kazoos and funnels featured. Perhaps the best example of her set-up can be heard on the washboard solo to be found on the City Ramblers' recording of 'Mama Don't Allow'.

Shirley had joined the City Ramblers in October 1956, replacing Alan 'Little Bear' Sutton. Before joining the group she had been a professional ballet dancer, and before that one of the 'Glamour Garage Girls'. For a while she was married to Jimmie MacGregor and she and Jimmie made three appearances on 'Saturday Skiffle Club' as a duo, singing mainly folk material. She also featured in the folk group, the Galliards.

Her memories of the City Ramblers give us a fair insight into what life was like on the road for such a mixed group:

> We travelled the continent in a Canadian ex-army ambulance, which was pretty beat up and painted all over the outside 'Russell Quaye's City Ramblers'. We managed to break down on the autobahn, and had to be towed into Berlin by the army. As I recall the big end had gone and was going to cost a hell of a lot to replace. This meant that we had to busk every day for over a week, and almost starve ourselves of food and drink. The ambulance remained parked on the Reinbank for many weeks afterwards;

Shirley Bland

most of us slept outside the van throughout the winter and it was
bloody cold.

During the day, Russell and Hylda would creep into the van for
a little of what you fancy. The van was parked perilously close to
the water's edge on a downward slope. To the intense interest of
all those also camping nearby, the van would start rocking back
and forth violently, while we watched gleefully, half hoping that it
would slide into the river.

Russell and Hylda were obviously demonstrating to one and all the original meaning of the term rock and roll.

Chris Bateson, a young art student, was the group's original blue blower, playing a trumpet mouthpiece through a paraffin funnel and, in Shirley's opinion, was 'bloody good'. A 'Little Englander' by nature, he refused to learn a word of French or any other language for that matter.

> Every morning he used to go off to a little restaurant near where we were staying, for fried egg and crispy bacon, none of this continental coffee and croissants shit for him. I was naturally curious as to how he managed to get his message across and asked him; he produced a beautifully executed drawing of one fried egg with crispy streaky bacon, which would be shown to the waiter in any country he happened to be in, with the desired results! Such initiative had to be admired.

The City Ramblers played all over Europe, from Moscow to Brussels and Berlin. They made numerous television appearances where, much to her annoyance, Shirley was often described as a *Reinmaiden*, due to her long golden tresses falling around her shoulders. On one occasion it was not her hair that was the focus of attention, but her feet. She always wore sandals and it

John and Tena Pilgrim jiving to the City Ramblers at their wedding reception. (J. Pilgrim)

transpired that while playing the washboard she beat time with her big toes, independently from the other digits. The TV cameramen were fascinated by this phenomenon and zoomed in for a close-up over the opening bars of music. Marc Sharratt had his fingers insured with Lloyds. Shirley should have insured her big toes; they were obviously a major commercial asset.

When the City Ramblers broke up as a unit, Shirley and Jimmie carried on as a duo and when Jimmie teamed up with Robin Hall (a partnership that lasted 14 years), they occasionally included Shirley in the line-up as well as Leon Rosselson on guitar and banjo to form the Galliards. When she and Jimmie finally split, for a while Shirley lived on the south coast in Brighton. In recent years, however, she has made her home in Numansdorp, Holland.

John Pilgrim

John was the original washboard player on all the Vipers skiffle group hit records. His interest in the washboard stems back to his youth when he was a regular at the jazz club held at the Regent Street Polytechnic on Sunday lunchtimes. It was here that he had heard Beryl Bryden sit in on washboard with the Mick Mulligan Band.

Like all wacky washboard players he is proud of his washboard's pedigree. It was a gift from his granny, who had acquired it from a lady who had been in service as a housekeeper for John Stuart Mill, and swore that it had been used to wash the smalls of the famous. The wooden frame is warped but the metal ridged plate has never been replaced, having survived the years of scraping and banging with amazing resilience; which unfortunately is more than can be said for John himself. After a catalogue of personal tragedies, he suffered a nervous breakdown. He is now recovered and broadcasting regularly with his own programme, devoted to the blues, on BBC Radio Suffolk.

His career as a washboard player began with a short stint with Johnny Yorke's group at the Breadbasket. He was sacked by Yorke after an altercation he had with Lonnie Donegan, who had come down looking for material. Lonnie got a little upset when John said he'd never heard his records. He reckons that this was the occasion when Donegan first heard 'Don't You Rock Me Daddy O'.

As at this time he was living in the same house as Russell Quaye and Hylda Sims, it was ideal for him to play with their group which then included John Lepthorn on cheese-box bass. On clarinet was Harry Jackson, later a diplomatic correspondent for the *Guardian*. It was Harry who wrote,

> A young man is improperly dressed these days in the West End unless he wears a washboard or a guitar.

They used to play down the Nucleus coffee bar, the all-night haunt for jazz musicians and sundry characters. Sunday lunch-times would find the group at the Perseverance pub and it was here, almost on his own doorstep, that Wally Whyton would hear them play. No money changed hands for the gig; but a form of payment was made in liberal measures of rum and blackcurrant. The landlord must have had a surplus of this particular libation.

This was the period when Johnny Yorke's Alleycats and the Cavemen played around such coffee bars as the Breadbasket and the Gyre and Gimble.

Johnny Yorke's group included John Brasacier (Armstrong) on guitar; Les Rawlings, bass; Jack Buddis, drums and Isobel Street and Rosella on vocals. The Cavemen included, variously, Mike Pratt, Lionel Bart, Tommy Steele and Wally Whyton. It was into this milieu that John Pilgrim was thrust and he emerged as washboard player for the Vipers. His place with the City Ramblers was taken by 'Little Bear' Sutton. John remained with the Vipers during their heyday only leaving to be replaced by a drummer shortly before they broke up.

John Pilgrim together with Johnny Martyn were the zoo-keepers for the Vipers' menagerie of pets, which included monkeys, a coati-mundi, a skunk, various rabbits and a snake.

Pilgrim's monkey was Higgins or, to be more precise, Iggins, who was not averse to causing mayhem. On one occasion, guitarist Diz Disley found an excuse to crash-out round their flat, only to be rudely awakened by the monkey peeing on him from his cage, strategically positioned over Disley's bed.

One day Lonnie Donegan was visiting and said to Pilgrim, 'Give us a go of your monkey.'

Pilgrim replied haughtily, 'You don't "have goes" at monkeys.'

Suddenly Donegan jumped up and shouted, 'Here, your monkey's shit all over me!'

Wally Whyton was later to remark, 'That's something we'd always wanted to do.'

For which riposte Pilgrim said he was able to forgive Wally for all their previous disagreements.

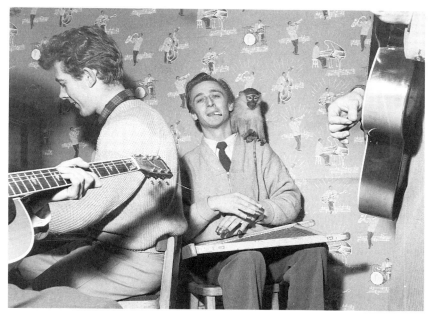

John Pilgrim and 'Iggins. (Terry Cryer)

After his time with the Vipers, Pilgrim took his degree at Hull University and later taught in Liverpool. It was here that he became really involved with the emerging folk and blues scene and even toured playing washboard with Sonny Terry and Brownie McGhee. He recalls that they were constantly bickering, sometimes not talking to each other for days on end; John was the messenger boy and often the butt of a tongue lashing from Sonny Terry. Brownie would tell John the key of the next song, and John would pass this on to Sonny, so that he could have the appropriate harmonica ready. One day John relayed the message from Brownie and Sonny retorted, 'I've been playing this instrument all my life, I don't need no white boy to tell me in which key to play.'

At this stage John decided it was time to leave the blues duo. Later he accompanied the first lady of British folk blues, Jo Ann Kelly, and even recorded with her on 'Do It'. For a while he ran a successful wholesale record business and even today his mammoth collection of records provides him with the ideal library for his broadcasts.

Washboards Today

If anyone should doubt that a washboard player doesn't take his art seriously, perhaps the following few extracts, culled from the Internet Dixieland Newsgroup, will dispel the notion:

At 3:44 pm on 26 March 1996, Bill Gunter wrote:

> The nights we washboardists spend being concerned with the gauge of the metal or the frequency of the corrugations or even the metal itself (galvanized or stainless) indicates the concern toward art which we feel. That doesn't even touch upon the question of thimbles! How quickly do they wear out, where do you find the correct sizes and who manufactures the most musical ones?
>
> My washboard is a Columbus Washboard Maid Rite. The metal is tinplate. I am serious enough to have visited the factory and discussed the history and construction of the washboard with a member of the family that owns Columbus Washboard (the last remaining US manufacturer of washboards). My thimbles are house brand from G Street Fabrics of Rockville.

Later Ralf contributed some advice from Florida:

> I just got in from another day playing with the Rhythm Rascals at Walt Disney World, only to find all these subject postings on the 'Washboard'. Now that is what I like to see! I could go on and on about the washboard; for those that don't know me, I play washboard five days a week with the Rascals at Disney World, Florida. It's a great band with Bill Allred on trombone, Jim Snyder on clarinet, Lee Floyd on banjo and Hank Greve on tuba. It is a fun band and we do have a good time, if any of you are in the Orlando area, please stop by. And now for anyone who is interested, I have played on all types of board inserts: brass, tin, glass, galvanized, porcelain enamel and stainless steel. I prefer the sound of the galvanized board, but, they just don't last. I used the Standard Family Size Galvanized No. 2090, manufactured by the Columbus Washboard Co. Ohio, for years replacing the insert about every four weeks. So I found a Mexican washboard that I really liked and had the machine shop at Disney make a filler out of stainless steel. I've been using the same washboard since 1977. Stainless steel does last but the thimbles don't. I use size 11 and 12 heavy English thimbles, they only last about three weeks. I believe all drummers will eventually mature to the washboard and become one with their instrument.

So there we are, tips for future skifflers from some modern washboard maniacs.

9
Record Charts, Radio, TV and Films

The record charts published in the 1950s were quite diverse and often reflected a strange disparity in the choice of hit records.

Radio Luxembourg was very popular and the only regular weekly chart to be heard on the air. Over the years, the *New Musical Express* has proved to be a reliable and fairly accurate source of chart information, particularly for the period in which we are interested. In the 1950s they would print a six-monthly chart, awarding artists points for their weekly position in their hit parade. For the first six months of 1957, only three skiffle groups appear in the compilation: Donegan, McDevitt and the Vipers. Nevertheless they acquit themselves well considering the hefty opposition.

The *Record Mirror* at that time published a weekly Top Twenty Chart of international artists as well as a similar chart of British ones. It also printed the top ten selling records in a selection of shops as well as publishing the address of each shop from which the choice was made – a highly suspicious system, leaving itsef wide open to manipulation.

An even more bizarre method was used by the *Melody Maker*, which printed the names and addresses of record shops in the major cities together with their best-selling jazz records. Skiffle records were included in this classification, much to the annoyance of many a jazz fan. Because the skiffle records were

BRITAIN'S TOP DISCS and TUNES

A GUIDE to the best selling discs for the week ended May 4, derived from information supplied by 21 leading record stores. ★

This week	Last week	Title	Artist	Label
1	(1)	CUMBERLAND GAP	Lonnie Donegan	Pye-Nixa
		Other discs—Vipers (Par) ; Dick Bishop (Dec).		
2	(6)	BUTTERFLY	Andy Williams	London
		Billy Williams (V-Cor) ; Charlie Gracie (Par) ; Tony Brent (Col).		
3	(4)	BABY, BABY	Teenagers	Columbia
		Don Lang (HMV)		
4	(10)	ROCK-A-BILLY	Guy Mitchell	Philips
		Vic Chester (Dec) ; Don Lang (HMV).		
5	(8)	I'LL TAKE YOU HOME AGAIN KATHLEEN	Slim Whitman	London
		Josef Locke (HMV).		
	(3)	YOUNG LOVE	Tab Hunter	London
		Sonny James (Cap); Tommy Steele (Dec) ; Crew Cuts (Mer).		
	(2)	THE BANANA BOAT SONG	Harry Belafonte	HMV
		Inia Te Wiata (HMV) ; Steve Lawrence (V-Cor) ; Sarah Vaughan (Mer) ; Fontane Sisters (Lon) ; Dorothy Squires (P-Nix) ; Zack Matalon (P-Nix) ; Shirley Bassey (Phi) ; Tarriers (Col) ; Peter Lowe (Par) ; Freddy (Poly) ; Lilli Verona (HMV) ; Stan Freberg (Cap).		
8	(5)	LONG, TALL SALLY	Little Richard	London
		Pat Boone (Lon) ; Marty Robbins (Phi).		
9	(8)	NINETY-NINE WAYS	Tab Hunter	London
		Charlie Gracie (Par).		
10	(12)	LOOK HOMEWARD, ANGEL	Johnnie Ray	Philips
11	(11)	WHEN I FALL IN LOVE	Nat " King " Cole	Capitol
		Doris Day (Col) ; Jeri Southern (Bruns) ; Ron Goodwin (Par).		
12	(17)	FREIGHT TRAIN	Chas. McDevitt	Oriole
		Bob Cort (Dec).		
13	(13)	THE GIRL CAN'T HELP IT	Little Richard	London
		Alan Dale (V-Cor).		
14	(—)	YES TONIGHT, JOSEPHINE	Johnnie Ray	Philips
15	(19)	BUTTERFINGERS	Tommy Steele	Decca
16	(—)	TOO MUCH	Elvis Presley	HMV
	(6)	DON'T FORBID ME	Pat Boone	London
		Glen Mason (Par) ; Freddy (Poly).		
18	(15)	HEART	Max Bygraves	Decca
		Tony Bennett (Phi) ; Johnston Bros (Dec.) ; McGuire Sisters (V-Cor) ; Ronnie Hilton (HMV) ; Dennis Lotis (P-Nix) ; Ruby Murray (Col) ; Joe Loss (HMV) ; King Bros (Par) ; Four Aces (Bruns).		
19	(—)	WHY, BABY, WHY	Pat Boone	London
		Denny Dennis (Emb.)		
20	(—)	ONLY YOU	Platters	Mercury
		Hilltoppers (Lon) ; Louis Armstrong (Bruns) ; Malcolm Vaughan (HMV) ; Steve Martin (Col) ; Annie Ross (Dec) ; Victor Silvester (Col).		

Three records " tied " for 5th position.
Two records " tied " for 16th position.

★STORES SUPPLYING INFORMATION FOR RECORD CHART
Sykes' Record Shop, Middlesbrough ; Duwe Wholesale, Ltd., Manchester, 1 ; R. C. Mansell, Ltd., Birmingham, 2 ; Glyn Lewis, Blackwood ; Sydney Scarborough, Ltd., Hull ; Boyds, Cardiff ; Nems, Ltd., Liverpool, 4 ; Bandparts Music Stores, Ltd., Edinburgh, 1 ; Imhofs, Ltd., London, W.C.1 ; W. A. Clarke, London, S.W.6 ; Engineering Service Co., Bolton ; McCormack's, Glasgow, C.2 ; A. R. Tipple, London, S.E.15 ; Popular Music Stores, London, E.6 ; J. W. Mansfield, Ltd., Worthing ; H. J. Carroll, Manchester, 18 ; Saville Bros. Ltd., South Shields ; Leading Lighting, London, N.1 ; Hickies, Slough ; Paish & Co., Torquay ; Rolo For Records, London, E.10.

THIS copyright list of the 24 best-selling songs for the week ended May 4, 1957, is supplied by the Popular Publishers' Committee of the Music Publishers' Association, Ltd. (Last week's placings in parentheses.)

1. (1) HEART (A) (2/-) .. Frank
2. (2) YOUNG LOVE (A) (2/-) .... Cromwell
3. (3) THE BANANA BOAT SONG (A) (2/-) .... Morris
4. (6) TRUE LOVE (A) (2/-) .... Chappell
5. (5) SINGING THE BLUES (A) (2/-) .... Frank
6. (4) DON'T FORBID ME (A) (2/-) .. Campbell Connelly
7. (7) MARIANNE (A) (2/-) .... Montclare
8. (9) LOOK HOMEWARD, ANGEL (A) (2/-) .... Kassner
9. (8) KNEE-DEEP IN THE BLUES (A) (2/-) .... Leeds
10. (10) MANGOS (A) (2/-) .. Bron
11. (19) BUTTERFLY (A) (2/-) .... Aberbach
12. (12) ADORATION WALTZ (A) (2/-) .... Bron
13. (13) CUMBERLAND GAP (B) (2/-) .... Essex
14. (11) THE WISDOM OF A FOOL (A) (2/-) .... Leeds
15. (—) NINETY-NINE WAYS (A) (2/-) .... Good Music
16. (22) I'LL FIND YOU (B) (2/-) .... Robbins
17. (—) ROCK-A-BILLY (A) (2/-) .... Joy Music
18. (20) THE GOOD COMPANIONS (B) (2/-) .. Peter Maurice
19. (16) ALL (B) (2/-) .... Anglo-Continental
    (17) BY YOU, BY YOU, BY YOU (A) (2/-) .... Cinephonic
21. (23) CHAPEL OF THE ROSES (A) (2/-) .... Victoria
22. (14) I DREAMED (A) (2/-) .... Duchess
23. (18) FRIENDLY PERSUASION (A) (2/-) .... Robbins
24. (15) DON'T YOU ROCK ME, DADDY-O (B) (2/-) Essex

Two titles " tied " for 19th position.
A—American; B—British;
(All rights reserved.)

getting a wider exposure than many a jazz record, it was not unusual to see skiffle groups at the top of the lists above such revered artists as Ella Fitzgerald and Louis Armstrong.

The showman's weekly, the *World's Fair*, calculated its chart on jukebox plays taken from selected sites. Their Top 100 often included obscure records that just happened to be advertised in the paper that particular week.

When a noted skiffle leader was at lunch with the editor of a well-known music weekly, he was asked how his latest record was faring. The skiffler replied, 'It's not showing in your chart yet.'

To which the riposte was, 'Wait until next week.'

Sure enough there it was, for one week, at number 19.

In America, *Variety*, *Billboard* and *Cash Box* all published their own charts, based variously on disc jockey plays, jukebox plays, record requests and record sales; again, a system wide open to manipulation.

Only Lonnie Donegan, and the Chas McDevitt Group with Nancy Whiskey, were to carry the flag for British skiffle in the USA.

The skiffle fan had few radio programmes on which he could hear his favourite music. As far as getting a record aired, the daily 'Housewives Choice' and the weekly 'Family Favourites' were essential plugs. They would nearly always play a record if they had sufficient requests to do so, bona fide or otherwise. Fan clubs were kept very busy.

Radio Luxembourg played an important part in showcasing recent releases and their DJs were fêted by one and all.

It was still the era of the song-plugger, nowadays almost a relic of yesteryear's Tin Pan Alley. The song-plugger, often a publisher himself, would try to persuade bands and singers with their own radio shows to record and cover their current promotion; failing that they might at least broadcast an arrangement of the song.

When Gerry Benson, the plugger and publisher of 'Freight Train', encountered resistance to the songs he carried in his little black briefcase, he would close it up, open a second case and try to sell the 'mark', a selection of costume jewellery, made by his brother-in-law.

In the USA the payola scandal surfaced at the end of 1959. Supposedly the practice had been rife since 1954. It manifested itself in many ways, from distributors wrongly filling in the chart forms with their favourites and returning them to *Cash Box*, to publishers giving the disc jockey a piece of the song from the composer's royalties, and even to the blatant exchange of cash for favours. The scandal virtually ruined Alan Freed, the man who almost single-handedly promoted rock and roll. Many other DJs escaped prosecution by the skin of their teeth.

As early as 1955, when Chuck Berry received his first royalty statement for 'Maybellene', he discovered that Russ Fratto, a Chicago record distributor, and Alan Freed 'had written the song with me'. When he confronted Leonard Chess, the head of his record company, he was told that the song 'would get more attention' if it included the names of Freed and Fratto. It proved a wise move; on one night alone it received a two-hour airing on Alan Freed's 'Rock 'n' Roll Party'. At a time when a good blues record sold tens of thousands and a hit R&R record sold hundreds of thousands, 'Mabellene' sold over a million.

The process also worked in reverse. Name recording artists realized that their returns could be increased by acquiring a piece of the action. In 1957 Elvis Presley said,

> I made over a million dollars this year. But I'm no musician at all. I can't play the guitar and I never wrote a song in my life. Yet I get my name on songs and I collect a third interest of all the songs I sing.

This practice was not apparent and seldom publicized in the UK. However, it did manifest its presence when a music publisher confessed to an investigative reporter, who had hidden a microphone, KGB-style in a bowl of flowers in the lobby of the Savoy Hotel. Still it did not create the upheaval that occurred in the USA. After all, what was called payola in the music business, over here, in Parliament, was referred to as lobbying.

There was still the odd television show where a few well-placed greenback dollars would ensure exposure for a particular artist. Such goings on were still going on throughout the 1960s and 1970s. Even Brian Epstein, when trying to secure a recording contract for the Beatles with Decca Records, suggested that if they were signed up he would purchase the first 5,000 records. The message never got through to Dick Rowe at Decca. He signed Brian Poole and the Tremelos instead.

As an alternative to having their records played, the skiffle groups had to pass a BBC audition to appear live on a broadcast. In many cases this proved a stumbling block. Jimmy Grant, the producer of the 'Saturday Skiffle Club', said:

> The trouble with most amateur skiffle groups is that they lack sufficient basic musicianship, which is the first essential.

Failing the audition, however, was not restricted to skiffle groups; Bruce Turner's band caused astonishment when they failed. Bruce was a highly respected jazz musician and each member of his band had all broadcast before, so one couldn't predict the standards required by the producers.

Having passed the audition there were few radio shows on which the groups could get exposure. These were mainly variety programmes: often a relic of wartime broadcasting like 'Workers' Playtime', and 'Mid-day Music Hall'. Groups would share the bill with sopranos, instrumentalists and stand-up comedians.

Eventually specialist shows began to take the air. 'Break for Jazz', broadcast on the BBC Light Programme, featured a name jazz band and a skiffle group. All these shows went out at about lunchtime.

Skiffle was at last to have its own show. On 1 June 1957, an initial series of eight programmes was scheduled. It was to replace the traditional organ recital aired at 10–10.30 am on a Saturday morning, which usually featured such doyens of the theatre organ as Reginald Dixon or Robinson Cleaver, and had been running for the last eight years. 'Saturday Skiffle Club' was to become one of the most successful minority interest radio shows of the late 1950s.

10.0 Greenwich Time Signal

SATURDAY SKIFFLE CLUB

Johnny Duncan
and his Blue Grass Boys
and The Pete Curtis
Folk and Blues Quintet
With guest appearances by
Bob Cort, Lonnie Donegan,
Chas McDevitt, Russell Quaye
Nancy Whiskey and Wally Whyton
who are invited to choose
their favourite skiffle record
Introduced by Brian Matthew
Produced by Jimmy Grant
and Jack Dabbs
(BBC recording)

News Summary at 10.30

Produced by Jimmy Grant and introduced by Brian Matthew, the programme proved to be much more successful than anticipated and ran for 61 consecutive weeks, missing out only Saturday 9 November 1957. In that time it featured over 40 skiffle groups and a dozen or more guests. Each show would include a name skiffle group plus support, usually a solo artist or a boogie piano player. The occasional folk singer would also get an airing. The main recording groups like Duncan, McDevitt, Bishop, Cort and the Vipers made at least eight or nine appearances each; surprisingly, Donegan, Colyer and the Worried Men only appeared once. The Avon Cities and the 2.19 Skiffle Group each received two spots. The fee from the BBC for broadcasting was quite negligible and presumably Donegan was getting sufficient exposure for his records elsewhere, without having to resort to live radio broadcasts.

By October 1957, 'Saturday Skiffle Club' had pulled in an unprecedented audience of two and a half million listeners. It continued to grow in popularity throughout 1957.

'Yes, there it is, the folksy jazz we call skiffle.' Brian Matthew's introduction was quite precise and apt, when one thinks about it. Brian's distinctive plummy BBC voice belied the jazz fan that lurked within; even so he was not averse to indulging in some banter of the type one now associates with the likes of Terry Wogan and Jimmy Young.

When Brian Matthew was about to go on holiday for a few weeks, he handed his regular spot over to Michael Brooke. The ensuing repartee was decidedly over the top:

Michael Brooke: 'I thought I'd come equipped actually for the first show.'

Brian Matthew: 'It was jolly noble of you, but I do feel I ought to point out, when we said drainpipes, we meant those made out of jeans and not out of drainpipes.'

Michael Brooke: 'Now look here, this skiffle, I haven't met it before. I've heard it and some of it I like and some of it I don't like awfully. Have I got to be terribly enthusiastic about it?'

Brian replies that he should at least try to keep it going until he gets back from his vacation. If Lead Belly hadn't already turned in his grave at the interpretation given to many of his songs, then this would surely have made this world-wise man spin like a top . . .

The programme did last until Brian got back, in fact it lasted another two months until 27 September 1958. From 4 October it was renamed 'Saturday Club', reflecting the gradual abandoning of the epithet by most of the groups. Still featuring the occasional skiffle group the show now encompassed a wider range of musical styles. One of the first programmes in the new format included such pop acts as the Five Dallas Boys, Marion Ryan and trad jazz bands like the Mick Mulligan Band with George Melly. It also included a record request spot and the show was spread over two hours, from 10 to 12 midnight.

The 'Saturday Skiffle Club' was nevertheless a milestone in broadcasting: a programme essentially aimed at teenagers without the restrictions and dryness of traditional BBC programmes. It gave a platform to lesser-known groups like the Bill Bailey Skiffle Group, who had been around for years in one form or another, without having broadcast, and to the new groups like the Martians, Pete Curtis, the 2.19 Skiffle Group, the Hi-Fi Skiffle Group, the Brett Brothers, Jimmy Jackson, the Eden Street Skiffle Group, Brian Newey, Westcott Skiffle and, from Scotland, Joe Gordon, the Black Diamonds, the Delta and Creole Skiffle Groups.

The Black Diamonds were: Jim Scott, guitar and leader, Joe Gordon, guitar, vocal, Jack Taylor, washboard, vocal and Dick Campbell on bass. Joe Gordon went on to front his Folk Four and later formed a double act with his wife Sally Logan, appearing in concert throughout the world, even playing the prestigious Carnegie Hall in New York. He currently hosts his own radio show 'Joe Gordon's Musical Mixture' on West Sound Radio. Other notable Scottish groups included The Spyders and The Kalamazoo Skiffle Group.

The BBC never retained any of the recordings of these early Saturday Skiffle programmes. One complete show has survived on tape, recorded by an astute fan. It features Dickie Bishop and his Sidekicks and George Melly with his Bubbling Over Four, including, on vocal and washboard, Beryl Bryden. Dickie Bishop's choice of numbers included:

'Raise the Ruckus', 'Closer Walk With Thee', 'The Prisoner's Song', 'Shorty George', 'Cindy' and 'Dang My Rowdy Ties' (vocal, Pete Korrison).

George Melly and his Bubbling Over Four's contribution was:

'This Train', 'Sportin' Life', 'Big Butter and Egg Man', 'Kansas City' and 'Casey Jones'.

The only other extracts from the show known to be available are the various numbers on Chas McDevitt's CD 'Freight Train' on Rollercoaster records, mainly from the broadcast on 5 July 1958.

Recently discovered are tapes and acetates featuring the Westcott Skiffle Group, recorded in 1956–57–58. The group consisted of: Maurice Foley, guitar and vocal; Pete Brider, lead guitar and vocal; Jean Foley, washboard; Clive Godden (Clive the Jive) tea-chest and bass, and Keith on rhythm guitar. Later the group included John Clark on double bass and Terry Minor, guitar and vocals. Titles featured are 'Face in the Rain', 'Goodmornin' Blues', 'Railroad Steamboat', 'Greenback Dollar', 'This Little Light o' Mine' and 'Hey Liley Lo'. The standard of musicianship and arrangements on these songs was certainly above average and it is surprising that the Westcotts didn't acquire a recording contract, particularly after their exposure on the BBC 'Saturday Skiffle Club'. This should soon be rectified, as Rollercoaster plan to include some tracks on one of their Skiffle Compilation CDs.

═NOVEMBER═

16 SATURDAY

MORNING AND AFTERNOON

10.0 Greenwich Time Signal
SATURDAY SKIFFLE CLUB
The Chas McDevitt Skiffle Group
with Shirley Douglas
The Hi-Fi Skiffle Group
Produced by Jimmy Grant
(BBC recording)

5.57   THE WEATHER

6.0   NEWS
and
SPORTS NEWS

6.5 SIX-FIVE SPECIAL
From the Scottish Radio
and Television Exhibition
with
Josephine Douglas
and Pete Murray
introducing
among others
Lita Roza, David Hughes
Jimmy Logan
The Eric Delaney Band
The Chas McDevitt
Skiffle Group
with Nancy Whiskey
Art Baxter and his Sinners
The Burt Twins
The Clyde Valley Stompers
The Glasgow
Rock 'n' Roll Sinners
Featuring Sport:
Freddie Mills
Script by Trevor Peacock
Additional research
by Kenneth Midwood
Produced by Josephine Douglas
(David Hughes and Jimmy Logan appear by permission of Howard and Wyndham Ltd.)

6.5 SIX-FIVE SPECIAL
From the
TWO I's COFFEE BAR,
Old Compton Street, London
with
Josephine Douglas and Pete Murray
introducing among others
Freddie Mills
Don Lang and his Frantic Five
Lucille Mapp
The King Brothers
Mike and Bernie Winters
Chas. McDevitt
and his Skiffle Group
with Shirley Douglas
The Worried Men
Wee Willy Harris
Disc Spot of the Week:
Terry Dene
in an excerpt from ' The Golden Disc '
by permission of
Butchers Film Distributors, Ltd.
Script by Trevor Peacock
Produced by Jack Good
(Chas. McDevitt and his Skiffle Group, with Shirley Douglas, are appearing at the Metropolitan Theatre, Edgware Road, London)

See facing page and page 11

As for the new medium of television, still only in black and white, there were few if any shows that could provide exposure to the up and coming groups. The best they could hope for would be a guest spot in a variety show. The McDevitt Skiffle Group, without Nancy Whiskey, made their television debut on the 'Fred Emney Show'. Even then they were subordinate to the rotund comedian who led the group in a spirited version of 'Don't You Rock Me Daddy O', playing a 'prop' guitar, with rubber strings.

It was another minor revolution in TV programming that came to the rescue of the new teenage musical acts and gave them a platform on which to expose their wares. In 1957, and indeed until 1972, television was restricted by the government to specific hours. Originally planned as a 'filler' programme to take up the extra hour which had been sanctioned between 6 pm and 7 pm the 'Six–Five Special' was aired immediately after the 'Six O'clock News', hence Six–Five. In no time at all it commanded a large and fanlike following.

In an era when television was still finding its feet, it turned the whole process on its head. No attempt was made to hide the cameras, the audience was part of the show and a genuine air of excitement was generated, marred only by the rather stilted performance of the main presenter and co-producer, Josephine Douglas. The brain behind the show was Jack Good, who later went on to produce the classic TV series for ATV, 'The Oh Boy Show', and, years later, the seminal US television music show 'Shindig'. Radio Luxembourg disc jockey, Pete Murray, was brought in as a presenter to give the proceedings an authentic pedigree and comedy was supplied by Mike and Bernie Winters, with interpolations from the former champion boxer, Freddie Mills. A great deal of the excitement came from the fact that this was a live broadcast and few filmed extracts were ever included. This is most unfortunate because nothing remains of the show on film; this was long before the days of the ubiquitous video. The only clip one can see nowadays is that of the opening credits to the movie *Six–Five Special*, a train rumbling over the rails to Don Lang's version of the title song. Without the luxury of film for reference, in hindsight the 'Six–Five Special' was probably much blander that it is remembered to be. Nevertheless, it revolutionized the manner of presenting the music of that era, be it skiffle or rock and roll and helped establish many of the name groups. On a couple of occasions it was produced on tour, as far afield as Glasgow, and featured variously the Donegan and the McDevitt groups as well as local skiffle groups like the Black Diamonds, who had reached the Scottish finals of the International Skiffle Competition.

One such memorable event was when the show came from the actual 2 I's. To see the technicians scrambling about the confined space with their cameras and microphones; to hear the excitable floor manager trying to rescue the proceedings from chaos is a piece of television history that should have been committed to film. In a space 25ft x 12ft they were able to film the audience, the jivers, the presenters and the groups, which included Don Lang's Frantic Five, the King Brothers, Chas McDevitt's Skiffle Group with Shirley Douglas, Wee Willie Harris, Larry Page (later to become a renowned record producer to the Kinks and the Troggs) and Laurie London. Use was made of the ground-floor coffee bar area, which housed a long counter with Gaggia machines, a large jukebox and various fixed seating. All in all, a cameraman's nightmare.

With the success of this show, more and more programmes opened their doors. Even the prestigious 'Sunday Night at the London Palladium' played host to the groups. Jack Payne's 'Off the Record' and 'The Jack Jackson Show' all contributed to the promotion of the groups' recordings and at last it looked as if the Establishment was becoming a little less condescending. The Chas McDevitt Group even had a resident guest spot, in a coffee-bar setting, on the Tessie O'Shea show, 'See You Soho'. Each week they would feature one full-length number as well as provide a constant flow of skiffle-type background music.

It was Lonnie Donegan who naturally benefited most from this new approach by the television moguls. He was riding high on the crest of the wave and his inclusion in a show would enhance its ratings. It was not long before he was to headline his own television series with his skiffle group and regular guests, Miki and Griff.

In 1956, the McDevitt Group had provided the soundtrack for an NBC documentary about London by night called *Nice Time* but, by the time the general film industry had woken up to skiffle's potential, the music had passed its peak and rock and roll in the shape of Tommy Steele and Cliff Richard had cornered the market.

The first British pop film, *The Tommy Steele Story* (a rather premature life story, presented by Nat Cohen and Stuart Levy), tried to cash in on all the current musical themes. In the final scenes Tommy Steele hosts a concert that features the Humphrey

On set of The Tommy Steele Story.

Lyttelton jazz band, Tommy Eytle's calypso band, Chris O'Brian's Caribbeans and the Chas McDevitt Skiffle Group. In late 1957, *The Golden Disc*, starring Terry Dene and his Dene Aces, featured Nancy Whiskey singing her last recording with the McDevitt Group, 'Johnny Oh', accompanied in the film by Sonny Stewart's Skiffle Kings. The Sonny Stewart boys played 'Let Me Lie' on their own, and Les Hobeaux gave a spirited rendering of 'Dynamo'.

The only other film to include skiffle material is *The Six–Five Special* in which Lonnie Donegan performed, 'Jack o' Diamonds' and 'Grand Coulee Dam'.

10

Skiffle Contests

The early New Orleans jazz bands used to delight in contests where they would try to carve-up the opposition. By outplaying their rivals they established a reputation for themselves and enhanced their commercial appeal. So too with the skiffle groups, who were suckers for a talent competition.

The normal talent show, featuring a variety of entertainers, gave way to the skiffle contest, which was open only to skiffle groups. Some of the contests had bizarre rules: no full-drum kits, only a snare drum could be played with brushes, and this had to be done standing up; there had to be a least one guitar in the line-up and one such rule required that everything had to be played in 'strict tempo for rock and roll'.

Very often the contests were no more than a ruse by the promoter to get free entertainment as well as ensuring a full house, made up mainly of the groups' followers. The groups were aware of this but didn't care; the contests were an opportunity of being heard by a larger audience and there was always the chance that a recording contract might come their way.

However, they were also fraught with danger, especially if the verdict displeased a faction in the audience. The *Jazz News* reported in November 1957:

SKIFFLE AND JAZZ CONTESTS GIVE CAUSE FOR ALARM

Amazing scenes of a kind which one reliable reporter described as 'near riotous' greeted the judges' verdict at a world skiffle contest, promoted under the auspices of the *Weekend Mail* which was held at the Mecca Ballroom, Leeds. This further incident concerning the seemingly ill-starred skiffle movement in Great Britain has ironic implications in that the 'trouble' arose when a section of the audience decided to quarrel alarmingly with the winner's and runner's-up placings arrived at by the adjudicators: tuba player Bob Barclay of the Yorkshire Jazz Band and three members of the Leeds United soccer team.

So discouraging and, to an unseasoned band, potentially demoralising was the attitude by sections of the crowd, that we feel inclined to say to all amateur skifflers with ambitions to enter contests: 'DON'T!' Not without weighing up the pros and cons very carefully in advance, and certainly not without checking the actual substance of unspecified cash prizes and theatrical engagements offered as 'bait' to would-be competitors.

Nevertheless these competitions flourished. Contests were held all over the country, from such large venues as the Hammersmith Palais and the Tottenham Royal, to the small rock and jazz clubs, even including the vicar's village fête. The national press, in the form of the *Daily Herald*, always ready to jump on the band-wagon, sponsored a skiffle contest to be held at all the Butlin's holiday camps. The contests continued even after the period when skiffle was apparently no longer commercial. In June 1959, when the McDevitt Group, now a four-piece including drums, piano and bass-guitar, played the Metropole Theatre in Glasgow, they were still supported by a skiffle contest: 'Semi-final first house Friday, final, second house.'

On 3 February 1958, the promoter Stanley Dale launched the National Skiffle Contest at the Empire Theatre, Glasgow. It was to be tied in with a nationwide tour headlined by Jim Dale and the Vipers. The tour covered most of the major cities, including Leicester, Derby Hippodrome, Nottingham Empire, Sheffield Empire, Leeds Empire and even the Metropolitan Theatre, Edgware Road, London.

Many people thought that skiffle, in a do-it-yourself style by local teenagers, would not make for good music. Fraser White reported in the *Weekly Sporting Review and Showbusiness* that critics, both expert and otherwise, condemned the show from the beginning. However, Stanley Dale defended his enterprise right from the start:

Skiffle may or may not be music, I don't know. I do know, however, that it is good entertainment and the sort that Joe public wants to see. Furthermore, he can bring his wife and kids to the show without embarrassing them. I do not employ nudes to boost business nor allow comics to crack dubious jokes for cheap laughs. The local groups who enter the competition get a great deal of fun out of doing so. They don't seem to care whether they win or not. They range from compact little groups of four to gangling outfits of up to ten. Many people tell me they are mostly Teddy Boys; some may be but I have had no trouble with them. Surely it is right to give them a moment of glory when they probably get a lot of the so-called Teddy Boy out of their systems. They are far better off strumming a guitar and rehearsing in Mum's parlour than roaming the streets with knives, looking for trouble.

From the heats held during the week, a winner would be chosen on the Saturday night to go forward to the eventual grand final. The winners were nearly always chosen by audience reaction, so if you had a large family and a lot of support, your success was guaranteed; the promoters would be too intimidated to go against powerful support, even if the group was not up to scratch. However, this was all academic; for after many weeks the tour was concluded without a final choice having been made. No prizes were given and interest just faded along with the skiffle boom.

Nevertheless when Stanley Dale put on his National Skiffle Contest at Finsbury Park Empire, the first week of December 1957, he was overwhelmed with applications. Of the 78 groups that wanted to participate, he was only able to accommodate 50, the rest were promised the opportunity of entering at a later date. The groups appearing, their leaders and their home territory were:

1	Romsiders	F. Warley	Romford
2	Krocketts	R. Greatbanks	Clapham
3	Medallions	B. Halsey	Edmonton
4	Silver Dollars	T. Silver	Hackney
5	Southerney	W. Mardell	Enfield
6	Riverside Ramblers	J. Kobell	Tottenham
7	Lucky Six	R. Betney	Hackney
8	Pete Abbott	P. Abbott	Highbury
9	Moonlite	W. Harvey	Barking
10	Bryan Newey	B. Newey	Enfield
11	Adders	R. K. Higdon	Barnet
12	Moonshiney	S. Rey	Edmonton
13	Hurricanes	M. Burton	Holborn
14	Ace Five	D. F. Stewart	Poplar
15	Dave Elliot	D. Elliot	Cheshunt
16	Muskrat Ramblers	T. Watts	Romford
17	Flophouse 4 + 1	D. G. Simmonds	Enfield
18	Alley Kats	P. E. Hubbard	Enfield
19	Black Cats	M. A. Bradshaw	Wanstead
20	Hornets	M. Powell	Winchmore
21	Forty Niners	N. Webster	Dalston
22	Skeletons	A. Engey	Highgate
23	Spirits	F. Miller	Highgate
24	Kilowats	J. Maitland	Finchley
25	Gordon Rd Ramblers	R. Cotton	Tufnell Park
26	Monarchs	B. Lloyd	Dagenham

27	Metropolitan	D. Bergin	Harrow
28	Jyants	D. Steele	Royston
29	Valley Ramblers	H. Allen	Cheshunt
30	Jimmy Wheeler	R. Arnitt	Edgware
31	Nomads	K. Dedman	Stamford
32	Kordas	W. Turnbull	Hornsey
33	Heather and Toothbrush Ensemble	P. De Villiers	Regents Park
34	Senators	B. Burns	Highbury
35	Bob Stokes	B. Stokes	Tottenham
36	Spiders	N. A. Stewart	Camden Town
37	Streamliners	B. Cornes	Enfield
38	Satellites	V. Mitchell	Stamford
39	Grasshoppers	A. Roberts	Hornsey
40	Rhythm Kings	D. Duggan	Islington
41	Scorpions	T. Abrahams	Tottenham
42	Sinners	A. J. Barr	Upminster
43	Bob Western	B. Western	Edmonton
44	Sky Blue	R. Docherty	Islington
45	Railroad	T. Bowen	Enfield
46	Pirates	F. Dobson	Shoreditch
47	Blue Stars	E. F. Pearce	Highbury
48	Bob Corrie Five	T. Guyver	Tufnell Park
49	Saints	F. Walker	Finchley
50	Jesters	T. Gover	Tottenham

When one considers that the average group consisted of about six members, there would be about 300 skifflers from one area all appearing at the local theatre, all toting their guitars, tea-chest bass or double bass and drum kits or washboards. Multiply this nationwide in all the local venues, and the enormity of this phenomenon becomes evident.

Just imagine the logistics of this lot turning up for the competition. This was the era before the car was king. Few groups had their own vehicles and either had to travel on foot or use public transport. One group even walked the 75 miles from London to Bury St Edmunds to enter the National Competition. The big red London double-decker bus was a godsend for the skiffler; at least they could stow the tea-chest in the ample luggage compartment, under the stairs. However, in Leeds they were banned from the buses and had to travel by tram. In London the underground was awash with skiffle groups, particularly late at night when the pubs and clubs turned out. Walking across the metropolis at one in the morning with a guitar under your arm, while your mate carried a tea-chest bass over his shoulder, was sure to prompt the local bobby to question your motives. Groups naturally searched for a residential booking to avoid this problem. It was not long before the coffee bars provided this refuge.

Another event, also billed as the First National Skiffle Contest, had a chequered background. This was a one-day promotion held in Bury St Edmunds on Whit Monday in June 1957, organized by the Bury St Edmunds Round Table with the help of Sam Benjamin, the vice-president of the International Jazz Club, who in fact was one of the judges. Hundreds of groups tried to enter, but in the end after most of the non-skiffle groups were weeded out, 44 groups were listed. In the end only 34 took part, but considering the inclement weather – it rained most of the time – this was still an amazing turn-out. The annual fête normally drew a crowd of 12,000, but even though this year's attendance was down all the groups went through their paces. The judges, apart from Benjamin, included Johnny Duncan, Paul Oliver, the renowned collector and blues authority and Graham Boatfield, who confessed he was a little tired of listening to 'Cumberland Gap' for the twentieth time. Their final decision:

1 The 2.19 Skiffle Group
2 The Station Skiffle Group
3 The Delta Skiffle Group
4 The Lea Valley Skiffle Group

The winners originally came from Rochester in Kent and grew out of Dave Chandler's Riverside Ramblers Jazz Band. Billed as 'A threat to the best, from Chatham', the 2.19 Skiffle Group built up quite a following, even appearing on 'Saturday Skiffle Club' and ATV's 'Saturday Spectacular'. Joint leaders of the group were guitarists, Mike Wallace and Mik Lauder. They had started singing and playing folk songs together the previous September while on holiday in Paris. Mike was doing his National Service, so too was Dave Chandler, the washboard player, an outsider from Ilfracombe. Mik was an art student; and one of their bass players, Len Harris, was a wages clerk.

Two of the group were in the band of the Royal Engineers in Chatham and eventually left to continue their studies at the Royal College of Music. Jack McCormack, on bass in the original group, is now principal bass player with the Royal Philharmonic

Orchestra and Dave Chandler, the original washboard player, now plays trombone with the Orchestra of the Royal Opera House, Covent Garden. On Sundays he still leads his own jazz band at the Lamb and Flag in Covent Garden. With this sort of potential talent on tap, the group's attitude to skiffle was much more ambitious than that of the average group.

At first, after the contest, all seemed well but soon a certain amount of discontent surfaced, particularly over the distribution of prizes and the promise of paid engagements for the winners.

The Delta Skiffle Group, who had already taken part successfully in the Scottish Skiffle Championships, had travelled down from Glasgow for the event and were upset at only receiving £5 and not even a trophy, as they had been promised. They had also been offered paid engagements on 'The Rock across the Channel', but this too was not forthcoming. As a sop all three groups were given a free trip, sponsored by the co-promoter, Freddy Irani, owner of the Côte d'Azur Club, formerly of the 2 Is. Doug Taylor, the leader of the group said:

> We were told that we had been booked to play on the 'Rock across the Channel' and assumed that this was one of the 'theatrical engagements' promised to the winners and runners up of the contest. We assumed naturally that this would be a paid engagement and arranged to travel to London for this job and the recording session on the Whit weekend.
>
> We took a chance in coming with no money, but believed that work was waiting for us in London. Mr Irani gave us a £1 between us, Carlo Kramer of Esquire Records bought our train tickets back to Glasgow as well as paying us for the recording session.

The group consisted of Douglas Taylor, an art student at the Glasgow School of Art, guitar and banjo; Don Finlayson, a radio and TV salesman in Sauchiehall Street, who had once played the bagpipes in a world champion band; his brother Tom Finlayson on guitar, Ian Couper on bass, also a bagpipe player, and Hank Smith on washboard, a merchant seaman, and the only sassenach in the group.

The line-up of the Lea Valley Skiffle Group shows precisely how an average group was made up. Hailing from Hackney Wick in the East End, it included an ambulance driver, a tailor's cutter, a progress chaser, an insurance broker and two market porters. Their enthusiasm for the music is apparent in the few recordings they made for Esquire Records. Enthusiasm is what skiffle groups had in abundance.

The Station Skiffle Group perhaps made the most progress of all the finalists. The group fragmented into two sections: one section reaching the semi-finals of Stanley Dale's National Skiffle Contest and appearing on the 'Six–Five Special' on 29 March 1958, the other forming Jimmy Miller's Barbecues and recording twice for the legendary Joe Meek, in 1957 and 1958.

At this point it might be appropriate to examine the background, pressures and influences on a budding skiffler from that era – the semi-pro who just loved the music. This age of innocence is far removed from the cut-throat world of pop today. Derek Mason, still playing washboard to this day, recalls:

My early influences were traditional jazz and blues singers like Lead Belly and Snooks Eaglin. I started playing at a friend's house, his brother played guitar and there was a washboard there, left behind by someone else. I put the thimbles on and just played it. I found that I had a sense of rhythm. We used to play along to the records of Donegan, Duncan, McDevitt and Ray Bush.

My first band was with my mate's brother, Pat O'Malley, we called ourselves the Ravens and played a few gigs at local clubs. Pat joined another local group, the Saints, who were at that time considered the best group in the area. Fortunately for me they were soon to lose their washboard player to the powers of the opposite sex. I was asked to join and for several months played some good gigs, including the Odeon in Tooting, which used to put on regular Sunday evening concerts.

There was a lot of swapping of musicians in those days. Singers without a group would contact whoever they could just to fulfil the booking they had arranged. My mates at the local boys' club had suddenly become guitar players or tea-chest bass players and were practising madly or taking music lessons.

As for the New Station Skiffle Group, originally called the Station Skiffle Group, their progress was typical of the trend at that time. They came from West Kensington and took their name from the Underground station, as they practised in the tunnels because of the excellent acoustics. When they disbanded in 1957, their lead singer, Mike Jarvie, formed his new band. My mates from the boys' club had joined him and were busy fulfilling gigs that had been booked through Mike's old band. The washboard player with the New Station had been taking guitar lessons as well, so when it was decided that he should 'move up', I joined the band on a regular basis. Without doubt they were the best band in south-west London. We had our own regular Friday night at the Constitutional Club in Shorrolds Road, Fulham, and on Thursday and Sunday

Presenting the prize cheque to the John Henry Skiffle Group.

evenings we had a regular booking at the Prince of Wales pub in Ravenscourt Park, Hammersmith.

The original Station Band had won their way through two rounds of Stanley Dale's National Skiffle Competition. The new band was fortunate enough to continue with this competition; more so as the next round, the quarter final, was to be screened on BBC's flagship, 'Six–Five Special'. This was in March 1958 and our opponents that night were the Wild Five from Manchester. Viewers were asked to vote by sending in their postcards. We must have known more people because we won that round. In July of 1958 we appeared again in the semi-final. Our opponents this time were the Moonshiners from Sheffield and the Saxons from Barking. Unfortunately we came second, losing to the Saxons. In the Final they came second, which we all felt was an injustice as they were by far the better of the three finalists.

How or why it all came to an end I don't really know. Mike was the inspiration of the band and when in 1959 he decided to get married and skiffle itself was being forced out by the influence of the likes of Bill Haley, we just stopped playing. Rather sad because they were great times. I am privileged, I feel, to have been part of those happy innocent days. The 1950s and 1960s will never be equalled for the atmosphere that prevailed and way of life that existed.

Derek Mason still plays washboard with the Lonnigan Brothers and Loose Chippings, who all hail from Greenwich. He wears gloves to which is attached some velcro; to this he fixes a strip of 'chain mail' and plays a tray with ridges, stuck to a cushion and mounted on a zimmer frame.

It is with the likes of Derek and his mates that skiffle will continue to be played and enjoyed as a goodtime happy musical escape from the woes and troubles of this present era.

11
They All Played Skiffle

Van Morrison, the Beatles, the Shadows, Adam Faith, Joe Brown, Chris Farlowe, Johnny Kidd, Ralph McTell, Chas Hodges of Chas and Dave, Tony Davies and Mick Groves of the Spinners, Brian Gregg of the Pirates and Tornados, artist David Oxtoby, comedian and broadcaster, Roy Hudd, they all played skiffle. Skiffle is the key that opened up their lives to the excitement of music and song. From such humble beginnings many an impressive career was carved.

Tony Meehan and Brian Bennett, both drummers with the Shadows, had served their apprenticeships with such groups as the Worried Men and the Vipers. Brian 'Liquorice' Locking their erstwhile bass guitarist had started on tea-chest bass with The Vagabonds in 1957. This group included Vince Eager on guitar and vocals. Vince was later to star in Jack Good's seminal TV show 'Oh Boy!'. Andy Summers of the Police and Deep Purple's Roger Glover both started in skiffle groups. Even modern guitar heroes like Albert Lee and Mark Knopfler acknowledge the influence that skiffle had on their initial interest in the guitar.

Van Morrison

George Ivan Morrison was born in Belfast, 31 August 1945. Because of his father's vast record collection his interest in music had already been whetted at an early age by listening to Lead Belly and Woody Guthrie. When he later heard Lonnie Donegan singing these same songs, he was determined to learn guitar.

Nearly 40 years later he would duet with Lonnie, singing 'Muleskinner Blues' and 'Alabammy Bound'.

In 1957, at the age of 12, he formed his first group with some of his neighbours. They called themselves the Sputniks and began playing at youth clubs and school concerts. The peak of the group's career came in 1958 when they were featured at a local cinema during a Saturday morning kid's matinee. With Van in the group at that time were Walter Blakey on washboard, Billy Ruth on guitar, John McLean, tea-chest bass and Gil Irvine playing a type of kazoo they called the zobo.

From those tentative steps came the Van Morrison we all know. He made his way through various beat groups and show bands, before in the mid-1960s forming the bluesy rock group, Them. With 'Gloria' and 'Baby Please Don't Go' they charted at number ten and later that year, 'Here Comes the Night' hit the number two position.

An introvert and somewhat reclusive person, he seemed to lie low for a while before re-emerging with the seminal album, his second, *Astral Weeks*, in 1969. From that moment on he has gone from success to triumphal success, establishing himself as a truly international superstar. But had it not been for skiffle . . .

Brian Gregg

Originally with Les Hobeaux on tea-chest then double bass, Brian Gregg went on to become one of the most sought-after bassists in the country. He played with Terry Dene, Billy Fury, Vince Eager, Dickie Valentine, Colin Hicks, the Tornados and with Johnny Kidd and the Pirates. He was playing on the latter's number one hit, 'Shakin' All Over'. This record, as well as Vince Taylor's 'Brand New Cadillac' and Cliff Richard's 'Move It', are recognized as being the three classic original contributions made by British musicians to the rock and roll catalogue of hits.

Realizing that at 1 am the night before their recording session, they hadn't yet got a song for the B side, Brian and Johnny Kidd disappeared into the basement of Chas McDevitt's Freight Train coffee bar in Berwick Street and, in half an hour, re-emerged with the song complete. They didn't even have a guitar to help them. It became the A side and an astounding success. The definitive riff on the guitar was by the Pirates' regular guitarist, Alan Caddy, but the tear-away solo was played by Joe Moretti, specifically brought in for the session.

With Colin Hicks and the Playboys, Brian introduced the Italians to rock and roll when, in 1958, he toured Italy on a package show with the Platters and Ramblin' Jack Elliott as compère link-man. Jack was completely miscast in this company: the Italians didn't know what he was all about, singing his Guthrie songs and 'Talking Blues'. In the end the agent insisted that Jack would have to sing such songs as 'Cigareets and Whisky and Wild, Wild Women' and 'Muleskinner Blues', forcing him to become almost a parody of himself.

Still it took a lot to get Jack riled; he seemed such a placid dude, resplendent in his Stetson, jeans and western boots – the original urban cowboy. However, Brian has vivid memories of one occasion when Jack's resolve was severely tested:

Whilst riding on a gondola on the Grand Canal in Venice, Jack was sitting aft on the barge playing his guitar. His first wife, June, was brow-beating him as usual when Jack, without missing a note, raised his fancy western boot and with a swift prod dumped the offending lady into the canal. While all around were trying to retrieve her with poles and grappling hooks, Jack just carried on playing, oblivious to the surrounding chaos!

It was obvious that Jack and June were not exactly kindred spirits. Poor Jack was harangued incessantly even when on stage. On one occasion she was shouting to Jack from the audience, telling him what to play, 'Pick it in G, Jack, pick it in G.'

He endeared himself to one and all when he called back, 'Why don't you pick your nose in G and piss off!'

Today Brian Gregg is still playing bass-guitar and has recently produced a CD for Rollercoaster of previously unreleased tracks by Terry Dene. Some of the tracks date from the early days when Brian and Terry used to work in the packing department of HMV Records in Oxford Street and feature Les Bennetts on guitar – skiffle with a Presley-style vocal.

Hank Marvin and Bruce Welch

Letter to Hank Marvin from Fred Lowe, the secretary of South Shields Jazz Club, May 1957:

> Dear Hank
> Very pleased to receive your entry for the skiffle contest. Just a reminder that it will be held in the Pier Pavilion, South Shields (near the lifeboat) on Saturday 18 May, so could you try to be there about 6.45 pm.
>
> Tickets are available at 2s. 6d. or 3d. 6d. or pay at the door if there are any tickets left.
>
> I am enclosing the complimentary tickets to admit each member of your group.
>
> The whole contest is being recorded and copies of any group will be available if you want them. So far we have entries from:
>
> | | |
> |---|---|
> | Team Valley Skiffle | Peter Bond Skiffle |
> | Rumjunglers | Brian Bainbridge Skiffle |
> | Santa Cruz Skiffle | Saints Skiffle |
> | Black Cats | |
>
> Tickets are on sale at 'Jeavons' Bigg Mart. See you on Saturday and here's wishing you the best of luck in the concert.

The Crescent City Skiffle Group won that contest on 18 May 1957. Hank was over the moon. They had played 'Stackolee', with Hank on banjo, an idea he said he nicked from watching Ken Colyer and he was convinced that this is what had swayed the judgement in their favour.

Hank and Bruce Welch both attended the same school. Having heard Hank play, Bruce asked him to join his own group, the Railroaders. They played working men's clubs and even a week at the Newcastle Palace. By now Hank was playing an electric Hofner guitar, Bruce and George Williams were on acoustic guitars, and Jim on drums and tea-chest bass. Bruce admits his debt to Lonnie Donegan and to the repertoire of Lead Belly and Big Bill Broonzy; they sang all the skiffle standards. As they began to include more rock numbers, Eddie Silva, another guitarist, joined, and George switched to bass.

The Railroaders Skiffle Group. (B. Welch)

Bruce used to be a regular patron at the Newcastle Empire where all the top recording acts would play a week's engagement. It was on the Moss Empire theatre circuit, known as the 'number ones'. There he had seen Slim Whitman, Johnny Ray, Lonnie Donegan, Jim Dale and the Vipers. The Chas McDevitt Skiffle Group played there the week of 26 August, Nancy Whiskey's last week with the group. On Saturday 31 August 1957, Hank and Bruce invited them all to come and hear the Railroaders play at a wedding. The lads, never known to turn down the opportunity of free drinks, went along enthusiastically. Chas remembers being pleasantly surprised by the proficiency of the group, particularly with their vocal sound and that they had such a good lead guitar, and he advised them that they should move south to get more recognition. It took them another eight months to make that move.

The *Newcastle Evening Chronicle* reported:

NORTH SKIFFLE BOYS GET RECORDING TEST

Four north-east youths today get their chance to make their names with a recording company.

They are members of the Railroaders Skiffle Group, which left Newcastle for London a fortnight ago at the invitation of skiffler Chas McDevitt.

Since they arrived in London they have had a busy time and many exciting moments.

They have played a four-hour session in the 2 Is club, where Tommy Steele, who has his own column in the *Evening Chronicle* every Saturday, began his career.

'It was the most wonderful and exciting thing that has ever happened to us,' they say.

And they add: 'We knocked them flat, Americans, Frenchmen and our own clan.'

Then they were given an audition by an agent, who immediately telephoned a recording company and arranged today's test.

'He also made us promise to keep away from any other agents until after the test.'

Meanwhile he is looking for part-time jobs for the boys.

Who are they? George Williams, aged 20, of East Street, High Spen (guitar); 15-year-old Bruce Cripps (Welch) of Westmorland Road, Newcastle (guitar and vocals); Fred Elliott, of Engle Street, Highfield (washboard) and 23-year-old Jed Watson of Park Road, Newcastle (tea-chest).

It was not as easygoing as the newspaper made it out to be. They had a fair amount of hardship before they eventually got their big break. By April 1958, the Railroaders were all in London and Hank and Bruce entered more talent contests and sang together as a duo in such coffee bars as Chaquito's, in Hanway Street.

Eventually the group disbanded. Various other combinations were tried, notably the Chesternuts, with Peter Chester, before they drifted into the Drifters.

When Chas first met Bruce he remembers that, at Bruce's request, Chas etched his signature, with a biro, into the body of Bruce's cello guitar. Little did either of them know that, in five years' time, Chas on tour, supporting the Shadows, would step into Bruce's shoes, when he was unable to appear in Liverpool and Peterborough on 28 and 29 April 1962. For two nights Chas was a Shadow. At least he didn't have to learn their renowned 'five-step' for the occasion and he was able to use his own Fender Stratocaster guitar.

Harry Webb (Cliff Richard to be) was a reluctant skiffler. He had been persuaded by a friend, drummer Terry Smart, to learn a few guitar chords and join him in the Dick Teague Skiffle Group. He stayed with the group a couple of months before his penchant for Presley eventually got the better of him. Both Harry and Terry broke away and formed the Drifters. Harry became Cliff, the Drifters became the Shadows and within 18 months they were both dominating the hit parade. Today they are still household names: Hank, living in Australia but nevertheless undertaking worldwide concert tours; Bruce living the life of luxury on the Thames at Richmond, still writing great songs and, as an A&R producer, making hit records and Cliff, reincarnated once again, this time as Heathcliff.

Cliff Richard and the Shadows, Bruce and Hank. (M. Sharratt/C. McD)

Chris Farlowe

The progress from skiffle group to rock, blues and jazz singer, to top recording artist, is precisely defined in the career of Chris Farlowe, John Deighton as was.

At the beginning of October 1957, the John Henry Skiffle Group won the final of the All England Skiffle Contest, held at the Royal Ballroom, Tottenham. John Deighton, their leader, was presented with a cheque for £25 by the judges who included bandleader Teddy Foster, Diz Disley, Don Wedge, Bill Varley, Shirley Douglas and Chas McDevitt. The musical press reported:

> The judges were unanimous in their decision, which should mean a lot of scope for these lads in the future.

For once this cliché was not to ring hollow. The group continued to develop and at one contest, held at the Harlequin Ballroom, Harlow, they turned up in their lamee suits and tore into a spirited version of Barrett Strong's 'Money'. The organizer halted their performance almost immediately, saying that they were disqualified as they were not playing skiffle. Later he confided

Chris Farlowe and the John Henry Skiffle Group.

that the group was too good and would have discouraged the others from entering.

From these initial stirrings, John was to become Chris, develop an interest in rhythm and blues, and eventually gain international renown with 'Out of Time', written for him by the Rolling Stones, number one in the hit parade in June 1966.

He still performs to this day touring overseas and on the continent fronting a magnificent big blues band, Coliseum. He also runs an antique business based in Canonbury Lane, London, specializing in Americana and 1950s memorabilia, quite appropriate for an ex-skiffler.

Joe Brown

If ever an artist deserved the tag 'all round entertainer', it's Joe Brown: West End musicals, starring with Dame Anna Neagle in *Georgie Girl*; directing and appearing in *Pump Boys and Dinettes*; numerous pantomimes; acting roles in such prestigious plays as *Sleuth*; hosting his own radio and record programmes, TV game-show panellist and, above all, talented multi-instrumentalist. He has had considerable chart success with his 'Bruvvers' and critical acclaim with his ambitious group, Brown's Home Brew. He still broadcasts regularly and, in January 1996, hosted a series put out by BBC Scotland called 'Skiffle', which defined skiffle in the context of other 1950s music.

Even with such a varied career it is the image of the 'cheeky chappie' with the guitar that is best remembered. From an early age he had learned the guitar and by the time that skiffle claimed him he was already quite proficient. While still at school he had started a skiffle group, the Ace of Clubs Rhythm Group. He remembers,

> We had an argument about how we should spell rhythm and in the end I got my way, which is why the cards we had printed said 'The Ace of Clubs Rhythim Group'; I was good at getting what I wanted.

On 23 November 1957, the *Melody Maker* reported:

> The Spacemen, a skiffle group including five members of Wanstead Aero-Modelling Club, last week, made their third appearance at London's Skiffle Cellar.

The same week the club calendar advertised:

BRIXTON ROLLER RINK
Fri. Dec.6
THE SPACEMEN SKIFFLE GROUP
Skating till 8.45

The Spacemen Skiffle Group was run by Pete and Tony Oakman and, having heard Joe play, they asked him to join them. Joe fondly recalls,

> It was probably the first break I'd had, especially as it brought me into contact with their parents. Albert and Frances Oakman had a small newsagent-tobacconist shop in Leyton, and it was here that I found the only real encouragement I'd had as far as music was concerned. Mrs O. was a wonderful pianist, she was a real inspiration.

The attitude of the adults, and particularly the ones in a position to assist the young in their appreciation of music, is a real bone of contention with Joe. He has said about those times,

> Kids were not encouraged to play music or form groups, no grants or prizes were forthcoming from official sources for this purpose. Local councils and government bodies would fork out pots of money to finance some obscure overseas ethnic group and put on festivals and concerts, yet home-grown talent was usually put down and neglected.

Talent obviously ran in the Oakman family for it was Pete Oakman who was co-writer of 'Picture of You', number two in the hit parade for Joe in May 1962. Notwithstanding this, Joe had risked losing Pete's friendship in the early days when Pete was a victim of Joe's dictatorial ways:

> In the Spacemen I decided we needed a proper bass rather than the standard tea-chest job; so while Pete Oakman was out at work one day, I took his guitar down to the local music store and traded it for a bass. When Pete came home he discovered that he had a new role in life!

Pete soon became proficient on the double bass and in fact Joe had done him a favour, for today he is a highly regarded and sought-after backing musician, often providing accompaniment for visiting American country artists and occasionally playing for Lonnie Donegan.

Joe Brown and the Spacemen. (J. Brown)

In his autobiography *Brown Sauce*, Joe says,

The Spacemen Skiffle Group started off good and we got better all the time. Playing around the local pubs and clubs and appearing in talent shows, we were earning quite a name for the group, even if we weren't earning much money. But nobody cared about money as long as we were enjoying ourselves. Then skiffle turned to rock and roll and it wasn't long before I was spending more time on stage than I was on the footplate [Joe worked as a fireman for British Rail, based at Plaistow loco yard]. I wasn't aware of it happening, but the music simply caught up with me and before I knew it, I was a professional musician.

On 18 October 1957, Derek Allaway, organizer of the Leyton and East London Skiffle Clubs, presented on of his Skiffle Nites. The show included eight groups. The programme details were as follows:

The Stan Philips Skiffle Group

Stan Philips, guitar   Len Ridge, guitar   Roy Gordan, guitar
Len Johnson, banjo   Bob Pensiver, banjo   Ray Stotter, drums
'Dees' Anderton, bass   Bob Sach, washboard
    'A Blue Ridge Round My Heart'   'Puttin' on the Style'
    'John Henry'   'You Don't Care'

The A.1 Skifflers

'Trev' Westall, guitar   Ken Mizen, guitar   Ed Ryan, guitar
Al Hart, bass   'Biff' Jeffery, washboard
    'Ain't It a Shame'   'Valerie'
    'Down by the Riverside'   'Green Back Dollar'

Cleveland Skiffle Group

Harry Murray, guitar   Ted Short, guitar   Ken Cook, guitar
Brian Downs, bass   Terry Bowan, washboard
    'Little Light of Mine'   'House of Rising Sun'
    'Fisherman's Blues'   'Trust in God'

The Paramount Ramblers

Terry Yarnell, guitar   John Wood, guitar   Tony Hunt, bass
Brian Edwards, guitar   'Toots' Smith, washboard
    'Goin' Down The Road'   'Mind Your Own Business'
    'Stackalee'   'Sister Kate'

Lea Valley Skiffle Group

Brian Coford, guitar   Mike Warwick, guitar   Brian Warwick, banjo
Brian Kohler, bass   Trevor Morgan, guitar   Sid Herbert, washboard
    'Where Shall I Be'   'True and Trembling'
    'Doin' My Time'   'Streamline Train'

Pentagon Skiffle Group

Jerry Ward, guitar   Ron Mears, guitar   Gwyn Lloyd, guitar
Mick Walters, bass   'Tel' Larkin, washboard
    'Mr Ratty Went a Wooing'   'In the Book'
    'Long Gone Dean'   'The Saints'

The Valley Ramblers

Bert Allen, guitar	Bill Morter, guitar	Derek Casey, guitar
'Binx', banjo	Colin Hares, bass	Ron Wallace, drums

'Railroad Steamboat' 'Pull On Down'
'No Other Baby' 'Maggie May'

The Spacemen

Toni Oakman, guitar	Peter Oakman, guitar	Joe Brown, elec. guitar
George Staff, guitar	Gary Gleed, bass	'Sid', drums

'Railroad Bill' 'Trace Little Footprints'
'Gypsy Davy' 'Toll the Bell Easy'

It is interesting to note that out of almost fifty skifflers, Joe was the only one playing the electric guitar. The story of his metamorphosis from skiffler into guitar wizard is typical of the success many achieved by being fired by their initial enthusiasm for skiffle music.

Currently Joe is touring with the 1990s version of the 'Bruvvers', including on guitar Neil Gauntlett, Phil Capaldi on drums and 'Rico', Dave Nilo, on bass. He has a close musical relationship with Roger Cook, the song writer, originally of 'David and Jonathan' and 'Blue Mink', who has more than 70 hit songs to his credit. It was Roger who produced *Together*, Joe's album with Brown's Home Brew.

Recently Joe and Roger have collaborated in writing a musical with skiffle as the theme. Set in a coffee bar run by Daddy O (Joe), it concerns the problems faced by a young group entering the National Skiffle Competition. With background recordings by Lead Belly and others, featuring songs like 'Rock Island Line', the show includes some memorable melodies contributed by Roger and Joe. It is a nostalgic glance back to his own roots; a colourful foot-stomping musical, acknowledging the influence that these early days exerted on all who experienced this phenomenon called skiffle.

Roy Hudd

It is not only the rock musician who can look back on skiffle as the spark that ignited a promising career in the entertainment world. Broadcasters like Richard Stilgoe and Bernard Falk started their careers in a skiffle group; the Liverpool-based, Tony Snow and the Blizzards. And one of Britain's best loved comedians had

SAC Hudd R. 2765225. (R. Hudd)

a similar 'enlightenment': Roy Hudd, the star of the long running (21 years) BBC radio programme, 'The News Huddlines'.

Roy Hudd was born in Croydon on 16 May 1936. His first step on the ladder of success was as a Butlin's red coat in 1957. Since those early days he has established himself as one of the country's best loved comedians. In 1989, he was elected to the prestigious office of King Rat, in the Grand Order of Water Rats, an exclusive charitable organization, and is currently the president of the British Music Hall Society. His stage appearances range from *The Merchant of Venice* to *Run For Your Wife*, and in recent years he has starred in both Dennis Potter's controversial TV series, *Lipstick On Your Collar* and *Karaoke*.

He started playing banjo while doing his National Service with the RAF. Let him describe how he got into skiffle:

> I used the G banjo in our Station Band, The Waterbeach Imperial Jazz Band, circa 1956. I used this in the skiffle group as well. I was stationed at RAF Waterbeach near Cambridge and there were lots of American Air Force bases nearby. Whenever I returned from a 48-hour pass from London, there were always plenty of American servicemen on the train. They would see the banjo, which I took

everywhere with me, and 'borrow' it. I learned more songs on those train journeys than I ever have since. Lots of blues and folk songs and cracking semi-vaudeville ones like, 'Blues My Naughty Sweetie Gives To Me', 'Huggin' an' a Chalkin'', 'Ace in the Hole', etc.

The first gig I ever got paid for was at the Corn Exchange, March. We got five bob each for playing from 8 pm till 10.30 pm with just one break. Ah happy days!

My inspiration, like so many others, was Lonnie Donegan. I first saw him during a lunchtime at the Fleet Street Jazz Club. He was the banjo player with Chris Barber then. He did a couple of songs and paralysed them. It was the first time I heard 'Rock Island Line'. The rest is history.

Had Roy only realized that if he had wandered a block further with his banjo under his arm, from Ludgate Circus to Blackfriars Bridge, he could have joined the Chas McDevitt Skiffle Group, rehearsing in the archives of Unilever House. On second thoughts perhaps he did realize and steered well clear!

David Oxtoby

David Sandison, in the foreword to his book *Oxtoby's Rockers*, describes Oxtoby as:

The first modern painter to devote his working life completely to translating the images created by music in a way which is accessible both to the layman and the critic . . . throughout his career he has concentrated on capturing the aural and visual excitement of rock 'n' roll and its performers.

The advent of rock 'n' roll in the mid-fifties changed a whole generation's way of life. Few were as deeply affected as Oxtoby himself: He became and remains, the subtitle of this book: The Eternal Fan.

David Jowett Greaves Oxtoby was born in Horsforth, Yorkshire on 23 January 1938. From his early days at the Bradford Art School, to the Royal Academy of Art, and on to international acclaim, as the definitive artist of rock 'n' roll, he has maintained the image of the 'Wild Man of the Art World'. Particularly when roaring around on his motorbike, a 650cc Triumph Thunderbird.

Before being engulfed in the music of Jerry Lee Lewis, Elvis Presley and Buddy Holly he was influenced by both skiffle and jazz. This provided the foundation for his future devotion to rock 'n' roll. He recalls fondly his contribution to the Bradford Rag Skiffle Group:

> The group was formed during our last year at Bradford College of Art, 1957, and included Norman Stevens, vocal, John Loker, washboard, Bernard Woodward, banjo and Pete Kay and myself both on tea-chest bass, we also had three guitars! We played various venues and college dances, and on Rag Day we played all day long, unpaid! Happy days!

George Harrison, John Lennon, Paul McCartney and Ringo Starr

It was early 1957, when John Lennon, a pupil at Quarry Bank High School in Harthill Road, Liverpool, decided to form a skiffle group. At first he called the group the Blackjacks but, in March 1957, he changed the name to the Quarry Men, in deference to the school most of the group attended. With John were Eric Griffiths (guitar), Colin Harton (drums), Pete Shotton (wash-board), Rod Davis (banjo), and on tea-chest bass, Bill Smith, Ivan Vaughan and Nigel Whalley (each occupied that post at various times). Pete was one of John's best friends: their friendship even surviving the occasion when John got drunk at a party and smashed the washboard over Pete's head!

In those early days their programme would consist of the usual skiffle favourites: 'Worried Man', 'Freight Train', 'Maggie May', 'No Other Baby' and 'Come Go With Me'. The latter, a hit for the Dell Vikings in 1957, indicated that John was broadening his horizons.

In June 1957, they entered the Carroll Levis 'Search for a Star' Talent Show at the Liverpool Empire. However, on this occasion, the heat was won by the Sunnyside Skiffle Group.

In 1957, the Cavern was strictly a jazz club; they tolerated skiffle groups but rock and roll was anathema. When the Quarry Men

The Quarry Men, 6 July 1957. (G. Rhind)

first played there on 7 August 1957, John sang some Presley numbers. The owner of the club, Alan Synter, sent them round a note, which said, 'Cut the bloody rock.'

Len 'Duff' Garry on tea-chest had augmented the group to a six piece by 6 July 1957, the 'Red Letter' day that Paul McCartney met John Lennon for the first time. From little acorns, etc. Paul first played with the group on 18 October 1957 at a Conservative Club in Liverpool. He was on lead guitar.

In the Hunter Davies book on the Beatles, George Harrison recalls:

> Paul came round to my house one evening to look at the guitar manual I had, which I could never work out. We learned a few things and managed to play 'Don't You Rock Me Daddy O' with two chords.

George's first group, the Rebels, rehearsed and played one gig, for which they received 10s., 50p in today's coinage. The group included George's brother Peter and a friend, Arthur Kelly, on guitars, a mouth organ and a tea-chest bass with the Rebels painted across it. George said:

> I remember the Rebels had a tea-chest with a lot of gnomes around it. One of my brothers had a five-shilling guitar, which had the back off. Apart from that it was all fine. Just my brother, some mates and me.

From February 1958 the Quarry Men included George Harrison and John Lowe on piano. In mid-1958, Garry and Griffiths left the group and although they entered the odd skiffle contest the gigs were not forthcoming. The group virtually disbanded. George had joined the Les Stewart Quartet but, when this too broke up, he and Ken Brown, a fellow member of the Quartet, contacted John and Paul and re-formed the Quarry Men. They took up residency at the Casbah Club in Liverpool, receiving £3 per night between the four of them. Their weekly spot lasted seven weeks before they fell out over their fee. By January 1959 they no longer worked as a group.

Ringo Starr played in the Eddie Clayton Skiffle Group during 1957–8. Apart from Ringo, the group included his next-door neighbour Eddie Miles (guitar and vocals), Roy Trafford (tea-chest), John Dougherty (washboard), and Frank Walsh (guitar). They appeared in local clubs and skiffle contests. At one stage Ringo also played with the Darktown Skiffle Group.

In the summer of 1958, the Quarry Men had paid 17s. 6d. to use the Kensington Recording Studios in Liverpool to make a demo of 'That'll Be the Day' and a McCartney–Harrison original, 'In Spite of all the Danger'. On the session were Colin Hanton and John Lowe, as well as John, Paul and George. They could only afford one acetate of the session and this was kept by John Lowe, who eventually sold it to Paul McCartney in July 1981. Having at first

The Beatles, ABC Blackpool, 25 August 1963.

refused £5,000 for the record, anticipating he could get more for it at auction, Lowe received a court order obtained by Paul McCartney banning the sale of the record. This can now be heard on the *Beatles Anthology*, issued in 1995.

Sotheby's can claim to hold the record for the sale of skiffle-related memorabilia. In 1994 they sold a portable Grundig TK 8 reel-to-reel tape recorder together with a 3¾ i.p.s. Emitape for £78,500. This tape had been recorded by Bob Molyneux on 6 July 1957 (the day Lennon and McCartney first met), at the dance which closed proceedings at St Peter's fête in the Liverpool suburb of Woolton. John Lennon was leading the Quarry Men skiffle group in spirited versions of Lonnie Donegan songs. Paul McCartney remembers John's breath smelling of beer, no wonder he sounds a little inebriated singing 'Putting on the Style'. EMI paid this record price for these four minutes of pop history and it was anticipated that this would be included in the *Beatles Anthology*, but so far nothing has been issued.

George Harrison summed up the influences that skiffle had on him and hundreds of his generation:

> Lonnie Donegan was the first music star to make an impression on me. Donegan and skiffle music just seemed made for me.

Other Liverpool skiffle groups that made the transition to rock and roll were the James Boys (King Size Taylor and the Dominoes), the Ralph Ellis Skiffle Group (Swinging Blue Jeans) and the Raving Texans (Rory Storm and the Hurricanes).

Chas Hodges

Chas Hodges, the piano-playing half of 'Chas and Dave', was born in the North Middlesex Hospital, Edmonton, on 28 December 1943. His was a particularly musical family and Chas was encouraged in this interest, notably by his mother, Daisy, who was a fine piano player. To earn a little extra cash she would often play at the Exhibition Pub on Edmonton Green and on some occasions would go out busking on harmonium, with Chas's great granddad accompanying her on clarinet or penny whistle.

At first Chas resisted his mother's wishes and preferred fishing and playing football to sitting down and learning the piano; but he was soon to succumb to the influences of this musical environment.

In the pre-television era, radio played an important part in one's musical education. Radio Luxembourg was immensely popular in the mid-1950s. Chas was to be turned on to rock and roll by hearing the wild playing of Little Richard. Before this he had become a Lonnie Donegan fan and remembers hearing the Chas McDevitt Skiffle Group when they made their first broadcasts in November and December 1956, on the Pye Radio Luxembourg Talent Show. As he had only previously heard the term skiffle in conjunction with Lonnie Donegan, he thought that Chas McDevitt had pinched the name for his own group.

Chas recalls that he was about to find out that taking up music wasn't as easy as taking up fishing or football and it was going to be harder to put down. He had tried the piano but couldn't make head or tail of it. He was excited by Little Richard, Fats Domino and all the other rocking maniacs, but it was the popularity of the skiffle groups that convinced him that he could master the guitar. Anxious that there should be another musician in the family, his mum promised to get one for him.

> It was an old Spanish guitar she got off my Uncle Alf. I went over to Uncle Alf's in Hackney to get it. I can still remember the smell of that guitar now. Uncle Alf had done it up. Filled all the cracks up with filler and given it a fresh coat of varnish.

It's a strange fact but every guitar player seems to experience that sensation: the smell of their first guitar, be it a brand new instrument in its velvet-lined case or a battered second-hand guitar yellow with nicotine stains.

Chas had returned home filled with pride, but how was he to tune it. His mum lent a hand and tuned it to a piano chord and Chas played it by placing his finger across all the strings to produce a chord. However, a neighbour, Bob Weston, had a skiffle group, and Chas got him to teach him the correct tuning. He got hold of a chord book and things began to look a little clearer. His mum worked out how to play the chords of 'Bring a Little Water Sylvie' and his next-door neighbour, Johnny Wright, played the banjo and taught Chas a few more chords.

> Mum noticed an advert in the sweetshop window round the corner that said 'Guitarist/Banjo player wanted for the Horseshoe Skiffle Group'. That was Bob Weston's Skiffle Group over the road.

Dave Peacock, Joe Brown and Chas Hodges, 1996. (J. Brown)

I not only passed the audition, but I had really impressed them with my guitar and banjo playing. (I had bought an old banjo for a shilling at a jumble sale.) I was in the group! The first playing gig I ever did ('playing jobs' you called them in those days) was a hall over the Britannia pub, Edmonton. Everyone remembers their first gig. We got paid as well! In my experience you got paid money for doing something you didn't like doing, not for something you loved doing and would have done anyway.

The band got better and we did more and more gigs in and around North London. The personnel changed as the band progressed. An electric guitar was added and I wanted to put rock and roll songs into the act. Little Richard's 'Rip It Up' was the first and it didn't sound bad. Skiffle had been a big help to me, but I was ready to move on. Now I was a rock and roller.

Skiffle had played its part and an important part. It got me started. Throughout pop history a relatively simple type of music every now and then becomes popular. It is good because it makes kids think, 'perhaps I can do that,' and they do, and in a short time some of them are sounding as good as the records. The serious ones move on from there, but that start is important.

The Horseshoe Skiffle Group was a Carroll Levis Junior Discovery at the Finsbury Park Empire. They began playing rock venues. Chas progressed from group to group; playing bass with Mike Berry and the Outlaws, even playing for his idol, Jerry Lee Lewis. He also played with Cliff Bennett and the Rebel Rousers as well as the seminal group Heads Hands and Feet, which included Albert Lee. From the humble beginnings of the Horseshoe Skiffle Group, Chas teamed up with Dave Peacock on bass-guitar to establish one of the best loved acts in the UK. With Micky Burt on drums, Chas and Dave have recreated the original Jerry Lee Lewis line-up and have delivered a unique style of cockney music with a boogie and blues beat originally dubbed 'Rockney', but which has now reached a universal and appreciative audience.

12

And the Band
Played On

By 1960, skiffle had passed its peak but the music was still being heard and performed. Hit records like 'Chewing Gum', 'Freight Train' and 'Daddy O' were still featured on record programmes and even to this day the same titles are regularly broadcast.

By 1961 most of the skiffle groups had disbanded; Lonnie Donegan continued to appear in variety and Shirley Douglas and myself carried on as a duo. We travelled from Iceland to Thailand, from New Zealand to New York and from Helsinki to Cape Town in concert and cabaret. During the period 1960–4 we played support to many groups, all former skifflers who acknowledged the influence our music had on their careers; notable among these were both the Shadows and the Beatles.

In 1965, we recorded some skiffle tracks for an album on Columbia Records and as late as 1975 I put out an album on President Records' Joy label, *Takes Ya Back Don't It*, which included 50 per cent skiffle with accompaniment from Marc Sharratt, Pete Stanley, Wizz Jones and Joe Brown. During the 1980s and early 1990s I regularly re-formed my group and renewed my acquaintance with Lonnie, playing concerts together, both in the UK and on the continent.

Every now and then skiffle in one guise or another has crept into the hit parade and into the limelight. Both the Springfields and the Seekers owed a great deal in their style and line-up to

The K.C. Moaners – Jenny and Alan Dailey, Ken Butler (obscured) John Wall, with Chas and Kerry McDevitt, New Orleans Jazz Fest, April 1994.

skiffle. Mungo Jerry with their 1970 hit 'In The Summertime' was not far removed from skiffle and 'Cotton Eyed Joe', which topped the charts in 1995, was pure 1950s skiffle. By a small stretch of the imagination the epithet could be applied to the Travelling Wilburys, surely a modern skiffle group par excellence. Bob Dylan, George Harrison, Jeff Lynne, Roy Orbison and Tom Petty all performed together with the enthusiasm and line-up of a skiffle group, but with modern techniques, both musical and mechanical. The Notting Hillbillies with Mark Knopfler have a similar approach.

By the early 1980s, skiffle had acquired a cult following not only in the UK but on the continent as well. As recently as 1996, Lonnie Donegan has played with great success in Germany filling a 20,000-seater stadium to capacity. My own group has played in France, Belgium and Holland to enthusiastic audiences, of whom many can go into the most detailed information concerning the early skiffle groups and their recordings. All these countries have a thriving underground of skiffle fans and groups, so much so that Holger Lührig, in Germany, is compiling a comprehensive directory of the groups currently playing and recording in Europe.

A short list of skiffle and jug bands that have recorded in Europe in recent years:

Chas, Lonnie Donegan and Joe Brown, London Palladium, 11 June 1989.

GERMANY
Heupferd Jug Band
Skiffle Syncopators
Havel City Ramblers
Owl City Washboard Men

FRANCE
Long Chris et les Cowden
Hugues Aufray Skiffle
Rocky Mountain Ol' Time Stompers

DENMARK
Freddy Fraek

AUSTRIA
Worried Man Skiffle Group

SWEDEN
Robans Skiffle Group
Chilos Skiffle Group
Storyville Creepers
Woodpeckers
Qwidde's Skiffle Boys

HOLLAND
Mozam Skiffle Group
Blue Star Skiffle
Silly Skiffle Group
Lightown Skiffle

BELGIUM
Ferre Grignard

SWITZERLAND
Sunday Skifflers

All these groups are influenced by the UK interpretation of skiffle and not so much by the original jug and spasm bands. In the USA there is a great following for skiffle but it draws more on the jazz and down-home blues of their native music. At the forefront in the USA are Henry B. Stinson, Dick Parks and the Sunshine Skiffle Band. Other current US bands are:

Asylum St Spankers of Austin Texas
Juggernaut Jug Band (as seen on the 'Today Show')
Washboard Slim and the Blue Lights of New Haven, Connecticut
White Lightning Washboard Band

Even in the antipodes the Captain Matchbox Whoopee Band have a fan-like following; one has only to hear their 'Mobile Line' to realize why they are still skiffling in New Zealand.

In the UK there are groups of enthusiasts who not only play but promote skiffle by every means possible: through newssheets, fanzines, memorabilia and skiffle clubs. Some notable organizations are *Rock You Sinners*, a rock 'n' skiffle magazine edited by Mick Hill; the Northern Skiffle Preservation Society, based in Leeds and run by John Wall of the K.C. Moaners; Days of Skiffle from Ely, promoted by Tony Ferrige and the Southern Skiffle Society, organized by Eddie Armer and Derek Mason of the Lonnigans.

The Southern Skiffle Society promoted a memorable party at London's 100 Club in March 1997 at which I played host. The doors of the 100 Club had to be locked by 9 pm as the premises were full to capacity. This reunion was held in order to celebrate over 40 years of skiffle and many of the faces featured in this book attended. Guests included: Bill Colyer, Beryl Bryden, Terry Dene, Wee Willie Harris, Tony Sheridan, Bruce Welch, Clinton Ford, Hylda Sims, Shirley Douglas, Jimmie MacGregor, Jack Fallon, Steve Benbow, Davey Graham, Duffy Power, John Pilgrim, Chas and Dave, Pete Stanley and Wizz Jones, The Quarry Men, some of the 2.19 and Station Skiffle Groups, Rick Richards, Freddy Lloyd, Tony Kohn, Dennis Carter, John Wall, Ray Foxley, Tex Makins, Brian Gregg and Garry Winkler. It was a gas to see the ancient skifflers peering through their spectacles, trying to put a name to a wizened, balding, grey-haired, face that had survived the previous 40 years.

No doubt skiffle will carry on as a minority-interest music. Its cult status will ensure that it will always have a following, if merely at the jazz club level. Because of its close relationship with both jazz and rock and roll, it can easily live alongside these art forms and surfaces nationwide in both jazz and rock promotions.

Whatever else, skiffle changed the course of popular music in this country. It made playing music accessible to the masses and helped break down the barriers that existed between the audience and the performer. Everyone could join in and become part of a skiffle group. It sired the early rockers, who in turn became the supergroups of the 1970s and 1980s. In the period of a generation, one experienced the transition from supernova to supergroup and all this with the assistance of just three guitar chords – E, A and B7 . . .

Lonnie Donegan with Buddy Holly and the Crickets, 'At the Crossroads'. (J. Chown/J. Breeder)

PART
FOUR
Discography

13

A–Z Discography

GROUP	LABEL	NUMBER	S/EP/LP/CD

Avon Cities Skiffle Group with Ray Bush

Tempo	A146		S
Tempo	A149		S
Tempo	A156		S
Tempo	A157		S
Tempo	EXA40		EP
Tempo	EXA50		EP
Tempo	TAP 18		LP
Storyville	SEP335		EP SCA.GER.
Decca	ACL 1250		LP
Decca	TAB 56		LP
Decca	DS 3212/1-2		LP GER.
Decca	6.28422DP		LP GER.
Decca	6.28422DP		LP GER.

Arthur Baird Skiffle Group

Beltona	BL 2669	S	

Kenny Ball (Al Young)

Jazz Collector	JDN 101		LP

Chris Barber Skiffle Group

Pye-Nixa	7NJ 2014		S
Pye-Nixa	7NJ 2017		S
Pye-Nixa	NJE 1025		EP
Marble Arch	MAL 1287		LP
Ace of Clubs	ACL 1037		LP
Decca	SPA 254		LP
Decca	6 24024		LP GER.

Boulevard	4110	LP
Everest	FS 224	LP
Limelight	820 878 2	CD GER.

Barnstormers Spasm Band

Parlophone	R 4416	S
Tempo	A 168	S
Tempo	EXA 95	EP

Graeme Bell and his Skiffle Gang

Columbia	DO 3877	S AUS.
Columbia	DO 3887	S AUS.
Columbia	DO 3875	S AUS.
Columbia	DO 3888	S AUS.

Dickie Bishop and his Sidekicks

Decca	F 10869	S
Decca	F 10959	S
Decca	F 10981	S
Decca	F 11028	S

Blue Jeans Skiffle Group

Decca	LF 1300	LP (10-inch)
Decca	6.28422	LP GER.
London	LL 3034	LP CAN.

Beryl Bryden's Backroom Skiffle

Decca	FJ 10823	S
Decca	D 18450	S

Bill Bramwell

Starlite	ST 45 004	S

Johnny Christmas and the Sunspots

Starlite	ST EP 5	EP

City Ramblers Skiffle Group

Tempo	A 158	S
Tempo	A 161	S
Tempo	A 165	S
Tempo	EXA 59	EP
Tempo	EXA 71	EP
Tempo	EXA 77	EP
Storyville	A 45 004	S SCA. GER.
Storyville	A 45 501	S SCA. GER.

Storyville	A 45 508	S SCA. GER.
Storyville	108 104 STF	S SCA. GER.
Storyville	108 112 STF	S SCA. GER.
Storyville	SEP 327	EP SCA. GER.
Storyville	SEP 345	EP SCA. GER.
Decca	ACL 1250	LP
Decca	TAB 56	LP
Decca	DS 3212/1–2	LP GER.
Decca	6. 28132 DP	LP GER.
Decca	6. 28422 DP	LP GER.
Elite	SOLP 336	LP GER.

Coffee Bar Skifflers

Embassy	WEP 1008	EP

Ken Colyer Skiffle Group

77	77 LEU 12/7	LP
Decca	F 10631	S
Decca	F 10711	S
Decca	FJ 10751	S
Decca	FJ 10772	S
Decca	FJ 10889	S
Decca	FJ 10926	S
Decca	FJ 10972	S
Decca	D 18449	S GER.
Decca	D 18752	S GER.
London	54–1674	S USA
Decca	DFE 6286	EP
Decca	DFE 6444	EP
Decca	DFEM 6444	EP NZ.
Decca	DFE 6563	EP
Decca	SDE 7076	EP SCA.
K.C.	KCS 11 EP	EP
Decca	LF 1196	EP (10-inch)
Decca	BLK 16092	LP GER.
Decca	ACL 1250	LP
Decca	TAB 56	LP
Decca	DS 3212/1–2	LP GER.
Decca	6.28132 DP	LP GER.
Decca	6.28422 DP	LP GER.
Decca	6.22319	LP GER.
Decca	DS 3271/1–2	LP GER.
Decca	6.25013	LP GER.
WAM	MLP 15399	LP GER.
Metronome	200194	LP GER.
Storyville	DALP 2/1941	LP GER.
Polydor	623 231	LP GER.
K.C.	KCS 1001	LP

K.C.	KC 2	LP
Lake	LA 5007 and LACD7	LP
Lake	LACD 68	CD

Bob Cort Skiffle Group

Decca	FJ 10831	SP
Decca	F 10878	SP
Decca	F 10892	SP
Decca	F 10899	SP
Decca	F 10905	SP
Decca	F 10951	SP
Decca	D 18433	SP GER.
Decca	D 18679	SP GER.
Decca	F 10989	SP
Decca	DFE 6409	EP
Decca	DX 1969	EP GER.
Decca	SDE 7075	EP SCA
Decca	SDE 7093	EP SCA
Decca	SDE 7094	EP SCA
Decca	LK 4222	LP
Decca	ACL 1959	LP
Decca	ACL 1250	LP
Decca	TAB 56	LP
Decca	DPA 3087/8	LP
Decca	6DS 3212/1-2	LP GER.
Decca	6. 28132 DP	LP GER.
Decca	6. 28422 DP	LP GER.
London	45 1713	SP USA
London	LL 1774	LP USA

The Cranes Skiffle Group

Embassy	W223	S
Embassy	W238	S

Lorrae Desmond and her Rebels

Parlophone	R 4287	S
Parlophone	R 4320	S
Parlophone	R 4361	S

Delta Skiffle Group

Esquire	10-504	S 78
Esquire	10-507	S 78
Esquire	10-517	S 78
Esquire	EP162	EP
Esquire	20-089	LP (10-inch)
Storyville	A 45505	S. SCA. GER.
Storyville	108 108 STF	S. SCA. GER.

Lonnie Donegan

This is a selection of Lonnie Donegan's skiffle recordings, including some of the more important non-skiffle tracks.

For a complete 130 page discography of Lonnie's recordings, contact:

Dave Radcliffe, 14 The Link, High Crompton, Shaw,
Nr Oldham, Lancs. OL2 7QN. Tel 01706 845554.

Decca	FJ 10647	S
Decca	FJ 10695	S
Decca	DFE 6345	EP
Decca	LF 1198	LP (10-inch)
Decca	LF 1299	LP (10-inch)
Decca	LK 4088	LP
Decca	ACL 1250	LP
Decca	TAB 56	LP
Decca	DPA 3087/8	LP
Storyville	A 45005	S SCA. GER.
Storyville	108 111 STF	S SCA. GER.
Storyville	SEP 306	EP SCA. GER.
Storyville	SLP 100	LP SCA. GER.
Old Gold	OG 9131	SP
Old Gold	OG 9902	SP
Old Gold	OG 7705	EP
Old Gold	OG 1502	LP
Polygon	JTE 107	EP
Metronome	200 194	LP GER.
Armando Curcio	GSR 38	LP ITA.
Pye-Nixa	N 15036	S (78)
Pye-Nixa	N 15071	S (78)
Pye-Nixa	N 15080	S (78)
Pye-Nixa	N 15087	S (78)
Pye-Nixa	N 15093	S (78)
Pye-Nixa	N 15108	S (78)
Pye-Nixa	7N 15116	S
Pye-Nixa	7N 15129	S
Pye-Nixa	7N 15148	S
Pye-Nixa	7NJ 2006	S
Pye-Nixa	7N 15158	S
Pye-Nixa	7N 15165	S
Pye-Nixa	7N 15172	S
Pye-Nixa	7N 15181	S
Pye-Nixa	7N 15198	S
Pye-Nixa	7N 15206	S
Pye-Nixa	7N 15219	S
Pye-Nixa	7N 15223	S
Pye-Nixa	7N 15237	S
Pye-Nixa	7N 15256	S
Pye-Nixa	7N 15267	S

Pye-Nixa	7N 15275	S
Pye-Nixa	7N 15315	S
Pye-Nixa	7N 15354	S
Pye-Nixa	7N 15371	S
Pye-Nixa	7N 15410	S
Pye-Nixa	7N 15424	S
Pye-Nixa	7N 15455	S
Pye-Nixa	NJE 1014	EP
Pye-Nixa	NJE 1017	EP
Pye-Nixa	NEP 24031	EP
Pye-Nixa	NEP 24040	EP
Pye-Nixa	NEP 24067	EP
Pye-Nixa	NEP 24075	EP
Pye-Nixa	NEP 24081	EP
Pye-Nixa	NEP 24104	EP
Pye-Nixa	NEP 24107	EP
Pye-Nixa	NEP 24114	EP
Pye-Nixa	NPT 19012	LP (10-inch)
Pye-Nixa	NPT 19027	LP (10-inch)
Pye-Nixa	NPL 18034	LP
Pye-Nixa	NPL 18043	LP
Pye-Nixa	NPL 18063	LP
Philips	6305 227	LP GER.
Philips	6305 288	LP GER.
Philips	6449 073	LP GER.
Chrysalis	CHR 1158	LP
Chrysalis	CHR 1205	LP
Cuba Libre/Virgin	VS 460	SP
Cube	ICSD 2001	LP
Bear Family	BFX 15170	LP GER.
Bear Family	BCD 15700 (8 x CD)	GER.
Rio Digital	RD LP 1201	LP
Timeless	CD TTD 553	CD HOL.

Johnny Duncan and his Blue Grass Boys

Columbia	DB 3925	S
Columbia	DB 3959	S
Columbia	DB 3996	S
Columbia	DB 4029	S
Columbia	DB 4074	S
Columbia	DB 4118	S
Columbia	DB 4167	S
Columbia	DB 4179	S
Columbia	DB 4282	S
Columbia	DB 4311	S
Columbia	DB 4415	S
Pye	7N 15358	S
Pye	7N 15380	S
Pye	7N 15420	S

Columbia	DB 7164	S
Columbia	DB 7334	S
Columbia	DB 7833	S
Old Gold	OG 9902-A	S
Columbia	SEG 7708	EP
Columbia	SEG 7773	EP
Columbia	SEG 7753	EP
Columbia	SEG 7850	EP
Columbia	33S 1122	LP(10-inch)
Columbia	33S 1129	LP(10-inch)
Columbia	33SX 1328	LP
Encore	ENC 190	LP
MFP	MFP 1032	LP
Lucky	LUS 3012	LP
Lucky	LUS 3014	LP
Lucky	LUS 100	LP
Decca	SPA 295	LP
Intercord	146 531	LP
Bear Family	BFX 15169	LP
Bear Family	BCD 15947(4 x CD)	CD GER.

Johnny Duncan with Chris Barber Skiffle Group

Pye	7NJ 2014	S
Pye	NJE 1025	EP
Marble Arch	MAL 1287	LP

Eden Street Skiffle Group

H&G General Supplies	1-10 flexi-discs	S

Frog Island Skiffle Group

77 Records	EP 4	EP

The Hallelujah Skiffle Group and Clinton Ford

Oriole	CB 1425	S
Oriole	CB 1427	S
Oriole	CB 1429	S

Les Hobeaux Skiffle Group

HMV	POP 337	S
HMV	POP 403	S
HMV	POP 444	S
HMV	7EG 8297	EP

Jimmy Jackson and his Rock 'n' Skiffle

Columbia	DB 3898	S

Columbia	DB 3937	S
Columbia	DB 3957	S
Columbia	DB 3988	S
Columbia	DB 4085	S
Columbia	DB 4153	S
Columbia	SEG 7750	EP
Columbia	SEG 7768	EP

Alexis Korner Skiffle Group

Tempo	A166	S
Tempo	EXA 76	EP
Tempo	EXA 102	EP
77 Records	LP 2	LP
Folklore	F.LEUT/9	LP
Krazy Kat	KK 789	LP
Decca	ACL 1250	LP
Decca	TAB 56	LP
Decca	DS 3212/1–2	LP GER
Decca	6.28132DP	LP GER.
Decca	6.28422DP	LP GER.
Decca	6.24475	LP GER.

Don Lang and his Skiffle Group

HMV	POP 335	S
HMV	DLP 1151	LP (10-inch)
See For Miles	CM 119	LP

Lea Valley Skiffle Group

Esquire	10-508	S
Esquire	10-518	S
Esquire	EP 163	EP
Storyville	A 45503	S. SCA. GER.
Storyville	108 106 STF	S. SCA. GER.

Alan Lomax and the Ramblers

Decca	F 10787	S
Decca	DFE 6367	EP
Decca	DS 3212/1–2	LP GER.
Decca	6. 28132DP	LP GER.

Chas McDevitt Skiffle Group

Oriole	CB 1352	S
Oriole	CB 1357	S
Oriole	CB 1371	S
Oriole	CB 1386	S
Oriole	CB 1395	S

Oriole	CB 1403	S
Oriole	CB 1405	S
Oriole	CB 1457	S
Oriole	CB 1511	S
Oriole	EP 7002	EP
Oriole	MG 10018	LP (10-inch)
Chic	45 1008	S USA
Sparton	4 369 R	S CAN.
Cupol	42	S SCA.
Cupol	CEP 174	EP SCA.
Versailles	9 5168	EP FRA.
Top Rank	JAR 338	S
HMV	POP 845	S
HMV	POP 928	S
HMV	POP 999	S
HMV	POP 1151	S
Columbia	DSA 711	S SA.
Columbia	DB 7595	S
Columbia	DB 7703	S
Columbia	DB 7846	S
Columbia	SEG 8468	EP
Columbia	SEG 8471	EP
Columbia	33SX 1738	LP
Columbia	33SX 6082	LP
Bell	644	S USA
Fontana	TF 957	S
Old Gold	OG 9052 A	S
President	PT 376	S
President	PT 410	S
Joy	JOYS 241	LP
Joy	JOYS 263	LP & Cas.
Rollercoaster	RCEP 113(33rpm)	EP
Rollercoaster	RCCD 3007	CD
Hallmark	301704	CD & Cas.
Hallmark	306032	CD & Cas.

Charlie McNair Skiffle Group

Beltona	BL 2670	S
Beltona	ABL 519	LP (10-inch)

George Melly

Tempo	A 98	S
Decca	LF 1299	LP (10-inch)
Decca	SPA 288	LP

Ian Menzies and the Clyde Valley Stompers

Decca	CES 2007	LP

Jimmy Miller and the Barbecues

Columbia	DB 4006	S
Columbia	DB 4081	S
Northwood	NW 45 001	S

Morris and Mitch

Decca	F 10900	S
Decca	F 1-0929	S
Decca	F 11086	S
Decca	DFE 6486	EP
Decca	6. 28422 DP	LP GER.

The Old Timers Skiffle Group

Fontana	H 105	S

Johnny Parker

Pye-Nixa	NJE 1000	EP
Metronome	MEP 1092	EP SCA. GER.
Pye-Nixa	NXNJT	LP

Betty Smith's Skiffle

Tempo	A 162	S

Soho Skiffle Group

Melodisc	1403	S
Melodisc	1421	S
Melodisc	EPM 7.72	EP

Sonny Stewart Skiffle Kings

Philips	PB 719	S
Philips	PB 773	S
Top Rank	JAR 430	S
Bellaphon	BL 1021	S GER.

Station Skiffle Group

Esquire	10–503	S
Esquire	10–516	S
Esquire	EP 161	EP
Esquire	20–089	LP (10-inch)
Storyville	A 45504	S. SCA. GER.
Storyville	108 107 STF	S. SCA. GER.

Tin Pan Skiffle Group

Hardy	NR 06	S

2.19 Skiffle Group

Esquire	10–497	S78
Esquire	10–502	S78
Esquire	10–509	S78
Esquire	10–512	S78
Esquire	10–515	S78
Esquire	EP 126	EP
Esquire	EP 146	EP
Esquire	EP 176	EP
Esquire	EP 196	EP
Esquire	20-089	LP
Storyville	A 45 506	S SCA. GER.
Storyville	108 109 STF	S SCA. GER.

The Vipers Skiffle Group

Parlophone	R 4238	S
Parlophone	R 4261	S
Parlophone	R 4286	S
Parlophone	R 4289	S
Parlophone	R 4308	S
Parlophone	R 4351	S
Parlophone	R 4356	S
Parlophone	R 4371	S
Parlophone	R 4393	S
Parlophone	R 4435	S
Parlophone	R 4484	S
Odeon	45 O 29106	S GER.
Odeon	45 O 29119	S GER.
Odeon	45 O 29158	S GER.
Odeon	45 O 29173	S GER.
Odeon	O 21 055	S GER.
Odeon	O 21 700	S GER.
Capitol	US 41 205	S USA
Pye-Nixa	7N 15304	EP
Parlophone	GEP 8615	EP
Parlophone	GEP 8626	EP
Parlophone	GEP 8655	EP
Parlophone	PMD 1050	LP (10-inch)
EMI	OU 2148	LP
Rollercoaster	ROLL 2011	LP
Rollercoaster	ROLL 2091	LP (10-inch)
Time ('Original Soho Skiffle Group')		
	T/70005	LP USA
Bear Family	BCD 15 954(3xCD)	CD GER.

Bob Wallis Washboard Beaters

Storyville	A45 502	S
Storyville	A45 036	S
Storyville	108 105 STF	S

Nancy Whiskey

Topic	7 T 10	LP (8-inch)
Oriole	CB 1394	S
Oriole	CB 1452	S
Oriole	CB 1485	S
Cupol	CEP 174	EP
CBS	3090	S

Worried Men Skiffle Group

Decca	LF 1299	LP
Decca	LF 1300	LP
Decca	6.28422–2	LP GER.
London	LL 30034	LP CAN.

14
Skiffle Groups

Avon Cities Skiffle Group with Ray Bush

Tempo Records

78 RPM

Recorded London 1957

'Green Corn'/'Hey Hey Daddy Blues'	A 146
'Fisherman's Blues'/'This Little Light o' Mine'	A 149
'How Long'/'Julian Johnson'	A 156
'Lonesome Day Blues'/'I Don't Know'	A 157

45 RPM

'How Long'/'Julian Johnson'
'Lonesome Day Blues'/'I Don't Know'   EXA 40

'Fisherman's Blues'/'This Little Light o' Mine'
'Hey Hey Daddy Blues'/'Green Corn'   EXA 50

33 RPM

Skiffle tracks recorded London, 26 April 1958, 'Lonesome Day Blues'/'I'm On My Way To Caanan Land'/'Roll 'em Pete'/'Hand Me Down My Silver Trumpet'/'House of the Rising Sun'   TAP 18

Compilation and Continental Releases

Storyville Records, Copenhagen

'Fisherman's Blues'/'Hey Hey Daddy Blues'
'This Little Light o' Mine'/'Green Corn'   SEP 335

Decca Germany

Kings of Skiffle 1975
'Green Corn'/'This Little Light o' Mine'
'How Long Blues'   6.28132 LP

Fantastic Skiffle Festival 1977
'I Don't Know'/'Hey Hey Daddy Blues'/'Lonesome Day Blues'
'Julian Johnson'/'Fisherman's Blues'   6.28422 LP

Ace of Clubs

Skiffle 1968
'Green Corn'/'This Little Light o' Mine'   ACL 1250

Decca (re-issue), 1982

'Green Corn'/'This Little Light o' Mine'   TAB 56

All tracks recorded London 1957 except TAP 18 recorded 26 April 1958

Ray Bush, guitar, vocal   Mike Hitchings, mandolin
Geoff Nichols, bass   Wayne Chandler, guitar, banjo
Basil Wright, washboard: (not playing on TAP 18)

Chris Barber Skiffle Group

Pye-Nixa Records

The Chris Barber Skiffle Group   NJE 1025
Recorded London 14 September 1956

'Doin' My Time'/'Where Could I Go'
'Can't You Line 'Em'/'Gypsy Davy'

'Doin' My Time'/'Where Could I Go'   7NJ 2014
'Can't You Line 'Em'/'Gypsy Davy'   7NJ 2017

Chris Barber, bass   Johnny Duncan, guitar, mandolin, voc.
Dickie Bishop, guitar, voc.   Ron Bowden, drums

The Golden Age of Skiffle   MAL 1287
Barber EP NJE 1025 plus two Donegan EPs

Decca Records (Ace of Clubs)

The Best of Chris Barber
Including early Donegan tracks
'Rock Island Line'/'John Henry'   ACL 1037

Re-issued 1972 on Decca World of Jazz   SPA 254

Issued on Everest 'Archive of Folk and Jazz'   FS 224

Chris Barber, bass   Beryl Bryden, washboard
Lonnie Donegan, guitar, voc.

Decca Records Germany

Chris Barber Jazz Band – Profile   6 24024
Recorded London 30 October 1954. Issued 1979
'Diggin' My Potatoes'. Other tracks by Chris Barber Jazz Band

Limelight Records Germany

Chris Barber Jazz Band – Live in 1954–55
Recorded as above. Issued Dixie Gold Series   CD 820 878 2
'Diggin' My Potatoes', as above

Chris Barber, bass   Pat Halcox, piano
Jim Bray, banjo   Lonnie Donegan, guitar, voc.
Ron Bowden, drums

Boulevard Records

Chris Barber and Lonnie Donegan 1976   4110
Recorded Copenhagen 10 October 1954
'New Burying Ground'/'Leaving Blues'

Other tracks by Chris Barber Jazz Band

Chris Barber, bass   Lonnie Donegan, guitar, voc.

Barnstormers Spasm Band

Parlophone Records

Recorded London 11 February 1958

'Whistling Rufus'*/'Won't You Come Home Bill Bailey'   R 4416

'Sugar Time'*/'I Never Knew'   (unissued)

Tempo Records

Recorded London 3 February 1959

'Storming the Barn'/'That's All There Is'†   A 168

The Barnstormers Spasm Band, 1959   EXA 95

'Storming the Barn'/'Tiger Rag'
'Shine'/'That's All There Is'

John Gunn, kazoo, voc*†   Johnny Wadley, harmonica, voc†
John Denning, banjo   Jim Robinson, guitar,
Pete Wadley, bass   Brian Rust, washboard, drums, voc†
Non recording members:
J.R.T. Davies, washboard   John Fry, washboard.

Dickie Bishop and his Sidekicks
Decca Records

Recorded London 1957

'No Other Baby'/'Cumberland Gap'	F 10869
'Please Remember Me'/'The Prisoner's Song'	F 10959
'No Other Baby'/'Skip To My Lou'	F 10981

Recorded London 1958

'Jumpin' Judy'/'They Can't Take That Away From Me'	F 11028

Dickie Bishop, guitar, voc.   Pete Korrison, guitar, mandolin
Don Wilson, bass   Stan Belwood, drums

Blue Jeans Skiffle Group
Decca Records

Rockin' at the 2 I's	LF 1300

Recorded London 1958

'Lonesome Traveller'/'When I Get to Glory'

Other tracks by Worried Men, etc.

Fantastic Skiffle Festival 1973	6. 28422

'Lonesome Traveller'

London Records (America/Canada)

Music for Hand Jiving 1961	LL 3034

'Lonesome Traveller'/'When I Get to Glory'

Beryl Bryden's Backroom Skiffle
Decca Records

Recorded London 9 November 1956

'Kansas City Blues'/'Casey Jones'	FJ 10823

Recorded London 25 January 1957
'Rock Me'/'This Train' (not issued)

Beryl Bryden, washboard, voc.   Dave Stevens, piano
Alexis Korner, guitar   Frank Clark, drums
Cyril Davis, 12-string guitar, harmonica

Johnny Christmas and the Sunspots
Starlite Records (Esquire subsidiary)

I'm Gonna Sing, Sing, Sing	ST EP 5

Recorded London 15 March 1958.

'Mister and Mississippi'/'Black, Brown and White'/'Lost Love'
'Harmonica Train Blues'/'Sing, Sing, Sing'

Johnny Christmas, guitar. voc.   Bob Neil, uke, banjo, voc.
Robby Robinson, harmonica,   Al Simmons, bass,
   bongos
John (Tubby) Hill, tea-chest bass.

City Ramblers Skiffle Group

Storyville Records

Recorded Copenhagen 12 September 1956

'When the Saints'/'Mama Don't Allow'*   A 45 004

'Midnight Special'†/'I Shall Not Be
   Moved'   108 103 STF and A 45 501

'I Want a Girl'*/'900 Miles'   108 112 STF and A 45 508

The City Ramblers Skiffle Group
'I Want a Girl'*/'2.19 Blues'*
'Mama Don't Allow'*/'900 Miles'   SEP 327

I Shall Not Be Moved'/'Picket Line'
'When the Saints'/'Midnight Special'†   SEP 345

Russell Quaye, quattro guitar,   Hylda Sims, guitar, voc.
   voc.   Chris Bateson, blue blowing
Anthony 'Bo-Bo' Buquet,   (tpt. mouthpiece)
   tub bass   Alan 'Little Bear' Sutton,
Henrik Johansen, clarinet,*   washboard
Jack Elliott, guitar, voc.†

Tempo Records

The City Ramblers Skiffle Group
Recorded Copenhagen 12 September 1956
'I Want A Girl'*/'2.19 Blues'*
'Mama Don't Allow'*/'900 Miles'   EXA 59

The group played as for Storyville Records above
Recorded London 1957

'Ella Speed'‡/'2.19 Blues'‡   A 158

'Mama Don't Allow'§/'Tom Dooley'   A 161

The City Ramblers Skiffle
'Good Morning Blues'/'Down by the Riverside'
'Grey Goose'/'Jubilee'   EXA 71
Russell Quaye, quattro guitar,   Hylda Sims, guitar, voc.
   kazoo, voc.   Pete Maynard, tub bass

Chris Bateson, jug§, blue
  blowing

Shirley Bland, washboard
Jimmie MacGregor, guitar, voc.
    (not on‡)

The City Ramblers Skiffle
'Delia's Gone'/'Keep Your Pistol Good and Loaded'
'Careless Love'/'Boodle-am-Shake'   EXA 77

'Delia's Gone'/'Boodle-am-Shake'   A 165

Russell Quaye, quattro
  guitar, voc.
Jimmie MacGregor, guitar, voc.
Eric Bunyan, fiddle

Hylda Sims, guitar, voc.
Shirley Bland, washboard
Vic Pitt, bass
Chris Bateson, blue blowing, jug

Compilation and Continental Releases

Ace of Clubs

Skiffle 1968   ACL125

Skiffle Re-issued 1982   TAB 56

'Good Morning Blues'/'Down by the Riverside'

Decca Records Germany

Kings of Skiffle 1973   6. 28132 DP
'Good Morning Blues'/'Down by the Riverside'   and DS 32 12/1–2

Fantastic Skiffle Festival 1977   6. 28422 DP
'Mama Don't Allow'/'Delia's Gone'/'Boodle-am-Shake'
'Careless Love'/'Keep Your Pistol Good and Loaded'

Elite Records Germany

Recorded Frankfurt Germany 1961
London City Ramblers 1961   SOLP 336
'Sheik of Araby'/'Everybody Loves My Baby'/'Blue Heaven'
'Five Foot Two'/'David Blues'/'Boodle-am-Shake'
'Darktown Strutters Ball'/'Yes Sir That's My Baby'/'Dallas Blues'
'If You Were the Only Girl in the World'/'Jelly Roll'
'I Wish I Could Shimmy'

Russell Quaye, quattro guitar,
  kazoo, voc.
Terry Hennessy, spasmophone (gramophone horn and mouthpiece)

Bob Taylor, funnel
Rose Ann Law, washboard,

Coffee Bar Skifflers

Embassy Records

Recorded London 1958
'River Line'/'He's Solid Gone'/'Frankie and Johnny'
'Steamboat Bill'/'Ella Speed'/'Bad Man Stack-o-Lee'   WEP 1008

Members of the group not known

Ken Colyer Skiffle Group

77 Records

Recorded Burnham, Bucks early 1950.   77 LEU 12/7
'Muddy Old River' (other tracks by the Original Crane River Jazz Band)

Ken Colyer, guitar, voc.   J.R.T. Davies, guitar
Bill Colyer, wire brushes on plank of wood, washboard effect

Decca Records

Back to the Delta 1954   LF 1196
Recorded London 25 June 1954
'Midnight Special'*/'Casey Jones'/'K.C. Moan'
Other tracks on album by Ken Colyer Jazzmen

Ken Colyer, guitar, voc.   Alexis Korner, guitar, mandolin,
Diz Disley, national steel guitar   Micky Ashman, bass
Bill Colyer, washboard

Recorded London 28 July 1955
'Take This Hammer'/'Down by the Riverside'
                              F 10631 and D 18158 GER.

'Go Down Old Hannah'/'Streamline Train'
                              F 10711 and D 18449 GER.

Ken Colyer Skiffle Group
'Take This Hammer'/'Down by the Riverside'
'Go Down Old Hannah'*/'Streamline Train'   Decca DFE 6286

Ken Colyer, guitar, voc.   John Bastable, banjo, guitar*
Alexis Korner, guitar, mandolin*   Dick Smith, bass
Bill Colyer, washboard

Recorded London 25 May 1956
'Downbound Train'/'Muleskinner Blues'   FJ 10751
'Old Riley'/'Stack-o-Lee Blues'   FJ 10772

Ken Colyer Skiffle Group
'Downbound Train'/'Muleskinner Blues'/
'Old Riley'/'Stack-o-Lee Blues'
                              SDE 7076 SWE.
                              DS 3271/1–2 GER.

Ken Colyer, guitar, voc.   John Bastable, banjo
Micky Ashman, bass   Colin Bowden, washboard

Decca Records

Recorded London 12 March 1957
'The Grey Goose'/'I Can't Sleep'   FJ 10889
'Sporting Life'/'House Rent Stomp'   FJ 10926

Ken Colyer, guitar, voc.   John Bastable, banjo
Ron Ward, bass   Bob Kelly, piano
Colin Bowden, washboard

'Ella Speed'/'Go Down Sunshine'   FJ 10972
                                                             18725 GER.

The Ken Colyer Skiffle Group
Recorded London 11 November 1957
'This Train'/'Midnight Hour Blues'
'Ella Speed'/'Go Down Sunshine'   DFE 6444

Ken Colyer, guitar, voc.   Ray Foxley, piano
Ron Ward, bass   John Bastable, banjo
Colin Bowden, washboard

The Ken Colyer Skiffle Group in Hamburg
Recorded 'Curio House', Hamburg 3 March 1958
'Ham and Eggs'/'Down by the Riverside'
'Nobody Knows The Trouble I've Seen'   DFE 6563

Ken Colyer, guitar, voc.   John Bastable, guitar, banjo
Ray Foxley, piano   Ron Ward, bass
Colin Bowden, drums   Mac Duncan, backing vocal.

Skiffle   1968   ACL 1250
            1982   TAB 56
'Midnight Hour Blues'/'Take This Hammer'

The group were as for previous releases

Compilation and Continental Releases

Metronome Records

The Best of Skiffle 1974   200 104
Recorded Hamburg 10 October 1966
'Alabamy Bound'/'House Rent Stomp'
These tracks are also on   Polydor 623 231
                                                  Philips 0664462
                                          Storyville DALP2/1941-2A

Recorded Hamburg 5 November 1968*
'Take This Hammer'/'Ballad Of The Grey Goose'

WAM MLP 15.399

Ken Colyer, guitar, voc.   John Bastable, banjo
Bill Cole, bass   Malcolm Murphy, washboard*

Limelight Records Germany   CD 820 879 2

Ken Colyer's Jazz and Skiffle Group 1953–4
'Midnight Special'/'Casey Jones'/'K.C. Moan' reissue of

Decca LF 1196

'Back to the Delta' plus extra tracks

K.C. Records

Ken Colyer Skiffle Group 1966   KCS 11 EP
Recorded Crown Hotel Twickenham 21 July 1965
'New York Town'/'Green Corn'
'Casey Jones'/'I Can't Sleep'

Wanderin' 1966   KCS 1001
'I'm Going to Walk and Talk with Jesus'/'No Letters Today'
'Colorado Trail'/'Ella Speed'/'Poor Howard'/'I Can't Sleep'
'Mule Skinner Blues'/'Wanderin''/'If I Could Hear My Mother Pray Again'/'Good
Morning Blues'/'Drop Down Baby'/'Easy Ridin' Buggy'

Ken Colyer, guitar, voc.   Sammy Rimington, mandolin
John Bastable, tenor banjo   Bill Cole, bass

Historic Recordings Vol. 2 1988   KC 2
*Recorded, Studio 51, London 31 May 1957
'How Long Blues'*/'Streamline Train'*/'Poor Howard'*
'Highway Blues'*/'This Train'*/'Sporting Life'
'House Rent Stomp'
Rest of tracks by Ken Colyer Jazzmen

Ken Colyer, guitar, voc.   John Bastable, banjo
Bob Kelly, piano   Ron Ward, bass
Colin Bowden, washboard

Lake Records

The Decca Skiffle Sessions   LA 5007 and LA CD 7
'Midnight Special'/'Casey Jones'/'K.C.Moan'/'Take This Hammer
'Down by the Riverside'/'Go Down Old Hannah'/'Streamline Train'/'Old
Riley'/'Downbound Train'/'Stack-o-Lee Blues'/
'Muleskinner Blues'/'The Grey Goose'/'Sporting Life'/'House Rent Stomp'/'I Can't
Sleep'/'This Train'/'Midnight Hour Blues'/'Go Down Sunshine'/'Ella Speed'

Decca Germany

Take This Hammer   6.22319
'Take This Hammer'/'Streamline Train'/'Stack-o-Lee'
'Midnight Special'/'Go Down Old Hannah'/'K.C.Moan'
'Ella Speed'/'Down by the Riverside'/'This Train'
'Casey Jones'/'Midnight Hour Blues'/'Go Down Sunshine'

Kings of Skiffle 2 x LP 1973   6.28132
'Take This Hammer'/'Midnight Special'/'K.C.Moan'
'This Train'/'Ella Speed'/'Casey Jones'/'Go Down Sunshine'

Fantastic Skiffle Festival 2 x LP 1977   6.28422
'Streamline Train'/'I Can't Sleep'/'Grey Goose'
'Down by the Riverside'/'Stack-o-Lee'/'House Rent Stomp'
'Sporting Life'/'Go Down Old Hannah'

An Interlude with Ken Colyer Vol.2
Recorded London November 1982
'Looky Looky Yonder'/'On a Monday'/'Meeting at the Building'
'Bourgeois Blues'/'John Henry'/'A Hundred Years From Now'
'Original Rags'/'When You Wish Upon a Star'/'Sentimental Journey'/'Sporting Life'/'Little Brother'/'Delta Blues'/'Feeling'

An Interlude with Ken Colyer Vol.3
Recorded London February 1983
'Hey There Nonny'/'It's Been a Long Time'/'Caribbean Sunset'
'Going Home'/'G and B Blues'/'Goodmornin' Blues'/'In the Evening'/'Casey Jones'/'K.C.Moan'/'Best to You'/'London Pride'

Ken Colyer, solo vocal, guitar

Both these last two volumes were issued as cassettes, without catalogue numbers.

Bob Cort Skiffle Group

Decca Records

Recorded London 1957
'It Takes a Worried Man'/'Don't You Rock Me Daddy O'
	1957	FJ 10831
'Freight Train'*/'Love Is Strange'*	1957	F 10878
'Maggie May'*/'Jessamine'*	1957	F 10899
'Six–Five Special'/'Roll Jen Jenkins'	1957	F 10892
'School Days'/'Ain't It a Shame'	1957	F 10905

Skiffle Party Parts 1 and 2 (Medley)   1957   F 10951
'Last Train to San Fernando'†/'Bring a Little Water Sylvie'†
'Rock Island Line'†/'Cumberland Gap'†/'Maggie May'‡

'Don't You Rock Me Daddy O'‡/'Puttin' on the Style'†/'Ain't It a Shame'‡/'The Ark'†/'Yes Suh'   1957   F 10989

Bob Cort, guitar,voc.	Ken Sykora, guitar
Liz Winters,voc.*	Neville Skrimshire, guitar
George Jennings, bass	Viv 'Clambake' Carter† or
	Bill Colyer‡, washboard

Bob Cort and Liz Winters 1957   DFE 6409
'Freight Train'/'Don't You Rock Me Daddy O'
'Maggie May'/'Six–Five Special'

Skiffle Music (German Decca)   DX 1969
'Six–Five Special'/'Freight Train'/'Ain't It a Shame'/'Jessamine'
The Bob Cort Skiffle (Swedish Decca)   SDE 7075
'School Days'/'Ain't It a Shame'
It Takes a Worried Man'/'Don't You Rock Me Daddy O'

The Bob Cort Skiffle (Swedish Decca)   SDE 7093
'Don't Stay Away'/'Eight More Miles to Louisville'
'West Virginia Snow'/'This Land Is Your Land'

The Bob Cort Skiffle (Swedish Decca)   SDE 7094
'Yes Suh'/'Where'd You Get Your Whiskey'
'Ain't It a Shame'/'Your Feets Too Big'

Ain't It a Shame 1957   LK 4222
Recorded London 28 June 1957. Also released on ACL 1959 and
LL 1774
'Eight More Miles to Louisville'/'Don't Stay Away'
'I'm Just a Country Boy'/'This Land Is Your Land'/'West Virginia Snow'/'The Streets of Laredo'/'I Can't Give You Anything But Love'/'Yes Suh'/'The Frozen Logger'/'Your Feets Too Big'
'Where'd You Get Your Whiskey'/'Lulu's Back In Town'
'Bouncing Around'/'Ain't It a Shame to Skiffle on a Sunday'

Compilation and Continental Releases

Music for Hand Jiving   LL 3034
They Called it Rock 'n' Roll   DPA 3087/8
Stars of the Six–Five Special (10-inch)   LF 1299
'Six–Five special'

Skiffle   TAB 56 and ACL 1250
'Freight Train'/'Don't You Rock Me Daddy O'

Kings of Skiffle 1973   6 28422 DP
                                                                         DS 3212/1–2
'Freight Train'/'Maggie May'/'Don't You Rock Me Daddy O'
Fantastic Skiffle Festival 1977   6.28422 DP

'Yes Suh'/'Where'd You Get Your Whiskey'
'Eight More Miles to Louisville'/'Ain't It a Shame'
'Six–Five Special'/'This Land Is Your Land'/'Don't Stay Away'

Members of the group as above. Other musicians featured live and on record:

Vic Flick, guitar
  (later with the John Barry 7)
Bryan Daly, guitar
  (the writer of 'Postman Pat'
  television theme)

Diz Disley, guitar
  (later with Stephan Grappelli)
Ivor Daniels, guitar
Ray Oliver, drums

The Cranes Skiffle Group

Embassy Records

Recorded March 1957 Levy's Sound Studios, London

'Banana Boat Song'*†/'Don't You Rock Me Daddy O'‡*	W223
'Freight Train'§/'Cumberland Gap'	W238

Chas McDevitt, guitar, voc.
  whistling
Alex Whitehouse, guitar, voc.
  lead vocal‡
Marc Sharratt, washboard

Dennis Carter, guitar, voc,
  2nd whistler§
John Paul, bass, voc.
Jimmie MacGregor, guitar, voc.*
Jack Baverstock (A&R producer),
  biscuit tin and brushes†

Delta Skiffle Group

Esquire Records

Recorded London 25 June 1957

'Skip to My Lou'/'John Brown's Body'	10-504
'K.C. Moan'/'Pick a Bale of Cotton'	10-507
'Open Up Them Pearly Gates'/'Ain't You Glad'	10-517
The Delta Skiffle Group	EP 162
'Skip to My Lou'/'Pick a Bale of Cotton'	
'K.C.Moan'/'John Brown's Body'	
The First National Skiffle Contest	20-089
'Skip to My Lou'/'John Brown's Body'	

Other tracks by Station and 2.19 Skiffle Groups

Storyville Records   108 108 STF and A 45505

'Skip to My Lou'/'John Brown's Body'

Douglas Taylor, banjo, guitar, voc.
Tom 'Tucker' Finlayson, guitar
Hank Smith, washboard

Don Finlayson, guitar
Ian 'Ogg' Couper, bass

Lonnie Donegan

Decca Records

New Orleans Joys (Chris Barber 10-inch LP)	LF 1198
Recorded London July 1954	
'Rock Island Line'/'John Henry'	1954

'Rock Island Line'/'John Henry' 1955	F 10647

Lonnie Donegan, guitar, voc.	Chris Barber, bass
Beryl Bryden, washboard	

'Diggin' My Potatoes'/'Bury My Body' 1956	F 10695

Lonnie Donegan, guitar, voc.	Chris Barber, bass
Pat Halcox, piano	Ron Bowden, drums

The Lonnie Donegan Skiffle Group
'Rock Island Line'/'John Henry'
'Diggin' My Potatoes'/'Bury My Body' 1956 — DFE 6345

Members of the group as above

Pye-Nixa Records

'Midnight Special'/'When the Sun Goes Down' 1956	NJS 2006
'Lost John'/'Stewball' 1956	N 15036
'Bring a Little Water Sylvie'/'Dead or Alive' 1956	N 15071
'Don't You Rock Me Daddy O'/'Alabammy Bound' 1957	N 15080
'Cumberland Gap'/'Love Is Strange' 1957	N 15087
'Putting on the Style'/'Gamblin' Man' 1957	N 15093
'My Dixie Darlin''/'I'm Just a Rollin' Stone' 1957	N 15108
'Jack o' Diamonds'/'Ham and Eggs' 1958	7N 15116
'Grand Coulee Dam'/'Nobody Loves Like an Irishman' 1958	7N 15129
'Sally Don't You Grieve'/'Betty Betty Betty' 1958	7N 15148
'Midnight Special'/'When the Sun Goes Down' 1958	7NJ 2006
'Lonesome Traveller'/'Times Are Getting Hard' 1958	7N 15158

Lonnie's Skiffle Party
'Little Liza Jane'/'Puttin' on the Style'/'Camptown Races'/'So Long'
'On Top of Old Smokey'/'Knees Up Mother Brown'

'Down in the Valley'/'So Long' 1958	7N 15165
'Tom Dooley'/'Rock o' My Soul' 1958	7N 15172
'Does Your Chewing Gum Lose Its Flavour'/'Aunt Rhody' 1959	7N 15181
'Fort Worth Jail'/'Whoa Buck' 1959	7N 15198
'Battle of New Orleans'/'Darling Corey' 1959	7N 15206

(Two versions of New Orleans issued, 'Ruddy' and 'Blooming British')

'Kevin Barry'/'My Laggan Love' (issued Ireland only) 1959   7N 15219
'Sal's Got a Sugar Lip'/'Chesapeake Bay'* 1959   7N 15223
'San Miguel'/'Talking Guitar Blues' 1959   7N 15237
'My Old Man's a Dustman'/'Golden Vanity' 1960   7N 15256
'I Wanna Go Home'/'Jimmy Brown the Newsboy' 1960   7N 15267
'Lorelei'/'In All My Wildest Dreams' 1960   7N 15275
'Lively'/'Black Cat' 1960   7N 15312
'Beyond the Sunset'/'The Virgin Mary' 1960   7N 15315
'Leave My Woman Alone'/'Beneath the Willow' 1961   7N 15330
'Have a Drink On Me'/'Seven Golden Daffodils' 1961   7N 15354
'Michael Row the Boat Ashore'/'Lumbered' 1961   7N 15371
'Commancheros'/'Rambling Around' 1962   7N 15410
'The Party's Over'/'Over the Rainbow' 1962   7N 15424
'I'll Never Fall in Love Again'/'Keep on the
    Sunnyside' 1962   7N 15446
'Pick a Bale of Cotton'/'Steal Away' 1962   7N 15455
'The Market Song'/'Tit Bits'† 1962   7N 15493
'Losing By a Hair'/'Trumpet Sounds' 1963   7N 15514
'Rise Up'/'It Was a Very Good Year' 1963   7N 15530
'Lemon Tree'/'I've Got a Gal So Fine' 1963   7N 15564
'This Train'/'500 Miles'‡ 1963   7N 15579
'It's a Long Road'/'Beans in My Ears' 1964   7N 15669
'There's a Big Wheel'/'Fisherman's Luck' 1964   7N 15679
'Won't You Tell Me'/'Get Out Of My Life' 1965   7N 15803
'Louisiana Man'/'Bound For Zion' 1965   7N 15893
'World Cup Willie'/'Where in This World Are
    We Going'   7N 15993
'I Wanna Go Home'/'Black Cat' 1966   7N 17109
'Auntie Maggie's Remedy'/'My Sweet Marie' 1966   7N 17232

* With Ian Menzies and his Clyde Valley Stompers
† With Max Miller, ‡ with the Kestrels

Backstairs Session 1956   NJE 1014
Re-issue of Polygon EP 1955   JTE 107
Recorded London 19 May 1955
'Midnight Special'/'When the Sun Goes Down'
'New Burying Ground'/'Worried Man Blues'*

Lonnie Donegan, guitar, voc.   Dick Bishop, guitar, voc.*
Chris Barber, harmonica   Pete Korrison, mandolin
Bob Watson, voc.   Jim Bray, bass

Skiffle Session 1956   NJE 1017
Recorded London 11 January 1956
'Railroad Bill'/'Stackolee'* (Recorded 4 April 1956)
'The Ballad of Jesse James'*/'Ol' Riley'

Lonnie Donegan, guitar, voc.   Dick bishop, guitar, voc.*
Chris Barber, bass   Ron Bowden, drums

Lonnie Donegan Hit Parade vol.1 1957   NEP 24031
Recorded London 20 February 1956
'Lost John'/'Stewball'

Members of the group as above

Recorded London 2 August 1956
'Bring a Little Water Sylvie'/'Dead Or Alive'

Lonnie Donegan, guitar, voc.   Denny Wright, guitar,
Micky Ashman, bass   Nick Nicholls, drums

Lonnie Donegan Hit Parade vol.2 1957   NEP 24040
Recorded London 22, 23 August 1956. 24 February 1957*
'Don't You Rock Me Daddy O'/'I'm Alabammy Bound'
'Cumberland Gap'*/'Love Is Strange'*

Lonnie Donegan, guitar, voc.   Denny Wright, guitar
Micky Ashman, bass   Nick Nicholls, drum

Lonnie Donegan Hit Parade vol.3 1958   NEP 24067
Recorded London 9 May 1957
'Putting on the Style'/'Gamblin' Man'
Recorded London 28 August 1957
'My Dixie Darling'*/'I'm Just a Rolling Stone

Lonnie Donegan, guitar, banjo, voc.
Jimmy Currie, guitar, voc.   Micky Ashman, bass
Nick Nicholls, drums   Miki and Griff, backing voc.*
Lonnie Donegan, guitar, voc.   Denny Wright, guitar
Micky Ashman, bass   Nick Nicholls, drums

Donegan On Stage 1958   NEP 24075
Recorded 25 January 1957
'Muleskinner Blues'/'Old Hannah'/'On a Monday'/'Glory'

Group as for NEP 24031, plus Dick Bishop, guitar, voc.

Lonnie Donegan Hit Parade vol.4 1958   NEP 24081
Recorded Pinewood Studios November 1957
Featured in *Six–Five Special* film.*
'Grand Coulee Dam'*/'Ham and Eggs'
'Nobody Loves Like an Irishman'/'Jack o' Diamonds'*

Lonnie Donegan, guitar, voc.   Jimmy Currie, guitar
Micky Ashman, bass   Nick Nicholls, drums
Miki and Griff, backing voc.

Lonnie Donegan Hit Parade vol.5 1959   NEP 24104
Recorded (1) November 1958. (2) October 1958. (3) November 1957 (4) March
1958

'Tom Dooley' (1)/'Rock o' My Soul' (2)
'Sally Don't You Grieve' (3)/'Betty Betty Betty' (4)

Lonnie Donegan, guitar, voc.   Les Bennetts guitar, voc. (1 and 2)
Jimmy Currie, guitar (3 and 4)   Pete Huggett, bass (1 and 2)
Micky Ashman, bass (3 and 4)   Nick Nicholls, drums
Miki and Griff, backing voc. (1, 3 and 4)

Relax With Lonnie 1959   NEP 24107
Recorded (1, 3 and 4) October 1958 (2) March 1959
'Bewildered' (1), 'Kevin Barry'* (2), 'It's No Secret' (3), My Laggan Love'† (4)

Lonnie Donegan, guitar, voc.   Les Bennetts, guitar, voc.
Pete Huggett, bass   Nick Nicholls, drums
* Lonnie Donegan, solo guitar, voc.
†Lonnie Donegan, voc. Les Bennetts, guitar

Lonnie Donegan Hit Parade vol.6 1959   NEP 24114
Recorded (1) May 1959. (2) April 1959 (3) 13 December 1958.
(4) October 1958
'The Battle of New Orleans'*/'Fort Worth Jail'†
'Does Your Chewing Gum Lose Its Flavour'‡/'Darling Corey'

Lonnie Donegan, guitar, banjo*, voc.
Pete Huggett, bass   Les Bennetts, guitar, voc.
Nick Nicholls, drums   Miki and Griff, backing voc.†
Brian Simmons, washboard‡

Lonnie Donegan Hit Parade vol.7 1961   NEP 24134
Recorded (1) February 1960. (2 and 4) 23 October 1959.
(3) September 1959
'My Old Man's a Dustman'*(1)/'The Golden Vanity' (2)
'Sal's Got a Sugar Lip'† (3)/'Talking Guitar Blues'‡(4)

Lonnie Donegan, guitar, voc.   Les Bennetts, guitar, bass*
Pete Huggett, bass, violin*   Nick Nicholls, drums
Miki and Griff, backing voc.†   Lonnie, voc. Les, guitar‡

Lonnie Donegan Hit Parade vol.8 1961   NEP 24149
Recorded (1 and 3) August 1961. (2) February 1960. (4) April 1961.
'Michael Row The Boat Ashore'/'I Want To Go Home'*
'Lumbered'/'Have A Drink On Me'†

Lonnie Donegan, guitar, banjo*, voc.
Les Bennetts, guitar   Pete Huggett, bass
Pete Appleby, drums   Miki and Griff, backing voc.
Orchestra directed by Wally Stott†

Showcase (10-inch LP) 1956   NPT 19012
Recorded London 22 and 23 August 1956
'Wabash Cannonball'/'How Long How Long Blues'/'Nobody's Child'/'I Shall Not Be Moved'/'I'm Alabammy Bound'/'I'm a Ramblin' Man'/'Wreck of the Old '97'/'Frankie and Johnny'

Lonnie Donegan, guitar, voc.   Nick Nicholls, drums
Denny Wright, guitar, piano. voc.   Micky Ashman, bass

Lonnie (10-inch LP) 1958   NPT 19027
Recorded London 11, 12 and 19 March 1958
'Lonesome Traveller'/'The Sunshine Of His Love'
'Ain't No More Cane on the Brazos'*/'Ain't You Glad You Got Religion'/'Times Are Getting Hard Boys'†/'Lazy John'*/'Light From the Lighthouse'/'I've Got Rocks in My Bed'/'Long Summer Day'*

Lonnie Donegan, guitar, voc. whistle†   Jimmy Currie, guitar,
Micky Ashman, bass   Nick Nicholls, drums
Miki and Griff, backing voc.   John Cole, harmonica*

Tops With Lonnie 1959   NPL 18034
'Don't You Rock Me Daddy O'/'Putting on the Style'/'Gamblin' Man'/'My Dixie Darlin''/'Bring a Little Water Sylvie'/'Cumberland Gap'/'Grand Coulee Dam'/'Sally Don't You Grieve'/'Nobody Loves Like an Irishman'/'Lost John'/'Does Your Chewing Gum Lose Its Flavour'/'Tom Dooley'

Group members and recording details as for *Lonnie Donegan Hit Parade Vols.1–6*

Sing Hallelujah 1962   NPL 18073
Recorded February and May 1962
'Sing Hallelujah'/'We Shall Walk Through the Valley'/'No Hiding Place'/'Good News! Chariots a' Comin''/'Steal Away'*/'Noah Found Grace in the Eyes of the Lord'/'Joshua Fit de Battle of Jericho'/'His Eye Is on the Sparrow'*/'Born in Bethlehem'/'This Train'/'New Burying Ground'/'Nobody Knows the Trouble I've Seen'*

Lonnie Donegan, guitar, banjo, voc.   Denny Wright, guitar
Pete Huggett, bass   Pete Appleby, drums
The Kestrels (Roger Greenaway, Tony Burrows etc), backing voc.
*Orchestra directed by Tony Hatch
*Backing voc. Mike Sammes Singers

The Lonnie Donegan Folk Album 1965   NPL 18126
Recorded Nashville, 7 May 1964*. 8 May 1964†
Rest London June 1965
'I'm Gonna Be a Bachelor'†/'Interstate 40'*/'After Taxes'‡
'Where in the World'/'Diamonds of Dew'†/'Bound For Zion'
'She Was a T-Bone Talking Woman'‡/'Wedding Bells'
'Reverend Mr Black'/'The Doctor's Daughter'/'Blistered'/'Farewell'

Lonnie Donegan, guitar, voc.   Denny Wright, guitar
Pete Oakman, bass, voc.   Mark Goodwin, drums
Cliff Hall, piano, organ. With chorus vocal.
Pete Sayers, banjo‡

*Lonnie Donegan, voc.
Floyd Chance, bass   Murray M. Harman, drums
Charlie McCoy, harmonica   Floyd Kramer, piano
The Jordanaires, backing voc.
Jerry Glenn Kennedy, Harold Ray Bradley, Ray Edenton, guitars

† As above plus Pete Drake, steel guitar and backing vocals by
Dolores D. Edgin, Priscilla Ann Hubbard

Lonnie Rides Again 1959   NPL 18043
Recorded London 22 and 23 October 1959
'Fancy Talking Tinker'/'Miss Otis Regrets'/'Gloryland'
'Jimmie Brown the Newsboy'/'Mr Froggy'/'Take This Hammer'
'The Gold Rush Is Over'/'You Pass Me By'/'Talking Guitar Blues'*
'John Hardy'/'The House of the Rising Sun'/'San Miguel'

Lonnie Donegan, guitar, banjo, voc.   Pete Huggett, bass
Les Bennetts, guitar, voc.   Nick Nicholls, drums
*Lonnie, voc. Les, guitar

More Tops With Lonnie 1960   NPL 18063
Recorded London 1959 and 1960. New York 10 March 1960*
'Battle of New Orleans'‡/'Lorelei'*/'Lively'†/'Sal's Got A Sugar Lip'‡/'I Wanna Go
home'§/'Leave My Woman Alone'/'My Old Man's a Dustman'/'Fort Worth
Jail'‡/'Have A Drink On Me'†
'Bury Me Beneath The Willow'¶

Lonnie's Skiffle Party Part 1
'Little Liza Jane'/'Putting on the Style'/'Camptown Races'/'Liza Jane'/'Knees Up
Mother Brown'

Lonnie's Skiffle Party Part 2 (So Long Medley)
'So Long'/'On Top of Old Smokey'/'Down in the Valley'/'So Long'

Lonnie Donegan, guitar, banjo, voc.   Pete Huggett, bass
Les Bennetts, guitar, voc.   Nick Nicholls, drums, voc.
Pete Appleby, drums†   Miki and Griff, backing voc.‡
*Lonnie Donegan, voc.   Allen Hanlon, guitar
George Barnes, guitar, banjo   George Duvivier, bass
Gary Chester, drums   Phil Kraus, percussion
Mike Stoller, piano   Leon Cohen, baritone sax
King Curtis, tenor sax   Taft Jordan, trumpet
Vocal chorus
§Orchestra directed by Wally Stott
¶Orchestra directed by Ralph Dollimore

Cuba Libre Virgin SP 1981   VS 460

'Cumberland Gap'/'Wabash Cannonball'/'Don't You Rock Me Daddy O'/'Only My Pillow'/'Grab It And Growl'

Lonnie Donegan, guitar, voc. with the Shakin' Pyramids

Philips Records Germany

Lonnie Donegan Meets Leineman
Recorded Germany 1974   6305 227
'Casey's Last Ride'/'Bottle of Wine'/'Dixie Darlin''/'Frankie and Johnny'/'Tops at Loving You'/'Gloryland'/'Leineman's Potatoes'
'Me and Bobby McGee'/'Does Your Chewing Gum Lose Its Flavour'/'Becky Deen'/'Jack o' Diamonds'

Lonnie Donegan, guitar,   Gottfried Bottger, piano
   banjo, voc.   Ulli Salm, bass, voc.
Chris Seelenmeyer, guitar,   Ulf Kruger, washboard,
   banjo. voc.   drums, voc.
Lorenza Westphal, Jerry Bahrs,
   guitar, voc.

Lonnie Donegan Meets Leineman –
Country Roads 1976   6305 288
Recorded Germany 1975
'Country Roads'/'Rock Island Line'/'Keep on the Sunny Side'
'Dixie Lily'/'Louisiana Man'/'Dead or Alive'/'Midnight Special'
'Muleskinner Blues'/'Roll in My Sweet Baby's Arms'/'Lost John'
'Have a Drink On Me'/'Dublin O'Shea'

Lonnie Donegan, guitar,   Gigo Seelenmeyer, guitar, banjo
   banjo, voc.   Ulli Salm, bass
Berry Sarluis, piano   Lonzo Westphal, fiddle
Jerry Bahs, harmonica, voc.   Ilf Kruger, washboard

Motive   6449 073
With Leineman, compiled from previous two LPs
'Midnight Special'/'Muleskinner Blues'/'Lost John'/'Have a Drink on Me'/'Country Roads'/'Rock Island Line'
'Dixie Darlin''/'Gloryland'/'Me and Bobby McGee'/'Does Your Chewing Gum Lose Its Flavour'/'Jack o' Diamonds'

Group as above. Both sessions included extra musicians

Chrysalis Records

Putting on the Style 1978   CHR 1158
Recorded London 1978
Produced by Adam Faith

'Rock Island Line'/'Have a Drink on Me'/'Ham and Eggs'
'I Wanna Go Home'/'Diggin' My Potatoes'/'Nobody's Child'
'Puttin' on the Style'/'Frankie and Johnny'
'Drop Down Baby'/'Lost John'

Lonnie Donegan, guitar, 12-string and banjo

Roger McKew, guitar	Rory Gallagher, guitar
Leo Sayer, harmonica	Henry Spinnetta, bass
Zoot Money, piano	Dave Wynter, guitar
Albert Lee, guitar	Pete Jameson, guitar
Pete Wingfield, guitar	Bruce Gary, drums
Ray Cooper, percussion	Gary Brooker, electric piano
Richard Hewson, strings	Frank Gibson, drums
Alan Jones, bass	Brian May, guitar
Elton John, piano	Jim Keltner, drums
Klaus Voorman, guitar	Ronnie Wood, guitar
Rev. James Cleveland, piano	Nicky Hopkins, piano
Colin Fairly, drums,	William D. Smith, organ
Mick Ralphs, guitar	Michele Phillips, backing voc.

Sundown 1978   CHR 1205
Recorded Westlake 1978
'All Out and Down'/'Home'/'Streamline Train'/'Sundown'
'Mama's Got to Know How'/'Morning Light'/'Louisiana Sun'
'The Battle of New Orleans'/'Cajun Stripper'/'Dreaming My Dreams'

Lonnie Donegan, guitar, banjo. voc.

Jim Keltner, guitar	Emery Gordy, bass
Jai Windong, piano	Albert Lee, guitar, mandolin, voc.
Scott Chambers, bass	Doug Kershaw, fiddle, accordion
Micky Raphael, harmonica	Richard Bennett, steel guitar
Ray Cooper, percussion	

Backing vocals by Becky Lopez, Ventta Fields, Shirley Matthews

Cube Records

Jubilee Concert 1981   ICSD 2001
Recorded Fairfield Hall Croydon 5 June 1981
'John Henry'*/'Take This Hammer'*/'Railroad Bill'*/'Tom Dooley'
'New Burying Ground'/'Grand Coulee Dam'/'New York Town'
'Miss Otis Regrets'/'Does Your Chewing Gum Lose Its Flavour'
'One Night of Love'/'Rock Island Line'/'Gloryland'/'Corrine Corrina'/'Goodnight Irene'

First LP features original jazz band line-up with Donegan on banjo.
Second LP features skiffle tracks

*Lonnie Donegan, guitar, voc.	Chris Barber, bass
Ken Colyer, guitar, voc.	Bill Colyer, washboard
Jim Bray, bass	

Other tracks feature the Donegan group of 1980:
Chris Hunt, drums with Jackie McCauley, Bill Scott, Ian Murray Sorbie

Rio Digital Records

Jubilee Concert Part 1   RD LP 1201
Re-issue of Cube ICSD 2001 *(Skiffle Album)*

Timeless Records Holland

The Great Reunion Concert 1975   CD TTD 553
Recorded Fairfield Hall Croydon 5 June 1975
'On a Monday'/'Bury My Body'/'Long Gone Lost John'

Lonnie Donegan, guitar, banjo   Chris Barber, voc.
Jim Bray, bass   Ron Bowden, drums
All other tracks on LP by Chris Barber's Jazz Band.
Lonnie plays banjo and sings on 'Jenny's Ball'

Bear Family Records Germany

Rare and Unissued Gems 1985   BFX 15170
Recorded Nashville, USA May 1964 Tracks 1–7.
'Cajun Joe'/'Louisiana Man'/'There's a Big Wheel'/'Fisherman's Luck'/'Lovey Told
Me Goodbye'/'Bad News'/'Nothing to Gain'

Lonnie Donegan, voc.   Harold Bradley, Jerry Kennedy,
Floyd Chance, bass   Ray Edenton, guitars
Pete Drake, pedal steel guitar   Floyd Cramer, piano
Charlie McCoy, harmonica   Buddy Harman, drums

Recorded London 1959–61 Tracks 8–16
'500 Miles from Home'*/'Tiger Rag'/'Keep on the Sunnyside'
'Red Berets'†/'Kevin Barry'‡/'The Commancheros'†
'Just a Wearying for You'/'Ding Ding'§/'Leaving Blues'§

Lonnie Donegan, guitar, banjo, voc.
Les Bennetts, guitar   Pete Huggett, bass
Pete Appleby, drums   Miki and Griff backing voc.
§ Pete Oakman, bass, voc. Mark Goodwin, drums
§ Cliff Hall, organ
† Orchestra directed by Tony Hatch
‡ Lonnie Donegan, guitar, voc.
* Denny Wright, guitar

More Than Pye In The Sky 1993   BCD 15700-H1
Tracks from the original Decca and Pye catalogue, including many rare and
previously unissued titles. In all, 209 tracks in an 8 x CD boxed set.
One example of the rare tracks:
Recorded 12 April 1953 Copenhagen

'Hard Time Blues'/'Nobody's Child'
'You Don't Know My Mind'/'Midnight Special'*

Lonnie Donegan, banjo, voc.   Chris Barber, bass
Ken Colyer, voc.*

Continental, Compilation and Reissued Albums

Country Style	Golden Guinea	GGL 0211
Lonnie Donegan's Golden Hour of Golden Hits vol.1	Golden Hour	GH 514
Lonnie Donegan's Golden Hour of Golden Hits vol.2	Golden Hour	GH 565
Golden Age of Donegan vol. 1	Golden Guinea	GGL 0135
Golden Age of Donegan vol. 2	Golden Guinea	GGL 0170
A Golden Age of Donegan vol. 1	Marble Arch	MAL 636
A Golden Age of Donegan vol. 2	Marble Arch	MAL 698
My Old Man's a Dustman	Hallmark	HMS 204
Lonnie Donegan	Hallmark	HMA 252
The Lonnie Donegan File (2 x LP)	Pye	FILD 011
Flash Backs – Rock Island Line	Flashbacks	FBLP 8071
The King of Skiffle – Hit Collection (2 x LP)	Pye (Ger.)	850 907 XBT
The Hit Singles Collection	PRT	PRL 7003
The Collection	Castle Comm.	CCSLP 7003
The Greatest Hits of Lonnie Donegan	Ronco	RTL 2017
	Bravo (cassette)	BRC 2530
The Hits of Lonnie Donegan	Music for Pleasure	
		MFP 50389
An Englishman Sings American Folksongs	Mercury (US)	MG 20229
La Grande Storia Del Rock	Curcio (ITA.)	GSR 38
Lonnie Donegan and his Group	Vogue (FRA.)	VPV 76002
Lonnie Donegan	Dot (CAN.US)	DLP 3159
	Dot (CAN.US)	DLP 3394
Lonnie Donegan	Tyler	LDNH 123

Johnny Duncan and his Bluegrass Boys

Columbia Records

'Kaw Liga'/'Ella Speed' 1957	DB 3925
'Last Train to San Fernando'/'Rockabilly Baby' 1957	DB 3959
'Blue Blue Heartache'/'Jig Along Home' 1957	DB 3996
'Get Along Home Cindy'/'Footprints in the Snow' 1957	DB 4029
'Goodnight Irene'/'If You Love Me Baby' 1957	DB 4074
'Itching For My Baby'/'I Heard the Bluebirds Sing' 1958	DB 4118

'All of the Monkeys Ain't In the Zoo'
   'More and More' 1958   DB 4167
'My Lucky Love'/'Geisha Girl' 1958   DB 4179
'Rosalie'/'This Train' 1959   DB 4282
'That's Alright Darlin''/'Kansas City' 1959   DB 4311
'Anytime'/'Yellow Yellow Moon' 1960   DB 4415
'Ballad of Jed Clampett'/'Will You Be Mine' 1963   DB 7164
'Dang Me'/'Which Way Did He Go' 1964   DB 7334
'My Little Baby'/'I Thank My Lucky Stars' 1966   DB 7833

Johnny Duncan and his Blue Grass Boys 1957   SEG 7708
'Freight Train Blues'/'Press On'
'Johnny's Blue Yodel'/'Out of Business'

Johnny Duncan and his Blue Grass Boys no. 2 1957   SEG 7733
'Last Train to San Fernando'/'Jig Along Home'
'Blue Blue Heartache'/'Ella Speed'

Footprints in the Snow 1958   SEG 7753
'Footprints in the Snow'/'Kaw Liga'
'Rockabilly Baby'/'Get Along Home Cindy'

Tennessee Song Bag 1958   SEG 7850
Medley: 'Rockabilly Baby'/'Raise a Ruckus Tonight'
'Pan American'/'I'm Moving on'/'Detour'
'Last Train to San Fernando'/'I'm Moving on'

Johnny Duncan, guitar,	Danny Levan, violin
mandolin, voc.	Jack Fallon, bass, violin
Denny Wright, guitar, piano	Lennie Hastings, drums

Later versions of the group included

Bryan Daly, guitar	Danny Craig, drums
Sandy Brown, clarinet	Pete Sayers, banjo
(on LP33 1122)	(on 'Jed Clampett', DB 7164)
Red Reece, drums	Boz Marsden, bass

DB 7164 released as *Johnny Duncan and The Kingpins*
DB 4415, DB 7833 released as *Johnny Duncan* with musical direction by Ivor Raymonde
DB 7334 released as *Johnny Duncan*

Tennessee Song Bag (10-inch LP) 1957   33S 1122
'Get Along Home Cindy'/'Old Blue'/'Travelin' Blues'
'St James Infirmary'/'Calamity Mose'/'More and More'
'Just a Little Lovin''/'Which Way Did He Go'
'Mind Your Own Business'/'Just a Closer Walk With Thee'

Salute to Hank Williams (10-inch LP) 1958   33S 1129
'Hey Good Lookin''/'Wedding Bells'/'Jambalaya'/'Moanin' the Blues'/'Cold Cold
Heart'/'Long Gone Lonesome Blues'/'Half As Much'/'May You Never Be
Alone'/'Salute to Hank Williams'

Beyond the Sunset 1961   33SX 1328
'Beyond the Sunset'/'Just a Little Walk With Jesus'/'Amazing Grace'
'Where Could I Go But to the Lord'/'Just a Closer Walk With Thee'
'Walking in Jerusalem Just Like John'/'Precious Lord Hold My Hand'/'No Hiding
Place'/'I've Just Told Mama Goodbye'/'Press On'
'In the Garden'/'When God Dips His Pen of Love in My Heart'

Johnny Duncan, guitar, voc.
Ivor Raymond directs orchestra and chorus

Encore Records

Salute to Hank Williams   ENC 190
'Kaw Liga'/'Mind Your Own Business'
plus tracks issued on 33S 1129

Music for Pleasure Records

Beyond the Sunset 1965   MFP 1032
Reissue of Columbia 33-SX-1328

Pye Records

'Sleepy Eyed John'/'Tobacco Road' 1961   7N 15358
'Hannah'/'The Legend of Gunga Din' 1961   7N 15380
'A Long Time Gone'/'Waiting for the Snowman' 1962   7N 15420*
*Orchestra directed by Tony Hatch

'Doin' My Time'/'Where Could I Go' 1958   NJ 2014

The Chris Barber Skiffle Group 1957   NJE 1025
'Doin' My Time'/'Where Could I Go' and two other tracks by Dickie Bishop
Johnny Duncan, guitar, mandolin voc.   Dick Bishop, guitar,voc.
Chris Barber, bass   Ron Bowden, drums.

Old Gold Records

'Last Train To San Fernando' 1989   OG 9902-A
backed with Donegan's 'Rock Island Line'

Lucky Records

Back in Town 1970   LUS 3012
'Last Train to San Fernando'/'Little Things'/'I Fought the Law'
'Joe and Mabel's 12th Street Bar and Grill'/'Margie's at the Lincoln Park Inn'/'Kaw

Liga'/'Out of Business'/'Footprints in the Snow'/'I Ain't Buyin''/'I Wonder Where You Are Tonight'/'Someone Stole My Steel Guitar'

The Best of Lucky 1970   LUS 3014
'Last Train to San Fernando'/'Joe and Mabel's 12th Street Bar and Grill'

The Country Music Story 2 x LPs 1971   LUS 100
'Kaw Liga'/'Margie's At The Lincoln Park Inn'

Other tracks by UK country artists on both LUS 3014 and LUS 100

Decca Records

The World of Country Music vol.2 1973   SPA 295
Recorded live at Nashville Rooms London
'Mustang Prang'/'Life Can Be Beautiful'/'Hello Heartache'/'If It Feels Good Do It'/'The Wild Side of Life'/'Just For What I Am'/'Salty Dog Blues'/'Just a Little Lovin''/'Footprints in the Snow'/'Blue Blue Heartache'/'Somebody to Give My Love To'

Tribute to Hank Williams: 'Hey Good Lookin''/'I Can't Help It'/'Jambalaya'/'Smoke Smoke Smoke That Cigarette'/'Tom Dooley'/'Last Train to San Fernando'/'Mustang Prang (Revisited)'

Johnny Duncan, guitar, voc.   Larry Allen, guitar
Eddie Seals, bass   Billy Talbot, drums
Pete Willshire, steel guitar

Continental Releases

Intercord Records

Rockabilly Baby   INTS 146 531
'Rockabilly Baby'/'Last Train to San Fernando'/'Freight Train Blues'
'Ella Speed'/'Old Blue'/'Footprints in the Snow'/'Blue Blue Heartache'/'I Heard the Bluebirds Sing'/'Jig Along Home'/'Get Along Home Cindy'/'Geisha Girl'/'Goodnight Irene'

Bear Family Records

Last Train to San Fernando 1985   BFX 15169
'Last Train to San Fernando'/'Itching For My Baby'/'Geisha Girl'/'Jig Along Home'/'Railroad Steamboat' (previously unissued)/'I Heard the Bluebirds Sing'/'Get Along Home Cindy'

Rockabilly Medley: 'Raise A Ruckus Tonight'/'Rockabilly Baby'/'Detour'/'Rockabilly Baby'/'Dang Me'/'Which Way Did He Go'/'Blue Blue Heartache'/'Footprints in the Snow'/'My Little Baby'/'Yellow Moon'

Railroad Medley: 'Pan American'/'I'm Movin' On'/'Last Train to San Fernando'

Last Train to San Fernando 1996   BCD 15947 DI
4 x CD boxed set 115 tracks

Eden Street Skiffle Group

Popular Skiffle Album no. 1 (gatefold album of ten records) 78 rpm
Recorded London 1958

1	'Man Taking Names'	6	'Old Smokey'
2	'Mary Don't You Weep'	7	'Raise the Ruckus Tonight'
3	'Gloryland'	8	'Heaven'
4	'Judy Drowned'	9	'Easy Rider'
5	'Black Girl'	10	'Ain't It a Shame'

Brian Jackman, guitar, voc.   Ron Lawrence, guitar, voc.
Hamish Maxwell, guitar, voc.   Micky Hopkins, mandolin
John Willard, bass   Bob Jones, washboard, drums

Frog Island Skiffle Group

77 Records

The Frog Island Skiffle 1957   77 EP 4
Recorded London 1957
'House of the Rising Sun'/'Going Down the Road Feeling Bad'
'Hand Me Down My Walking Cane'/'Another Man Done Gone'

Taff Price, guitar, voc.   Colin Edwards, guitar, voc.
Joan Bennett, banjo, voc.   Ian Green, washboard.

Les Hobeaux Skiffle Group

HMV Records

Recorded London 1957
'Oh Mary Don't You Weep'/'Toll the Bell Easy'   POP 377
'Mama Don't Allow'/'Hey Hey Daddy Blues'   POP 403
'Dynamo'/'Two Ships'   POP 444

Soho Skiffle   7EG 8297
'Hey Hey Daddy Blues'/'Mama Don't Allow'
'Toll the Bell Easy'/'Oh Mary Don't You Weep'

Northwood Records

'Mama Don't Allow'   NW45 001
coupled with Jimmy Miller's 'Barbecues'

Original Group
Les Bennetts, guitar, voc.   David Russell, washboard
Winky Wimbledon, box bass   Keith Lardner, voc.
Roger Smith, Alan Jones, voc.

Recording Group

Les Bennetts, guitar, voc.	Roger Smith, voc.
Darrell Lyte, guitar	Roy Tobin, guitar
Keith Lardner, voc.	Brian Gregg, bass

This group was augmented on recording sessions by
Bobby Kevin, drums   Roy Plummer, guitar
Joe Mudele, bass

In the film *The Golden Disc* the group was augmented by
Rory Blackwell, drums
Rex Rehak replaced Brian Gregg on bass
Red Reece came in on drums

Jimmy Jackson and his Rock 'n' Skiffle

Columbia Records

Recorded London 1957 and 1958

'California Zephyr'/'I Shall Not Be Moved' 1957	DB 3898
'Sitting on the Balcony'/'Good Morning Blues' 1957	DB 3937
'River Line'/'Lonely Road' 1957	DB 3957
'White Silver Sands'/'Build Your Love' 1957	DB 3988
'Love a Love a Love a'/'Photographs' 1958	DB 4085
'This Little Light of Mine'/'Swing Down Sweet Chariot' 1958	DB 4153

Rock 'n' Skiffle 1957	SEG 7750
'California Zephyr'/'I Shall Not Be Moved'	
'Good Morning Blues'/'Lonely Road'	

Country and Blues 1958	SEG 7768
'Midnight Train'/'Western Plains'	
'Reckon I'll Go'/'There's a Time For Moving'	

Jimmy Jackson, guitar, voc.	Neville Skrimshire, guitar
Pete Appleby, drums	Alan Duddington, bass,
Brian Horrey, lead guitar	
On some sessions Bill Wayne (Woodall), drums	

Alexis Korner Skiffle Group

77 Records

Blues from the Roundhouse	LP 2
Recorded Roundhouse, London, 13 February 1957	
'Leaving Blues'/'Roundhouse Stomp'/'Rotten Break'	
'Skip to My Lou'/'Alberta'/'Ella Speed'	
'Good Morning'/'Boll Weevil'	

Tempo Records

Blues from the Roundhouse vol. 1	EXA 76
Recorded Roundhouse, London, 22 July 1957	

'I Ain't Gonna Worry No More'/'Kid Man'/'County Jail'/'Easy Rider'

'I Ain't Gonna Worry No More'/'County Jail' 1958   A 166

Blues from the Roundhouse vol. 2   EXA 102
Recorded Roundhouse, London, 29 April 1958
'Sail On'/'National Defence Blues'/'Go Down Sunshine'/'Death Letter'

Folklore 77 Records

The Legendary Cyril Davies with Alexis Korner's Breakdown Group and the Roundhouse Jug Four 1970   F-LEUT 9
Same tracks as 77 LP 2, plus four tracks by the Roundhouse Jug Four.
'K.C. Moan'/'It's the Same Old Thing'
'Hesitation Blues'/'Short Legs Shuffle'

Krazy Kat Records

Alexis 1957 1984   KK 789
Same tracks as 77 LP 2 and F-LEUT 9 plus four previously unreleased tracks from February 1957 session
'Streamline Train'/'County Jail'
'Doggone My Good Luck Soul'/'Badly Mistreated Man'

Compilation and Continental Releases

Decca Records Germany

Skiffle	1968	ACL 1250
	1982	TAB 56
Kings of Skiffle	1973	DS 3212/1–2
	1975	6.28132 DP

'Sail On'/'I Ain't Gonna Worry No More'

Fantastic Skiffle Festival 1977   6.28422 DP
'Go Down Sunshine'/'Death Letter'/'National Defence Blues'

Alex Korner's Blues Incorporated 1981   6.24475
'Ain't Gonna Worry No More'/'Kid Man'
'County Jail'/'Go Down Sunshine'

Alexis Korner Skiffle Group

Alexis Korner, guitar, mandolin, voc.	Cyril Davies, 12-string guitar, harmonica, voc.
Terry Plant, bass	Mike Collins, washboard
London 13 February 1957	77 LP 2 and KK 789

Alexis Korner Skiffle Group
Alexis Korner, guitar, voc.   Chris Capon, bass
Cyril Davies, 12-string guitar, Dave Stevens, piano
 harmonica, voc.   Mike Collins, washboard
London 22 July 1957   EXA 76 and A 166

Alexis Korner's Blues Incorporated
Alexis Korner, guitar, voc.   Jim Bray bass
Cyril Davies, 6- and 12-string Dave Stevens, piano
guitar, harmonica, voc.   Mike Collins, washboard
London 29 April 1958   EXA 102

Roundhouse Jug Four
Cyril Davies, 12-string guitar, Jeff Bradford, mandolin, guitar,
 harmonica, voc.   kazoo
Lisa Turner, banjo, vocal   Reg Turner, jug
Kenton, Middlesex, 13 February 1961   F-LEUT9 and KK 789

Lea Valley Skiffle Group

Esquire Records

Recorded London 5 September 1957
'Streamline Train'/'Railroad Bill'   10-508
'I'm Gonna Walk and Talk'/'Oh Mary Don't You Weep' 10-518

The Lea Valley Skiffle Group   EP 163
'Streamline Train'/'Railroad Bill'
'I'm Gonna Walk and Talk'/'Oh Mary Don't You Weep'

Storyville Records   A 45503 and 108 106 STF

'Streamline Train'/'I'm Gonna Walk and Talk'

Ron Till, guitar, voc.   Trevor Morgan, guitar, voc.
Brian Coford, guitar   Mike Warwick, guitar
Brian Warwick, banjo   Sid Herbert, washboard
Brian Kohler, 2-string bass

Alan Lomax and the Ramblers

Decca Records

Recorded Lansdowne Studios London 2 August 1956. Dennis Preston
'Oh Lula'/'Railroad Man'
'Dirty Old Town'/'Hard Case' 1956   DFE 6367
'Dirty Old Town'/'Hard Case' 1956   45 F 10787
'Hard Case'/'Railroad Man'/'Oh Lula' 1956   DS 3212/1-2
      and 1956   6.28132DP

Alan Lomax, guitar, voc.   Ewan MacColl, voc.
Peggy Seeger, banjo, voc.   Shirley Collins, voc.

Sandy Brown, clarinet   John Cole, harmonica
Bryan Daly, guitar   Jim Bray, bass
Allan 'Little Bear' Sutton, washboard

Chas McDevitt Skiffle Group

Oriole Records

All recorded Levy's Sound Studios New Bond St London December 1956
Jack Baverstock, producer.

'Freight Train'/'Cotton Song'*	CB 1352
'New Orleans' ('House of Rising Sun')*/'Worried Man'*†	CB 1357

Chas McDevitt, guitar, voc.   John Paul, bass
   whistling   Dennis Carter, guitar, voc.
Nancy Whiskey, guitar, voc.   Marc Sharratt, washboard
Alex Whitehouse, guitar, voc.   Jimmie MacGregor, guitar,
                                   mandolin, voc.

*Nancy Whiskey not on these tracks.
†Jimmie MacGregor on this track only

'Greenback Dollar'/'I'm Satisfied'* May 1957	CB 1371
'Face in the Rain'/'Sportin' Life'* July 1957	CB 1386
'My Old Man'*/'Sing, Sing, Sing'* August 1957	CB 1395
'Johnnie O'/'Bad Man Stackolee'* August 1957	CB 1403
'Across the Bridge'†/'Deep Down'* August 1957	CB 1405
'Real Love'†/'Juke Box Jumble'‡ August 1958	CB 1457

Chas McDevitt, guitar, mandolin, whistling, voc.
Nancy Whiskey, guitar, voc.   Shirley Douglas†, guitar, voc.
Bill Bramwell, guitar; voc.   Tony Kohn, guitar, voc.
Lennie Harrison, bass   Marc Sharratt, washboard, drums
*Nancy Whiskey not on these tracks
‡Johnny Parker, piano.

The Intoxicating Miss Whiskey	MG 10018
'Poor Howard'/'The Fireman's Not For Me'§/'Sporting Life'	
'The Riddle Song'§/'I'm Satisfied'/'Face in the Rain'	
'Bad Man Stackolee'/'Farewell'§/'Every Day of the Week'	

The group as above except § Nancy Whiskey, voc. and solo guitar

Nancy and Chas	EP 7002
'Freight Train'/'Greenback Dollar'	
'Worried Man'/'I'm Satisfied'	

The group as above

'Sad Little Girl'*/'Teenage Letter'† November 1959	CB 1511

Chas McDevitt, guitar, voc.   Shirley Douglas*, bass-guitar†
†Eddie Warburton, trombone Keith Bird, tenor saxophone

Old Gold Records

'Freight Train'/'Greenback Dollar' (reissue)   OG 9052

Chic Records USA

'Freight Train'/'Cotton Song' May 1957   45 1008

Cupol Records, Sweden

'Freight Train'/'Cotton Song'   CS 45/23
'Johnny O'/'Bad Man Stackolee'   CEP 174
Two other tracks by Nancy Whiskey Skiffle Group
'He's Solid Gone'/'Ella Speed' (see Nancy Whiskey Discography)

Versailles Records, France

'Freight Train'/'Greenback Dollar'/'Worried Man'
'I'm Satisfied'   9 S 168
The group on all the above tracks as original Oriole recordings

Top Rank Records

Recorded London 1960 with Dick Rowe
'Dream Talk'/'Forever' 1960   JAR 338
Session musicians, musical director Johnny Douglas

HMV Records

Recorded 1961 Lansdowne Studios, Denis Preston
'One Love'/'Can It Be Love' 1961   POP 845

Chas McDevitt, guitar, voc. Shirley Douglas, voc.
Dave Sampson's Hunters
Norman Sheffield, drums   John Rogers, bass
Norman Stacey, guitar   Brian Parker, guitar

'Mommy out de Light'/'I've Got a Thing about You' POP 928
'Happy Family'/'Throwing Pebbles in a Pool' 1962 POP 999

Session musicians, musical director Harry Robinson (Lord Rockingham)

Lansdowne Studios 1963
'Cruel Love'/'I Never Will Marry' 1963   POP 1151

Session musicians, musical director Martin Slavin
Ossian Ellis, harp   John Williams, guitar

Columbia Records

Sixteen Big Folk Hits 1965   33SX 1738
Recorded London 1965 with Roy Pitt
'The Times They Are a' Changin''/'Walk Right In'
'Where Have All the Flowers Gone'/'Catch the Wind'
'If I Had a Hammer'/'House of the Rising Sun'
'Michael'/'San Francisco Bay Blues'/'Tom Dooley'
'Subterranean Homesick Blues'/'Little Boxes'/'Green Green'
'Blowin' in the Wind'/'Puff (the Magic Dragon)'
'Cotton Fields'/'Go Tell It on the Mountain'

Chas McDevitt, guitar, voc.	Pete Stanley, banjo/guitar,
Shirley Douglas, bass-guitar,	autoharp
voc.	Wizz Jones, guitar
Red Reece, drums	Marc Sharratt, washboard, drums

Six Folk Hits 1965   SEG 8468
Recorded London 1965 with Roy Pitt
'Blowin' in the Wind'/'Green Green'/'Tom Dooley'
'Walk Right In'/'If I Had a Hammer'/'Go Tell It on the Mountain'

The group as above

Columbia Records and Bell Records, USA

'The Most of What Is Least'*/'Don't Blame Me' 1966   DB 7703
'Don't Believe Them'/'Where Am I Goin''   DB 7595

Chas McDevitt, guitar, voc.	Shirley Douglas, guitar,
Wizz Jones, guitar and 12-string	bass-guitar, voc.
Pete Stanley, guitar, banjo,	Red Reece, drums
autoharp*	

'When the Good Times Come'/'Never Wed An Old Man'*   DB 7846

Session musicians, Chas McDevitt, guitar
*Shirley Douglas, guitar, voc. bass-guitar

Sixteen English Folksongs 1966   SX 6082
Recorded London 1966
'Seeds of Love'*†/'The Water Is Wide'‡/'Sweet Nightingale'†
'Let No Man Steal Your Thyme'/'The Tailor's Breeches'†
'Ophelia's Song'§/'Cattle Smock'¶/'Greensleeves'‡
'As I Roved Out'‡/'Kinrid's Garden'§/'Madeira M'Dear'
'My Mother Chose My Husband'§/'The Most of What Is Least'**§††
'Good Ale'/'Never Wed an Old Man'¶/'Leavin' Liverpool'¶

Chas McDevitt, guitar, voc.	Shirley Douglas, guitar, voc.,
†The Crofters, Gef and Martin,	autoharp,§ bass guitar,¶
guitars and voc.	Gef Lucena, kalimba,**

‡Jim Sullivan, 12-string guitar ocarina,¶
Wizz Jones, guitar** Pete Stanley, autoharp††

Naughty But Nice 1966 SEG 8471
Recorded Regent Sound Studios Denmark St London
'Mommy Out De Light'/'The Anvil at Gretna Green'/'Forbidden Fruit'*/'Naughty
But Nice'/'Follow Me'/'Night Food'*

Chas McDevitt, guitar, voc. Clem Cattini, drums
Shirley Douglas, guitar, bass-guitar, voc.

Columbia Records, South Africa

Recorded Johannesburg, 1967
'Mr Man'*/'Mummy out the Light' 1967 DSA 711

Chas McDevitt, guitar, voc. Shirley Douglas, bass-guitar, voc.
Session musicians*, musical director Gus Galbraith (flug. horn)

Fontana Records

Recorded Philips Studios Stanhope Place. Jack Baverstock.
'City Smoke'*/'One Man Band'† 1968 TF 957

Chas McDevitt, guitar, voc.† Red Reece, drums
Shirley Douglas, bass-guitar†, voc.
Session musicians*, musical director Ken Woodman

President Records

Recorded Pan studios Swiss Cottage London 1972
'Freight Train'/'Snowbird' 1972 PT 376

Chas McDevitt, guitar, voc. Pete Stanley, guitar, banjo
Shirley Douglas, bass-guitar, voc. Wizz Jones, guitar
Marc Sharratt, washboard

'A Boy Child Is Born'/'Amazing Grace' 1973 PT 410

Chas McDevitt, Shirley Irene Chanter backing vocal
  Douglas voc. Orchestra musical director
Martin Slavin

Joy Records

Recorded Pan Studios, Swiss Cottage London 1972
Old New Borrowed and Blue 1972 JOYS 241
'Rose Garden'/'Everything I Own'/'The First Time Ever I Saw Your Face'/'Kansas
City'/'I Could Say'/'La Bamba'/'Walk Right In'*/'Mummy out the Light'*/'She'll Be
There'/'Snowbird'*/'Try to Remember'*/'Freight Train'*

Orchestra musical director Gus Galbraith except for *

Chas McDevitt, guitar, voc.	Shirley Douglas, guitar, bass-
Wizz Jones, guitar	guitar, voc.
Pete Stanley, guitar, banjo	Marc Sharratt, washboard

Takes Ya Back Don't It 1976　　　　　　　　　　　　　　　JOYS 263
Recorded Grange Studios Chigwell. Regent Sound and Commodore
'Bloodshot Eyes'/'Thirty Days'*/'Crazy World'*/'La Bamba'*/'Peggy Sue'*/'Freight Train'/'Walk Right In'†/'Cottonfields'‡/'San Francisco Bay Blues'†/'Rock Island Line'‡/'Tom Dooley'†/'Wabash Cannonball'*

Chas McDevitt, guitar, voc.†	Wizz Jones, guitar
Pete Stanley, guitar, banjo	Marc Sharratt, washboard
Joe Brown, guitar, fiddle,	John Polwyn, guitar, banjo‡
autoharp*	
Other tracks	
Orchestra directed by Gus Galbraith	

Rollercoaster Records

Nancy and Chas 1993　　　　　　　　　　　　　　　　　RCEP 113
Recorded live at the Royal Festival Hall 22 April 1957
'Every Day of the Week'*/'I Saw the Light'†/'Ballad of the Titanic'‡/'Greenback Dollar'§/'Freight Train'§

Chas McDevitt, guitar, voc.*	Dennis Carter‡, guitar, voc.
Alex Whitehouse, guitar, voc.§	John Paul, bass
Marc Sharratt, washboard	Nancy Whiskey, guitar, voc.
	only on these two tracks*

Chas McDevitt Skiffle Group 1993　　　　　　　　　　　RCCD 3007
Recorded 1957–59
'Freight Train'*/'Badman Stackolee'/'County Jail'*/'I'm Satisfied (1)'/'I'm Satisfied (2)'/'She Moves through the Fair'*/'My Old Man (1)'**/'My Old Man (2)'**/'Poor Howard'/'Greenback Dollar'*/'Sing, Sing, Sing'‡/'BB Blues'**/'Deep Down'/'Born To Be With You'§/'I Want a Little Girl'‡/'Across the Bridge'§/'Come All Ye Fair and Tender Ladies'§/'Sportin' Life'‡/'Trottin' to the Fair'§/'Everyday of the Week'/'Face In The Rain'§/'Goin' Home'/'Tom Hark'/'It Makes No Difference Now'§/'Good Mornin' Blues'/'Real Love'§/'Pop Pourri'/'Everyday I Have the Blues'‡/'I Dig You Baby'¶#/'Ace in the Hole'/'Tom Hark'/'Teenage Letter'**

Hallmark Records

Skiffle Party 1995　　　　　　　　　　　　　　　　　　301704
'Freight Train'/'Everyday of the Week'/'My Old Man'/'Trottin' to the Fair'/'Sing, Sing, Sing'/'I Dig You Baby'/'County Jail'/'BB Blues'/'Poor Howard'/'Sportin' Life'/'She Moves through the Fair'/'Badman Stackolee'/'Come All Ye Fair and Tender Ladies'/'Greenback Dollar'

The group for both Rollercoaster and Hallmark CD

Chas McDevitt, guitar, mandolin, vocal, whistling
Nancy Whiskey, guitar, voc.*
Tony Kohn, guitar voc.‡
Bill Bramwell, guitar, voc.**
Marc Sharratt, washboard,
   drums

Shirley Douglas, guitar§,
   voc.+bass-guitar†
Lennie Harrison, bass
Les Bennetts, guitar, voc.#
Red Reece, drums¶

Big Folk and Protest Hits of the 60s 1997   306032
17 track CD. All titles and group same as *16 Big Folk Hits*
Columbia 33 SX 1738 and 'Freight Train' President PT 376

Old Timers Skiffle Group

Fontana Records   H 105

Recorded Philips Studios Stanhope Place London 1958
'The Woman Who Loved a Swine'/'The Lynching of Jeff Buckner'

Dennis Carter, guitar, voc.
John Paul, bass

Alex Whitehouse, guitar, voc.
'Little Joey' Jonkler, washboard

Soho Skifffle Group

Melodisc Records

Recorded London 1957
'Midnight Special'/'Give Me a Big Fat Woman'   1403
'Frankie and Johnny'/'Streamline Train'   1421

Soho Skiffle Group 1957   EPM 7.72
'I Shall Not Be Moved'/'Give Me a Big Fat Woman' (alternative take)/'Streamline Train'/'Frankie and Johnny'
John Audrey, guitar, voc.   Mike Naden, guitar, voc.
Plus unknown guitar, washboard and bass

Sonny Stewart Skiffle Kings

Philips Records

Recorded London 1957
'The Northern Line'/'Black Jack'   PB 719
'Let Me Lie'/'Mama Don't Allow'   PB 773

Top Rank Records

Recorded London 1960 (unissued, label defunct)
'A Year Ago'/'A Million Ways'   JAR 430

Bellaphon Records, Germany

'Come Along with Me'/'Beggar in Town'   BL 1021

The group includes at various times:

Pete Stewart, guitar, voc.
Sonny Stewart (Arthur
   Chamberlain), guitar, voc.
John Ebbles, bass

Steve O'Grady, guitar
Steve Benbow, guitar, voc.
Phil Ray, drums

Station Skiffle Group

Esquire Records

'Don't You Rock Me Daddy O'/'Hugged My Honey'	10-503
'Steamboat Bill'/'Titanic'	10-516

The Station Skiffle Group	EP 161
'Hugged My Honey'/'Greenback Dollar'/'Titanic'/'Steamboat Bill'	

The First National Skiffle Contest	LP 20-089
'Hugged My Honey'/'Titanic'/'Don't You Rock Me Daddy O'	

Storyville Records

'Titanic'/'Steamboat Bill'	A 45504 and 108 107 STF

Jim Miller, guitar, voc.
Pete Cozens, guitar
Johnnie Reid, one-string bass

Mike Jarvie, banjo, voc.
Pete Hions, washboard
Mike Hodge, vamp accordion

Jimmy Miller and the Barbecues

(Breakaway group. Station Group continued with Mike Jarvie as lead)

Columbia Records

'Sizzlin' Hot'/'Free Wheeling Baby'	DB 4006
'Jelly Baby'/'Cry Baby Cry' (without Barbecues)	DB 4081

Northwood Records

'Sizzlin' Hot' (coupled with Les Hobeaux)	NW 45 001

2.19 Skiffle Group

Esquire Records

Recorded London, 2 February 1957

'Railroad Bill'/'Freight Train'	10-497
'I'm Looking for a Home'/'When the Saints'	10-502
'In the Valley'/'Tom Dooley'	10-509
'Where Can I Go'/'Roll the Union On'	10-512
'This Little Light o' Mine'/'Union Maid'	10-515

2.19 Skiffle Group   EP 126
'Freight Train'/'Railroad Bill'
'I'm Looking For a Home'/'When the Saints'

Mik Lauder, guitar, voc.   Mike Wallace, guitar, voc.
Jack McCormack, bass   Dave Chandler, washboard

2.19 Skiffle Group   EP 146
Recorded 1 June 1957
'This Little Light o' Mine'*/'Union Maid'
'Where Can I Go'/'Roll the Union On'*

Mik Lauder, guitar, voc.   Mike Wallace, guitar, voc.
Idle Bill Smith, washboard, voc.*   Len Harris, bass

2.19 Skiffle Group   EP 176
Recorded 21 August 1957
'Trouble in Mind'/'Texas Lady'
'In the Valley'/'Tom Dooley'* (voc. Bill Smith)

The group as above but substitute Fred Cogger, bass
2.19 Skiffle Group   EP 196
'Hand Me Down My Walkin' Cane'/'Gypsy Davey'
'Oh Mary Don't You Weep'/'Black Girl'

The group as above but substitute Vic Pitt, bass

The First National Skiffle Contest   20-089 LP (10-inch)
'Freight Train'/'Union Maid'/'This Little Can o' Mine'
'Trouble in Mind'/'Texas Lady'
Other tracks by Station and Delta Skiffle Groups

Storyville Records

'Trouble In Mind'/'Hand Me Down My Walking Cane'
                                                                    A 45 506
                                                                    108 109 STF
The group for both recordings as above

The Vipers Skiffle Group

Parlophone Records

'Ain't You Glad'/'Pick a Bale of Cotton'
                                    November 1956   R 4238*
'Don't You Rock Me Daddy O'/'10,000 Years Ago'
                                    December 1956   R 4261*
'Hey Liley, Liley Lo'/'Jim Dandy'
                                    8 February 1957   R 4286†
'Cumberland Gap'‡/'Maggie May'‡
                                    28 February 1957   R 4289§

'Streamline Train'/'Railroad Steamboat'

          25 April 1957   R 4308§

'Homing Bird'/'Pay Me My Money Down'

          May 1957   R 4351§

Top Ten Special Other tracks by Jim Dale and King Bros.
'Puttin' on the Style'/'Last Train to San Fernando'

          July 1957   R 4356§

Skiffle Party   R 4371§
'Coming Round the Mountain'/'On Top of Old Smokey'
'Rock Island Line'/'Wabash Cannonball'
'Gimme Crack Corn'/'Skip to My Lou'

Wally Whyton, guitar, banjo‡, voc.	Jack Collier, bass*
Johnny Martyn (Booker), guitar, voc.	Joe Mudele, bass†
Jean Van Den Bosch, guitar, voc.	Tony Tolhurst, bass§
John Pilgrim, washboard	Jack Peach, drums

Skiffle Music   GEP 8615
'Cumberland Gap'/'Hey Liley Liley Lo'
'Don't You Rock Me Daddy O'/'It Takes a Worried Man'

Skiffle Music no.2   GEP 8626
'Streamline Train'/'Railroad Steamboat'
'Ain't You Glad'/'Pick a Bale of Cotton'

Skiffling Along   GEP 8655
'Homing Bird'/'Pay Me My Money Down'
'10,000 Years Ago'/'Maggie May'

The group as on singles

Coffee Bar Session   PMD 1050
Recorded IBC Studios London between 15 April and 5 September 1957
'Gloryland'/'John B. Sails'/'Wanderin''/'I Saw the Light'
'Precious Memories'/'Darlin''/'I Know the Lord Laid His Hands on Me'/'This Land Is Your Land'/'If I Had a Hammer'/'Easy Rider'

The group as above, plus Phil Seaman, drums

Recorded London 1958
'No Other Baby'/'Baby Why'*   R 4393
'Make Ready For Love'/'Nothing Will Ever Change'   R 4435

Wally Whyton, guitar, voc.	Johnny Martyn, guitar, voc.
Tony Tolhurst, bass	John Pilgrim, washboard,
Keith Bird, bass clarinet*	saxophone

'Summertime Blues'/'Liverpool Blues'   R 4484

Wally Whyton, guitar, voc.
Jet Harris, bass
Tony Meehan, drums

Hank Marvin, guitar,
Johnny Martyn and Zom (?),
  guitar, voc.

Pye Records

7N 15304

Recorded London 1960
'95 per cent of Me Loves You'*/'Marriage of Convenience'
'You're Going To Be Caught'/'It's a Rat Race'

Wally Whyton, guitar, voc.
Ian MacLeod, lead guitar
Bobby Orr, drums

Sally Miles, voc.*
Rex Dabinett (rehak), bass
John Pilgrim, washboard

EMI One-Up Records

Skiffle Hits 12-inch LP 1976

OU 2148

'Cumberland Gap'/'Don't You Rock Me Daddy O'/'Hey Liley, Liley Lo'/'If I Had a Hammer'/'Streamline Train'/'Maggie May'/'This Land Is Your Land'/'Ain't You Glad'/'Pay Me My Money Down'
'Easy Rider'/'10,000 Years Ago'/'John B. Sails'/'Pick a Bale of Cotton'/'Gloryland'/'It Takes a Worried Man'/'Railroad Steamboat'/'Homing Bird'/'Comin' Round the Mountain'/'On Top of Old Smokey'/'Rock Island Line'

Odeon Records Germany

'10,000 Years Ago'/'Don't You Rock Me Daddy O'	45 O 29106
'Cumberland Gap'/'Hey Liley, Liley Lo'	45 O 29119
'Skiffle Party Part 1'/'Skiffle Party Part 2'	45 O 29158
'Streamline Train'/'Railroad Steamboat'	45 O 29173
'Summertime Blues'/'Liverpool Blues'	O 21 055
'Jim Dandy'/'Maggie May'	O 21 700

Capitol Records USA

'10,000 Years Ago'

US 41 205

Time Records USA

British Blues Badmen Balladry

T/70005

'Sam Hall'/'Kevin Barry'/'Charlie Is My Darling'
'My Bonnie Lies Over the Ocean'/'I Know Where I'm Going'
'The Derby Ram'/'Liverpool Blues'/'The Ash Grove'
'She Was Poor but She Was Honest'/'Wild Colonial Boy'/'Spinning Wheel'/'Three Lovely Lassies'/'Greensleeves'/'Clementine'

Recorded as Original Soho Skiffle Group, while under contract to Parlophone, so probably 1958–9 group

Rollercoaster Records

Coffee Bar Session 1986   ROLL 2011
'Ain't You Glad'/'Pick a Bale of Cotton'/'It Takes a Worried Man'
'Don't You Rock Me Daddy O'/'10,000 Years Ago'/'Hey Liley, Liley Lo'/
'Cumberland Gap'/'Maggie May'/'Streamline Train'/'Railroad Steamboat'/
'Gloryland'/'John B. Sails'/'Wanderin''/'I Saw the Light'/'Precious Memories'/
'Darlin''/'This Land Is Your Land'/'I Know the Lord Laid His Hands on Me'/'If I
Had a Hammer'/'Easy Rider'

Skiffling Along With The Vipers 1997   ROLL 2019
'Hey Liley, Liley Lo'/'This Land Is Your Land'/'It Takes a Worried Man'/'John B.
Sails'/'Vipers Hangman'/'I Saw the Light'/'Pay Me My Money Down'/'Railroad
Steamboat'/'Streamline Train'/'Ain't You Glad'

Bear Family Records

10,000 Years Ago 1996   BCD 15954 C1
3xCD boxed set 64 tracks
1 Cl
'Ain't You Glad'/'Pick a Bale of Cotton'/'It Takes a Worried Man'/ Don't you Rock
Me Daddy O'/'10,000 Years Ago'/'Hey Liley Lo'/ Jim Dandy'/'Cumberland
Gap'/'Maggie May'/'Sam Hall'/'Kevin Barry'/'Charlie Is My Darling'/'My Bonnie
Lies Over the Ocean'/'I Know Where I'm Going'/'The Derby Ram'/'Liverpool
Blues'/'The Ash Grove'/'She Was Poor But She Was Honest'/'Wild Colonial
Boy'/'Spinning Wheel'/'Three Lovely Lasses'/'Greensleeves'/ 'Clementine'

2 Cl
'Darlin''/'Streamline Train'/'Railroad Steamboat'/'This Land Is Your Land'/'Poor
Lazarus'/'The Glory Land'/'Precious Memories'/'Pay Me My Money Down'/'I
Know The Lord Laid His Hands On Me'/'Easy Rider'/'Wanderin''/'Old Joe Clark
(l)'/'Old Joe Clark (2)'/'Homing Bird'/'If I Had a Hammer'/'I Saw the Light'/'John
B. Sails'/'All Shook Up'/'Last Train To San Fernando'/'Putting On the
Style'/'Wandering Eyes'/'Skiffle (1)'/'Comin' Round the Mountain'/'On Top Of
Old Smokey'/'Rock Island Line'/'Skiffle Party (2)'/'Wabash Cannonball'/'Gimme
Crack Corn'/'Skip To My Lou'

3 Cl
'Baby Why'/'No Other Baby'/'Make Ready For Love, Nothing Will Ever
Change'/'Banks of the Ohio'/'Trouble in Mind'/'Worried Man Blues'/
'Instrumental*'/'Summertime Blues Cool Gool**'/'The Horror Show**'/'Don't Tell
Me Your Troubles'/'It's All Over Now'/'All Over This World'/'Got Me a Girl'/'It's
a Rat Race'/'Marriage Of Convenience'/'95 Per Cent of Me Loves You'/'Your
Going To Be Caught'

* Experimental instrumental with Hank Marvin and Jet Harris
**Recorded as Sharkey Todd and the Monsters

The group as for *Coffee Bar Session* LP and Parlophone singles and EPs
Freddie Lloyd, guitar, voc. replaced Jean Van Den Bosch who, although he
toured with the group, did not record with them.

Nancy Whiskey

Topic Records

Recorded London 1956
Nancy Whiskey 1957   7 T10
'An Old Man Came Courtin' Me'/'Bonny Lad'/'The Bold Fenian Men'/'Poor Little
Turtle Dove'/'The Trooper and the Maid'/'The Farewell Song'

Nancy Whiskey, voc. guitar

Oriole Records

'He's Solid Gone'/'Ella Speed' 1958   CB 1394

Nancy Whiskey, voc. guitar   Diz Disley, guitar
Bryan Daly, guitar   Tony Kinsey, or Alan Ganley,
George Jennings, bass   drums
Bob Kelly, piano, washboard
Some of these musicians played in touring group, the Teetotalers

'I Know Where I'm Going'/'Hillside in Scotland' 1958   CB 1452
'Old Grey Goose'/'Johnny Blue' 1959   CB 1485

Session musicians, guitar, harp, bass, drums and vocals

Cupol Records Sweden

The Chas McDevitt Skiffle Group, Nancy Whiskey 1958   CEP 174
'Ella Speed'/'He's Solid Gone'
'Johnnie O'/'Badman Stackolee' (McDevitt Oriole tracks CB 1403)

The group as above and Oriole CB 1403 in McDevitt Discography

CBS Records

'Freight Train'/'The Game' 1967   CBS 3090

Session musicians

Worried Men Skiffle Group

Decca Records

Stars of the Six–Five Special 1958   LF 1299
Recorded London 1958
'Fraulein'

Other tracks by Donegan, Cort, etc.
Rockin' at the 2 Is 1958   LF 1300
Recorded London 1958
'This Little Light of Mine'/'900 Miles from Home'
Other tracks by Blue Jeans Skiffle Group, Wee Willie Harris, etc.

Decca Records Germany

The Fantastic Skiffle Festival 1973   6.28422–2
'This Little Light of Mine'

London Records America/Canada

Music for Hand Jiving 1961   LL 3034
'This Little Light of Mine'/'900 Miles From Home'

Terry Denver (Nelhams), guitar, voc.	Chas Beaumont, lead guitar
Dennis Nelhams, guitar, voc.	Roger Van Engel (Hurgy), washboard, drums

Later non-recording personnel includes:

Freddie Lloyd, guitar, voc.	Rick Richards, guitar, voc.
Tony Mehan, drums	Brian Bennett, drums

15

Skiffle in Traditional Jazz Bands

Avon Cities Jazz Band, *see* Ray Bush

Kenny Ball Jazzmen (Al Young and The Band Boys)
Jazz Collector Records   JDN 101

Recorded London 24 June 1957
'Wabash Cannonball'/'Waterloo'
Other tracks by Kenny Ball Jazz Band

Kenny Ball, voc.	Dick Bishop, banjo
Vic Pitt, bass	Tony Budd, drums

Chris Barber Jazz Band, *see* Chris Barber Skiffle Group

Graeme Bell and his Australian Jazz Band

Recorded as Graeme Bell and his Skiffle Gang

Columbia Records Australia

Recorded Sydney Australia 17 July 1957
'Sweet Georgia Brown'/'Freight Train Blues' (Freight Train)
                                                           DO 3877
'John Henry'/'Don't You Rock Me Daddy O'   DO 3887
Recorded Sydney Australia 8 August 1957
'Gamblin' Man'/'Skiffle Board Blues'   DO 3875
'The Gospel Train'/'Come Shiffle Chicken'   DO 3888

Graeme Bell, piano celeste
Charlie Morrow, guitar
Johnny Sangster, washboard

Geoff Kitchenn, clarinet, tenor sax
Jeff Mack, guitar
Vic Sabrino, voc.

Ken Colyer Jazz Band, *see* Ken Colyer Skiffle Group

Charlie McNair Jazz Band and Skiffle Group

Beltona Records (unknown personnel)

'Hiawatha'/'Meadow Lane Stomp'
'O Didn't He Ramble'

Beltona (78 rpm) BL 2670
Beltona (10-inch LP) ABL 519

Ian Menzies and the Clyde Valley Stompers

Decca Records

'Pearly Gates'/'Old Time Religion' 1956

ECS2007 LP

Mary McGowan, voc.
Norrie Brown, banjo

Louis Reddie, bass,
Bobby Shannon, washboard

Mick Mulligan Magnolia Jazz Band with George Melly

Tempo Records 1951

A 96

Recorded London 1951
'Rock Island Line'

George Melly, voc.
Stan Belwood, drums
Barry Longford, bass

Johnny Parker, piano
Johnny Lavender, banjo

Decca Records 1973

SPA 288

The World of George Melly
Recorded London 30 October 1954, 8–22 July 1957
'Sporting Life'*/'I'm Down in the Dumps'/'Frankie and Johnny'
'Loveless Love'†‡/'Michigan Water Blues'†
Other tracks with Mick Mulligan's Magnolia Jazz Band

George Melly, voc.
Fred Hunt, piano
Frank Thompson, bass
Ronald Duff, piano†‡

Denny Wright, guitar*
Neville Skrimshire, guitar
Pete Appleby, drums
Alan Duddington, bass‡

Johnny Parker

Pye-Nixa Records

Johnny Parker's Washboard Band

Recorded London 23 Sept 1955
'Canine Stomp'/'Number Sixty-Nine'
'The Fox's Tail'/'Up There'   EP NJE 1000
(Also released on Metronome Sweden, Germany)   MEP 1092

Johnny Parker, piano   Denny Wright, guitar
Jim Bray, bass   Stan Greig, washboard, drums

Johnny Parker's Barrelhouse Four
Recorded London 25 May 1956
'Mr Freddy Blues'/'Hold That Thing'   LP NXNJT 503
(Other tracks by Terry Lightfoot, Al Fairweather, Fawkes-Turner)

Johnny Parker, piano   Cedric West, guitar
Jim Bray, bass   Stan Greig, drums

Parlophone Records

Humphrey Lyttelton Jazz Band
Recorded London 17 and 20 April 1956
'Bad Penny Blues'/'Close Your Eyes'*   PA R4184

Johnny Parker, piano   Humphrey Lyttelton, trumpet
Jim Bray bass   Stan Greig, drums
John Picard, trombone*   Wally Fawkes, clarinet*
Bruce Turner, alto*   Freddy Legon, guitar*

Bob Wallis and his Storyville Jazzmen

Recorded as Bob Wallis Washboard Beaters

Storyville Records

Denmark 1955
'Tight Like That'/'Meeting at the Building'*   A45 502
'Juliana Johnson'/'K.C.Moan'   A45 036
'Meeting at the Building'*/'Tight Like That'   108 105 STF
*Although credited on sleeve and label, 'Crawdad Hole' is substituted

Bob Wallis, voc.   Freddie Poulsen, mandolin
Tove Karre, guitar   Ole Christiansen, bass
Ron MacKay, washboard

Bibliography

Asbury, Herbert: *The French Quarter* (Pocket Books)
Brown, Joe: *Brown Sauce* (Collins Willow)
Broonzy, Big Bill, with Yannick Bruynoghe: *Big Bill Blues* (Cassell)
Colyer, Ken: *When Dreams Are In The Dust* (K.C. Trust, Millbury)
Davies, Hunter: *The Beatles* (Arrow)
Faith, Adam: *Act Of Faith* (Bantam)
Godbolt, Jim: *The World Of Jazz* (Studio Editions)
Hammond, John: *John Hammond on Record* (Penguin)
Harry, Bill: *The Ultimate Beatles Encyclopaedia* (Virgin)
Hasted, John: *Alternative Memoirs* (Greengates)
Ives, Burl: *Wayfaring Stranger* (Whittlesey House)
Jackson, John: *A Big Beat Heat* (Schirmer)
Lomax, John A. with Alan Lomax:
    Best Loved American Folk Songs (Grosset & Dunlap)
    Negro Songs As Sung By Lead Belly (Macmillan)
McAleer, Dave: *Hit Parade Heroes* (Hamlyn)
Melly, George: *Owning Up* (Weidenfeld & Nicolson)
Oliver, Paul: *The Story Of The Blues* (Penguin)
Read, Mike, with The Shadows: *The Story Of The Shadows* (Sphere)
Rose, Al: *Remember Jazz* (Louisiana State University)
Turner, Steve: *Van Morrison, Too Late To Stop Now* (Bloomsbury)

Newsletters:
    The Southern Skiffle Society
    Lead Belly Society

Newspapers and periodicals:
    Melody Maker
    New Musical Express
    Jazz News
    Weekly Sporting Review & Showbusiness

Useful Addresses

Lead Belly Society
P.O. Box 6679
Ithaca N.Y. 14851
USA

Tel: (607) 273-6615
Fax: (603) 844-4810
e-mail: sk86@cornell.edu

Southern Skiffle Society
147 Tudor Drive
Kingston-upon-Thames
Surrey KT2 5NT
UK

Tel: 0181 546 2713
Fax: 0171 7211 7292

Ken Colyer Trust
24 Rosebery Avenue
Langley Vale
Epsom Downs
Surrey KT18 7HE

UK Washboards International
19840 S. Summerset Lane
Parker
CO 80138 USA

Tel: (303) 841 4229
Fax: (303) 840 0402
http://www.washboards.com

Columbus Washboard Co., Inc.
1372 Oxley Road
Columbus
OH 43212
USA

Tel: (800) 343 7967

Bear Family Records
P.O. Box 1154
D. 27727 Hambergen
Germany

Tel: 04794 9300 0
Fax: 04794 9300 20

Lake Records
Workington
Cumbria CA14 3EW
UK

Rollercoaster Records
Rock House
London Road
St Mary's
Stroud GL6 8PU
UK

Tel: 014531 886252
Fax: 01453 885361
e-mail rolle 38374@aol.com

Index